EMPLOYERS, AGENCIES AND IMMIGRATION

Research in Migration and Ethnic Relations Series

Series Editor:
Maykel Verkuyten, ERCOMER
Utrecht University

The Research in Migration and Ethnic Relations series has been at the forefront of research in the field for ten years. The series has built an international reputation for cutting edge theoretical work, for comparative research especially on Europe and for nationally-based studies with broader relevance to international issues. Published in association with the European Research Centre on Migration and Ethnic Relations (ERCOMER), Utrecht University, it draws contributions from the best international scholars in the field, offering an interdisciplinary perspective on some of the key issues of the contemporary world.

Also in series

European Immigration
A Sourcebook
Edited by Anna Triandafyllidou and Ruby Gropas
ISBN 978 1 4094 5363 5

Ethnic Diversity and Social Cohesion
Immigration, Ethnic Fractionalization and Potentials for Civic Action
Merlin Schaeffer
ISBN 978 1 4094 6938 4

Full series list at back of book

**EUROPEAN RESEARCH CENTRE
ON MIGRATION & ETHNIC RELATIONS**

Employers, Agencies and Immigration

Paying for Care

Edited by

Anna Triandafyllidou
European University Institute, Italy

and

Sabrina Marchetti
European University Institute, Italy

Routledge
Taylor & Francis Group

LONDON AND NEW YORK

First published 2015 by Ashgate Publishing

2 Park Square, Milton Park, Abingdon, Oxfordshire OX14 4RN
52 Vanderbilt Avenue, New York, NY 10017

Routledge is an imprint of the Taylor & Francis Group, an informa business

First issued in paperback 2020

British Library Cataloguing in Publication Data
A catalogue record for this book is available from the British Library

The Library of Congress has cataloged the printed edition as follows:
Employers, agencies and immigration : paying for care / [edited] by Anna Triandafyllidou and Sabrina Marchetti.
    pages cm. – (Research in migration and ethnic relations series)
  Includes bibliographical references and index.
  ISBN 978-1-4724-3321-3 (hardback)
  1. Household employees–Europe. 2. Foreign workers–Europe.
  3. Caregivers–Europe. 4. Immigrants–Employment–Europe. I. Triandafyllidou, Anna.
  II. Marchetti, Sabrina.
  HD8039.D52E9724 2015
  331.7'6164094–dc23

                                                                                    2014027936

ISBN 978-1-4724-3321-3 (hbk)
ISBN 978-0-367-59989-8 (pbk)

From Anna to Patty who often teaches more than what books can say

*From Sabrina to the people in Reggio Emilia who opened their homes
and their hearts to me*

Contents

List of Tables

Notes on Contributors

Maurizio Ambrosini is Professor of Sociology of Migration at the University of Milan, Department of Social and Political Sciences, and *chargé d'enseignement* at the University of Nice-Sophia Antipolis (France). He is the editor of the journal *Mondi Migranti* and the Scientific Director of the Centre Medì – Migrations in the Mediterranean, of Genoa and of the Italian Summer School of Sociology of Migrations. His main interests cover immigrants' labour market, transnational links and migration policies. He is the author of more than 200 books, articles and essays in these fields, published in several languages. His handbook, *Sociologia delle migrazioni*, is adopted as the textbook on migration in many Italian universities. A new book, *Irregular Immigration and Invisible Welfare*, has been recently published by Palgrave.

Beatriz Camargo is a PhD candidate at the Group for Research on Ethnic Relations, Migration and Equality – GERME, at the Sociology Institute of the Université Libre de Bruxelles (ULB), Belgium. Her doctoral thesis focuses on changes introduced in the domestic work relationships and the labour market in Brussels in view to implement a formal system for domestic work service. Her main areas of interest are migration studies, gender and labour issues and welfare economics. Prior to joining GERME, Beatriz obtained a European Master's Degree on Humanitarian Action (NOHA) from the Université Catholique de Louvain (UCL)/Université Aix-Marseille III and, more recently, a Complementary Master's on Human Rights from Université Saint-Louis, Brussels. She also holds a journalism degree from the University of São Paulo (USP), Brazil.

Pilar Goñalons-Pons is a sociology PhD candidate at the University of Wisconsin-Madison. Her research interests include social inequality, feminist theory, international migration and comparative social policy. Funded in part by several grants, including the National Science Foundation Dissertation Improvement Grant, her doctoral thesis *Care and Housework for Sale* examines how the marketisation of domestic and care labour affects gender and class inequalities in Spain. Pilar Goñalons-Pons is the author of *Practicing Intersectionality in Spain*, a review article published with Myra Marx Ferree. She has also written about housework, income inequality and the politics of paid domestic work. Pilar teaches courses on social stratification, sociology of gender and feminist theory. She has been a visiting research fellow at the European University Institute, Juan March Institute and Utrecht University.

Majda Hrženjak, PhD, is a Senior Research Fellow at the Peace Institute for Contemporary Social and Political Studies, in Ljubljana (Slovenia). Her current research interests are related to gender studies, including critical studies of masculinities, social politics, in particular issues related to labour markets, globalisation of care work and intersectional inequalities. From 2004 to 2007 she initiated a developmental partnership entitled the *System of Household Assistance* (*SIPA*) to explore the prospects for innovative approaches toward the organisation of care work within the social economy sector. From 2008 to 2010 she coordinated the first national study about the situation of (migrant) domestic workers in Slovenia in the ground-breaking research project, *Informal Reproductive Work: Trends in Slovenia and EU*. Currently she is exploring issues of socialisation of reproductive work through a research project entitled *Prospects for Desegmentation of the Labour Market* and acts as a manger of the Slovenian national focal point of the European Union Fundamental Rights Agency (2011–14). Among others, she is the author of *Invisible Work* (2007, PI) and editor of *Politics of Care* (2011, PI).

Živa Humer, PhD and sociologist, is a Research Fellow at the Peace Institute for Contemporary Social and Political Studies, in Ljubljana. Her research interests are related to gender studies, social policy and sociology of families, especially in relation to gender and care, division of domestic and care work and family life. She acted as a national evaluator of the Resolution on the National Programme for Equal Opportunities for Women and Men (2005–13) and acts as a researcher at the national focal point of the European Union Agency for Fundamental Rights. She is a co-author of two monographs: *New fatherhood in Slovenia* (2008) and *Faces of homophobia* (2012).

Anna Kordasiewicz is an Assistant Professor at the Centre for Migration Research, University of Warsaw, and works full time at the Polish NSC funded 'Unfinished migration transition and ageing population in Poland. Asynchronous population changes and the transformation of formal and informal care institutions' project. She collaborates with the Institute of Sociology, University of Warsaw, University of Lodz and with the Field of Dialogue Foundation. Her research interests pertain to paid domestic work, the transformations of contemporary social relationships, migratory processes and civic participation. She studied paid domestic work in Italy, Germany and Poland. Her PhD thesis concerning the role of migrants in the domestic service labour market in Poland was granted the 3rd prize from the Polish Ministry of Labour and Social Affairs in the competition for the best PhD thesis on labour and social affairs in 2011. She recently co-authored and co-edited a book on youth civic participation, *Edukacja obywatelska w dzialaniu*, with Przemyslaw Sadura).

Guro Korsnes Kristensen is a Post-Doctoral Fellow at the Norwegian University of Science and Technology's Department of Interdisciplinary Studies of Culture. She holds a PhD in Interdisciplinary Studies of Culture. Kristensen specialises in gender research, with a particular focus on the intersections of gender, ethnicity/

nationality, religion and social class. Her research is broadly focused on migration and family life. Kristensen's present research project focuses on Norwegian couples' reflections on and experiences with paid domestic work. Kristensen is the coordinator of the research project *Buying and Selling Gender Equality: Feminized Migration and Gender Equality in Contemporary Norway*. She has published several journal articles and book chapters in the field of gender equality and multiculturalism and in 2009 won the *Norwegian Journal of Gender Studies* 'Article of the Year' prize.

Sabrina Marchetti is currently a Jean Monnet Post-Doctoral Fellow at the Robert Schuman Centre of the European University Institute in Florence. She received her PhD in Gender and Ethnicity from the University of Utrecht in 2010. Sabrina was a visiting fellow at the University of Linköping, the University of Southern California and at Delhi University. She has worked for Kassel University and the Metropolitan University in London, and with various non-academic research centres such as ISFOL in Italy, and IIED in the UK. Sabrina has mainly specialised on issues of gender and migration, with a specific focus on the question of migrant domestic work. From a comparative perspective, she has studied the case of Filipino, Eritrean and Afro-Surinamese migrants in Italy and the Netherlands. Her current project focuses on the case of Eastern European home-carers in Italy on the basis of interviews with workers and their employers. She has recently published her book *Black Girls. Migrant Domestic Worker and Colonial Legacies* (Brill, 2014).

Adéla Souralová is an Assistant Professor in the Social Anthropology program and at the Office of Population Studies at the Faculty of Social Sciences, Masaryk University. In her research she specialises in the topics of migration, particularly the family relationships of Vietnamese immigrants in the CR, gender and generational conflict, and the demands of the second generation on citizenship. Her doctoral thesis (defended in June 2013, Department of Sociology, Masaryk University) dealt with caregiving work relationships among Vietnamese immigrant mothers, children and their Czech nannies in the Czech Republic. She lectures following courses: Anthropology of Migration; Belonging, Nationalism and Citizenship; Anthropology of Gender, and Ethnography and Field Work.

Bernhard Weicht has studied (Social) Economics at the University of Vienna and Social Policy at the University of Nottingham. He received his PhD in Sociology from the University of Nottingham, researching the social and moral construction of care for elderly people (2010). Since 2012 he has been working as a Marie Curie Fellow at Utrecht University in the Netherlands on a project on migration and care. Starting from an interdisciplinary, intersectional perspective this research focuses on the intersection of care and migration regimes in Austria, the UK and the Netherlands and the consequences of social policy arrangements for the people in question. Bernhard has published on the construction of care, ideas of dependency, migrant care workers, the intersection of migration and care regimes and the construction of ageing and older people. He is vice-chair of the European Sociological Association Research Network 'Ageing in Europe' and is a member of the editorial board of the *Journal of International and Comparative Social Policy*. Beside other projects he is currently co-editing a book on migrant care workers in Austria.

Lenka Pelechova recently completed a PhD thesis titled *Bringing Migrant Domestic Work Literature into Family Studies: The Intricate Dynamics of Au Pair Families*. She holds an MA in Research Methods with a Pathway in Sociology from the University of Nottingham (2009), where she also worked as a part-time seminar tutor for the undergraduate module Sociology in Contemporary Society in 2009/2010 and Culture in Contemporary Society in 2010/2011. She contributed to research on 'The role of class and family ideology in au pair recruitment' at the Intersecting Family Lives, Locales and Labours conference (London South Bank University 2012) and 'Host Parents and au pairs relationships: the context of gender in family roles' at the Centre for the Study of Women and Gender at the University of Warwick (2013). She worked as a journal editor of the postgraduate journal *ENQUIRE* at the University of Nottingham. Her research interests are: family ideology, family roles, gender, motherhood and domestic work.

Anna Triandafyllidou is Professor at the Global Governance Programme (GGP) of the Robert Schuman Centre for Advanced Studies (RSCAS), European University Institute, where she coordinates the Research Area on Cultural Pluralism. Before joining the Programme, she was a part-time professor at RSCAS (2010–12). During the period 2004–12 she was a Senior Fellow at the Hellenic Foundation for European and Foreign Policy (ELIAMEP) in Athens where she headed a successful migration research team. She has been a Visiting Professor at the College of Europe in Bruges since 2002 and is the Editor-in-Chief of the *Journal of Immigrant and Refugee Studies*. She has held teaching and research positions at the London School of Economics (1995–97), National Research Council in Rome (1997–99), EUI (1999–2004) and New York University (2001). Her recent books include *Migrant Smuggling* (with T. Maroukis, Palgrave, 2012); *Irregular Migrant Domestic Workers. Who Cares?* (Ashgate, 2013); *Circular Migration Between Europe and Its Neighbourhood* (Oxford University Press, 2013); *European Immigration: A Sourcebook* (Ashgate, 2014).

Cristina Vega Solis is a Professor at the Department of Sociology and Gender Studies, FLACSO, Ecuador. She has worked on several topics related to work and subjectivity, particularly domestic and care work. She has carried out extensive investigations of women in precarious sectors. Cristina is currently working on two projects: return migration from Spain to Ecuador and family strategies; and another on identity questions and plurinationality in migration, taking the two case studies of Ecuadorian and Ethiopian migrants in Spain and the USA. Relevant publications include: *Culturas del cuidado en transición* (2009) and *Por los circuitos de la precariedad femenina* (2004).

Chapter 1

The Employers' Perspective on Paid Domestic and Care Work

Anna Triandafyllidou and Sabrina Marchetti

Employers of paid domestic workers and home-carers are not employers like any others. They are not entrepreneurs or company owners. Very often, they have not hired anyone else in the past, nor have they received any training in business management. For most of them, employment dynamics are totally new, seen from the position of employers since normally they are or have been also workers, and they are themselves hired by someone else. In some instances, they are not directly paying the people working in their households, but this is done through an agency of which they become 'customers'. A further complication is that in some cases they might not pay these workers out of their own income, as happens often in elderly care where the salary of the worker is generally covered by the pension and the savings of the care-receiver, but still there are those who hire the care-givers and manage their work.

The perspective of these kinds of employers, who they are, their expectations and their values, are the object of this book. We look at all kinds of typologies: employers of nannies and housekeepers, relatives of dependent elders who need a care-giver, host-parents of international au pairs and finally clients of agencies that provide home-cleaning and care services. The majority of them currently employ migrant workers, but we are also interested in those who choose instead to hire their co-nationals for these jobs. In so doing, we adopt a variety of approaches, from policy oriented to narrative analysis, and we highlight the difference between employers in various European contexts since the realities of these jobs might be different.

The aim of this book is thus to illustrate who are these employers, and what is the specificity of their perspectives on migrant domestic and care work in contemporary Europe. This brings an important contribution to the debate that has developed during the last 20 years in international academia. Several scholars have investigated the phenomenon taking place in the increasing number of households that employ migrants in order to perform tasks related to the care of the house, of children, elders and other dependent persons. This debate intertwines broad research fields such as those on welfare, ageing and family, on gender, race/ethnicity and inequality and finally on globalisation and migration regimes.

So far, this scholarship has emphasised the importance of the international division of reproductive labour and of the 'global care chains'. For instance, scholars such as Rhacel Salazar Parreñas (2001, 2008), Bridget Anderson (2000), Pei Chia Lan (2006) and Nicole Constable (1997) who show how gender and ethnicity affect the formation of domestic work as a labour opportunity for Filipinas on a global scale. Along the same lines, Barbara Ehrenreich and Arlie Russell Hochschild (2002) have argued that this system has brought migrant women to be seen as those who embody 'traditional' gendered skills. Maurizio Ambrosini in his most recent book (2013) has analysed the 'invisible welfare' that migrant domestic workers provide for families and which covers for the gaps created out of the ageing of society and a decline in welfare services. Scholars such as Eleonore Kofman (2012), Fiona Williams (2012), Nicola Yeates (2009), Raffaella Sarti (2007) and Helma Lutz (2011), together with Sigrid Metz-Gockel, Mirjana Morokvasic-Muller and A. Senganata Munst (2008), have shown how the interconnection between gender and migration regimes shapes the experience of workers in this specific labour sector, in Europe and beyond, especially in the case of undocumented workers (Triandafyllidou 2013). These studies also show the importance of the fact that more often than not both the employer and the employee are women. This creates important dynamics of inequality where class, ethnicity and gender become intertwined, while it may also trigger feelings of mutual understanding and solidarity in terms of 'common' gender roles that have to be performed in the family context.

However, we believe that within this debate, the 'demand side' of paid domestic and care work still requires further elaboration. In fact, we are interested in bringing new analysis to a debate that takes employers as the object of analysis per se and which has been already developed by authors such as Helma Lutz (2011), Pierrete Hondagneu-Sotelo (2001), Claudia Alemani (2004), Bridget Anderson (2007), Lena Näre (2012) and Catrin Lundström (2012) in particular. Researching the standpoint of employers is very important in order to highlight the hierarchy between women employers and employees, as rooted in class and race/ethnicity inequalities of contemporary societies (see Cock 1989; Palmer 1989; Ray and Qayum 2009; Rollins 1985; Marchetti 2006). Importantly, employers talk about their competition with employees, especially for the case of employers of nannies and elderly carers, but also for those who worry about the possible seduction of their husbands from the side of the domestics (Lan 2006; Constable 1997). Finally, the perspective of employers is very important when talking about the transformation of welfare, families' needs and organisations (Vega Solis 2009).

It is by building on this debate that this book wants to offer the first edited volume, with intra-European comparisons, entirely devoted only to the figure of employers, with the aim to contribute not only to the specific debate on migrant domestic and care work, but also to understanding the response of middle-class European households to the changing intertwine between family life, the restructuring of welfare provision and the regulations pertaining to migrant work.

In the rest of this introduction, we elaborate on the debates that illustrate the context in which the experience of employers takes place. We focus on three main issues: the marketisation of care; the interconnection between family life and homes becoming workplaces; and finally the relationship between policies on welfare and on migration in Europe. In conclusion, we will briefly outline the structure of the book and the contribution brought by the authors of the chapters.

The Care We Pay For

Before entering into the discussion on who are the employers, it important to define what is the kind of work that they are buying from their employees. In other words, what is this 'care' that employers are willing to, although in different ways, pay for?

The employment of free or enslaved servants for care and cleaning chores goes back in history for a very long time (see Rollins 1985). Initially, however, masters did not actually 'pay' for the work of their servants but rather they provided them food and shelter. The monetarisation of care and domestic work is an increasing reality, as witnessed in the United States in the Seventeenth century (Hoerder 2014). This was the time in which slaves indeed started to be sold and therefore their workforce started to be something that employers needed to quantify. In other words, this is the time in which employers needed to assess the value of the care that they were buying, and thus also probably be more clear-minded about what they were actually buying.

The context in which employers live today is of course very different. In Europe, the monetarisation of domestic and care work has been in place since the nineteenth century (see Sarti 2007). Also, importantly, in countries like Italy, there has been a debate on remuneration for housewives, which takes into account their crucial role in the wellbeing of their families, something that had important repercussions on the valorisation of reproductive work in general (Repetto 2004).

Along these transformations, several attempts have been made to spell out what are the tasks that employers might expect their workers to perform. The recent ILO Convention n. 189 on the rights of domestic workers is only the last of these attempts in which a 'definition' of paid domestic work is provided by simply saying that domestic work 'means work performed in or for a household or households' (ILO 2011). Galotti (2009, p. 11) notes that it encompasses two broad areas of family care (whether for elderly or children) and household maintenance at large. The precise configuration of what domestic work means indeed varies from country to country.

In this volume, the emphasis is very much on the employer's attempt to buy something which goes beyond the performance of material chores, and which rather refers to their expectations and desires for the wellbeing of their households. This includes the cleaning and tidying of their living spaces, washing and ironing clothes, cooking meals, taking care of pets and plants as well as tending to children and assisting elderly family members. All these tasks equally affect the person that performs them as well as those who benefit from their accomplishment (Gutierrez-Rodriguez 2010). In other words, the buying of all this kind of work carries along an important emotional dimension, which leads us to group them all together as 'care'. Thus, as in the title of this book, we talk about 'paying for care' with reference to important stories that have to do with the monetarisation of all tasks that employers require from the people they employ, being this washing the dishes or playing with their children, for the wellbeing of their homes and their household members.

The relationship between domestic and care work and intimate life is of the utmost importance. Arlie Hochschild (2012) sees in the buying of care service a palpable example of what generally happens along the expansion of the service economy. She talks about the 'outsourcing of the self' to refer to a fundamental psychological dimension in employers' choices and expectations (see Chapter 6 by Marchetti, this volume). Also Eileen Boris and Rhacel Parreñas (2010) devote particular attention to employment in the domestic and care work fields, in their volume on 'intimate labours'. Viviane Zelizer (2010) talks about an 'economy of care' to refer to the specific market created by the delegation on others of tasks otherwise understood as intimate. Since this is a market based on the selling of 'relational services' (Cranford and Miller 2013), the figure of those who buy these services is more often seen as the one of 'customers', rather than, as we emphasise in this volume, of 'employers'.

Homes as Workplaces

In the debate on migrant domestic work, the importance of homes as workplaces has been widely discussed. Brenda Yeoh and Shirlena Huang (1999) see homes where migrant domestic workers are employed as 'contact zones', while Janet Momsen (1999) talks about 'culture-contact situations'. These scholars demonstrate how, in domestic and caring practices, employers are constantly negotiating with their employees and other members of their families' shared notions about gender which find their spatial context in their homes.

The home is a very special place of employment where the boundaries between the private and public are continuously renegotiated (Davidoff 2003). Homes are very much shaped by national culture and identities. Alison Blunt and Robin Dowlings (2006) talk about homes where discourses and practices related to the nation are reproduced. In what they call 'lived and metaphorical experiences of home', people create a sense of identity which then calls for an analysis of the power relations which make of homes an 'intensely political' site.

It is in this 'politicised' domestic space that the relationship between migrant domestic workers and their employers evolves. Employers are seeking in the workers someone who is able to take up domestic and caring practices, such practices are regulated by hidden principles and organised along axes of power. The 'home' is the site where those practices take place and identities are shaped, contested and reshaped over time.

In the perspective of this relationship, the house is considered not simply as a 'space', but rather as a 'place', that is a specific location where subjects' experience takes shape. The difference between 'space' and 'place' is emphasised by Doreen Massey who defines a 'place' as the result of particular interactions and of the meeting of certain social relations, which occur in that specific location (Massey 1994). For this reason, when looking at the interactions between employers and employees in the domestic sphere, one should see a 'place' rather than a 'space' being a specific location where different forces interact. The domestic 'place' where these encounters take place, practically and metaphorically, reflects the structure of the 'social space', where different subjects occupy and take up different positions. In this view, the organisation of these houses as workplaces is crossed by boundaries separating the upper-class in opposition to the working-class, and the European citizens versus the migrant (often undocumented) worker.

The debate on 'homes' as workplaces is very intertwined with the one on the role of women inside their households and the transformation in their commitment towards cleaning tasks. Already in 1994, in their classic book *Servicing the Middle Class*, Nicky Gregson and Michelle Lowe acknowledge that:

> In certain middle-class households cleaning is no longer being seen as a suitable use of middle-class women's time-space. ... Social transformations ... have restructured women's relations to the home in ways that have altered their traditional ties to domesticity (Gregson and Lowe 1994, p. 24).

We are talking here about the rejection of those commitments towards reproductive work which have to do with the maintenance of the homes themselves. Middle-class women are ready to dismiss the low-level abjected tasks (Kristeva 1980; Douglas 1979) in order achieve the ideal of respectable women (Mosse 1985).

Bridget Anderson suggests the image of Dr Jekyll and Mrs Hyde to represent two women united by interdependent representations. The domestic workers represent physicality and dirtiness because of the tasks they accomplish, while the employers confirm their superiority regarding femininity and managerial skills (Anderson 2000). The European middle-class employers, in Anderson's view, take the role of organising domestic work: they carefully choose the best employee; they assign her the tasks to fulfil and give her instructions about the education of the children. Therefore, the employers succeed in being domestic without being dirty (Ibid.).

This new model of femininity is closely related to the emergence, in contemporary Europe, of a very interesting female figure. She has been called the new traditionalist model that, as Leslie says, corresponds to the woman that 'was searching for something to believe in and look what she found: her husband, her children, herself' (Leslie 1993, p. 308). In fact, employers place a lot of effort in taking care of their house and in their family, which likely aims at the reproduction of a traditional household.

Thus while the entrance of women in the paid work sector outside the home is ever increasing, the tensions and gaps that this leaves by the 'care gap' that it creates do not disappear. While they are filled by migrant domestic workers, the transition to a commodified care is not as smooth as it may seem from a simple economic transaction perspective (the employer buys a service, the worker provides for the service, the need is addressed). This book emphasises the emotional and value tensions that this commodification of care creates for employers, particularly women, as well as on the new job arrangements that emerge out of the need to regulate the domestic work sector and help match offer with demand.

The issue is even more complicated in the case of elderly carers which individual families have to employ in order to compensate for the lack of public welfare provisions, as we will further discuss in the next section.

Welfare and Migration

The debate that has developed around care services and welfare has increasingly looked at four actors: the market, the state, the non-profit sector and the family (Kofman and Raghuram 2009). The employers whose experience we analyse in this volume belong to the first one of these four categories, covering the demand side of the private market of care services. However, they are also part of the last one of these four institutions, the family, since they are usually the relatives of those who are receiving the care services, especially in the case of care for elders, disabled and children. This book thus sheds light on the difficult positioning of employers as simultaneously market and family actors in the context of the changing welfare arrangements in contemporary Europe. The focus on these two dimensions, the market and the family, is very timely in relation to the evolution of national welfare towards privatisation and re-familiarisation, elements which are unsettling the borders between the different European welfare regimes as Esping-Andersen (1990, 1996) describes.

Care is probably the welfare sector which has been most privatised in Europe, in comparison to health, education, pension systems and so forth (Daly 2012; Ferrera 2005; Graziano, Jaquot and Palier 2011). The title of this book, *Paying for Care*, does reflect the condition of most European households that are asked to use their own family budget in order to purchase market-based services which were previously provided by public nurseries, rest homes and hospitals, or which were performed by members of the household itself (usually women). Once again, employers find themselves torn between the demands from family and the market when assessing the care which is needed and the resources available to afford it, they either buy care or mobilise their own time and energy to provide care. In other words, there is a very thin line separating the role of these employers as family care-givers or market-actors when they can afford to delegate this same caregiving to a paid worker. In this case, employers have to juggle meagre welfare allowances or service provisions for elderly or children with rising care needs (especially of the elderly as Europe's population is ageing), while women are increasingly engaged in full-time paid work outside the home.

Scholars explain how states have withdrawn from the field of personal care provision and have kept only a regulatory function. They are providing the normative framework and the working regulations that allow private companies or individuals to offer their services inside the households.[1] The way European states are doing that changes greatly from country to country. In some countries there is a strong intervention by the state in supporting employers to buy the service thanks to a monetarisation of allowances for households with disabled and seriously ill members, or for households with young children. In some other cases, the state intervenes in supporting the functioning of the market by emphasising the role of agencies. This is the case, for example, of the voucher system in Belgium which is analysed in this volume by Beatriz Camargo (Chapter 8).

Another important field of state policies for the private market of care services has to do with the issue of migration. The 'paying for care' entails indeed the search for a cheap and flexible workforce which is frequent to find amongst migrants, women especially, who are increasingly leaving their countries in order to find occupation in this specific sector. The reasons behind these tendencies have been widely analysed by the scholarship on the international division of reproductive labour that we have presented at the beginning of this introduction. The experiences of migrant domestic and care workers illustrate the divarication of care commitments between women from different parts of the world with women in the wealthy countries delegating the more menial and heavy tasks to migrants coming from poorer regions. This is especially so for women migrating from Asia towards Europe, Northern America and the Middle East, as well as for Eastern Europeans going towards Western Europe. Many of these women have caring commitments themselves towards their children or elderly parents which they are delegating to others, as is characteristic of transnational households.

State policies may strongly influence the employment of migrants for care and domestic work (Ruhs and Anderson 2010). Next to sending countries, also some receiving countries in Europe have adopted a mechanism to channel migrants into this specific occupation. Italy is a very well-known example for this tendency. In their regular decrees setting the limits of yearly on-call migrants' quotas, the Italian government provides a preferential quota for domestic and care workers. Countries of origin receive different allocations of vacancies depending on the agreements that Italy has in place. Also, in the regularisation procedures for undocumented migrants which Italy has launched in recent years, domestic and care workers received preferential treatment, thus favouring what Lena Näre (2013) calls the transnational familism of the Italian care sector.

Other countries have strongly contrasted this tendency instead. They are reluctant to welcome foreigners in this sector and it is therefore almost impossible to receive a residence permit when you are a migrant doing domestic and care work (Triandafyllidou 2013). Sarah Van Walsum explains that the internal pushes that put the Netherlands in this tough position against migrant domestic workers was an attempt to preserve this sector for working-class Dutch women or long-time

---

1   On the difference between individual and organisation-based provision of care services across Europe, see Barbara Da Roit and Bernard Weicht (2013).

residents (Van Walsum 2011). In some of these countries, however, the demand for full-time paid domestic work has been channelled into the au pair scheme, which is increasingly popular amongst families with young children that do not have other resources for the employment of foreigner workers (see Cox 2007; Isaksen 2010). This scheme will be discussed in the last two chapters of this book on the basis of interviews with Norwegian and British host-parents of international au pairs by Guro Kristensen and Lenka Pelechova.

These few examples show the resilient role of the state in the provision of home-care and domestic services. This takes a particularly interesting shape in the case of former socialist countries where the rampant growth of private services is sometimes contrasted by institutional attempts to direct the demand-offer dynamics to promote the occupation of unemployed local women, as in the case of Slovenia which is discussed in this book (see Chapter 10).

Contents of the Book

The book is divided into three parts. The first part entails a comparative analysis of the subjectivities of the employers and of the dynamics of the employer-employee relationship in the home, taking into account the different needs of different types of families. The contributions included in this part adopt qualitative methodologies, borrowing from social anthropology, sociology and gender studies. They focus on the negotiations that take place in the employer-employee relationship and the power relations that are inherent, even if often invisible, at first glance.

In Chapter 2, Maurizio Ambrosini reflects on the nature of the employment relationship between contracts, emotions and mutual obligations in a country such as Italy with a large care deficit and an increasing elderly population. Ambrosini introduces the notion of 'care-managers' to typify the profile of people who employ migrant workers in order to take care of their elderly parents and speaks of an invisible welfare regime that emerges silently to cover for the gaps of the formal welfare system.

The two chapters that follow by Pilar Goñalons Pons (Chapter 3) and by Anna Kordasiewicz (Chapter 4) examine the intersection of class in the personal and gendered relationship that exists between the employer and the migrant domestic worker/care-provider. Different views of equality and gender roles in Spain and Poland provide for different contextual understandings of this relationship. The Spanish employers value the contribution of migrant domestic workers in making their career outside the home possible, while the Polish employers view the notion of equality as problematic and express a sense of 'guilt' in employing a domestic worker. Both chapters deal with the unresolved tension between family and work in everyday life within a contemporary context of changing gender roles and dynamics.

The following two chapters by Cristina Vega Solis (Chapter 5) and by Sabrina Marchetti (Chapter 6) introduce a new element in the analysis of the employer-employee relationship; notably when it is the elderly family member that is being looked after. Vega Solis speaks about the dilemmas entailed in a triangular relationship between paid care-providers, care-recipients and families of the latter, from the perspective of the daughters of the care-recipients. Marchetti delves into the subjective perception of the work arrangement by the relatives of the care-receivers and the intertwining of the practical (working hours, full-time care) with the emotional concerns (that the service received will 'make mum happy'). The intimacy of the employer-employee relationship and the special nature of these 'care employers', as radically different from our usual understanding of the employer, come centre stage in these two chapters.

The second part of the book shifts the focus to the reorganisation of welfare and care arrangements that is currently taking place in several European countries in a combined effort to tackle informal work in the domestic and home-care sector, while also inventing mechanisms that match the labour supply and demand. These policies, often well-intentioned in their aim of providing a level playing field for employers and migrant domestic workers alike, only partly achieve their objectives. Indeed they are often faced with the contradiction between the personalised and intimate nature of domestic work and the need to create a professional profile and a job category for the benefit of both buyers and providers of the service. This part of the book starts with a discourse analysis of the debate around the Austrian reform of this sector, which has so far concealed the focus on the family or of the private individual as 'employer'. Bernhard Weicht (Chapter 7) shows how the policy discourse actually takes the Austrian citizen out of the equation of the employer-employee relationship.

Chapter 8 by Beatriz Camargo on Belgium scrutinises the 'voucher' system introduced in slightly different ways in the country with the aim of encouraging employers to declare their migrant domestic workers, pay the necessary welfare contributions and also receive tax relief when doing so. Chapter 9 by Adéla Souralová, instead, examines the Czech case looking at the emergence of job placement agencies in the paid childcare sector. Here the emphasis is less on the native or foreign nationality of the care worker but rather on the transformation of the employer-employee relationship within the sector. The placement agency emerges as the employer that guarantees a 'professional' service to the customer (the family) and holds all contacts with the employee (the care-provider).

Chapter 10, by Živa Humer and Majda Hrženjak, carries this issue further by looking at a concrete policy experiment that has taken place in Slovenia where the state has become the intermediary between the family as employer and the home-care worker/cleaner, subsidising this type of work as well as providing a concrete legal framework. While the aim of the intervention was to mobilise long-term unemployed women, the choice of the sector (notably that of domestic work) raises important issues on whether a state intervention is an appropriate policy measure in a sector that is characterised by intimate and individualised employment relationships.

Finally, the third section of the book concentrates on an emerging field in the wider area of migrant domestic and care work, looking at the transformation of the au pair scheme in the UK and Norway. Lenka Pelechova, in Chapter 11, considers au pair employment in the UK, focusing on the perspective of the employers and their effort to balance work and family life while keeping some 'free time' for themselves. The case of au pairs is an interesting example of similar dynamics (like those at play in the case of migrant domestic workers more generally) as the boundary between employment and free time, the informality of the arrangement and the practical as well as emotional aspects of the work are, here too, closely intertwined. The same issue is taken up by Guro Korsnes Kristensen (Chapter 12) in her own qualitative study of Norwegian families' experiences with home-cleaning and au pairing, paying special attention to inequalities within the rather informal and flexible arrangements of domestic work, which is often converted into informal domestic labour. These chapters look at both the work-related issues such as: where does the au pair 'experience' stop and real domestic work begins, what is the difference between employing a home-cleaner and hosting an au pair and so on. The chapter also examines the value tensions that these families experience: their commitment to equality and to being 'foster parents'; for an au pair vs their actual need for help in cleaning and caring; and the practical arrangement of having an au pair helper or employing a home-cleaner.

In the concluding chapter (Chapter 13), Anna Triandafyllidou and Sabrina Marchetti draw upon the new findings emerging from the individual chapters to discuss two main issues. First, they consider views and conceptions of gender roles (within the family and between the employer and the worker) and related notions of family, care, domestic work, comparing among the different countries and identifying, if possible, national patterns. Second, they reflect on how the welfare systems of the different countries studied in this volume affect the role of employers and the related labour market and other policy arrangements. This concluding chapter thus provides for a combined welfare and gender-sensitive typology of the countries and the 'type of employers' studied here, which will have also a wider validity for making sense of domestic work and care arrangements in Europe today.

References

Alemani, C., 2004. Le colf: ansie e desideri delle datrici di lavoro. *Polis*, 18, pp. 137–66.

Ambrosini, M., 2013. *Irregular Migration and Invisible Welfare*. New York: Palgrave Macmillan.

Anderson, B., 2007. A Very Private Business Exploring the Demand for Migrant Domestic Workers. *European Journal of Women's Studies*, 14, pp. 247–64.

Anderson, B., 2000. *Doing the Dirty Work? The Global Politics of Domestic Labor*. London, Zed Books.

Blunt, A. and Dowlings, R., 2006. *Home*. New York: Routledge.

Boris, E. and Parrenas, R.S., 2010. *Intimate Labors: Cultures, Technologies, and the Politics of Care*. Stanford, CA: Stanford University Press.

Cock, J., 1989. *Maids and Madams: Domestic Workers Under Apartheid*. London: Women's Press.

Constable, N., 1997. Sexuality and Discipline among Filipina Domestic Workers in Hong Kong. *American Ethnologist*, 24(3), pp. 539–58.

Cox, R. 2007. The au pair body: Sex object, sister or student? *European Journal of Women's Studies*, 14(3), pp. 281–96.

Cranford, C.J. and Miller, D., 2013. Emotion management from the client's perspective: the case of personal home care. *Work, Employment & Society*, 27(5), pp. 785–801.

Da Rott, B. and Weicht, B., 2013. Migrant care work and care, migration and employment regimes: A fuzzy-set analysis. *Journal of European Social Policy*, 23, pp. 469–86.

Daly, M., 2012. Making policy for care: experience in Europe and its implications in Asia. *International Journal of Sociology and Social Policy*, 32(11/12), pp. 623–35.

Davidoff, L., 2003. Gender and the 'Great Divide': Public and Private in British Gender History. *Journal of Women's History*, 15(1), pp. 11–26.

Douglas, M., 1979. *The World of Goods: Towards an Anthropology of Consumption*. New York/London: Routledge.

Ehrenreich, B. and Hochschild, A.R. (eds), 2002. *Global Women: Nannies, Maids and Sex Workers in the New Economy*. London: Granta Books.

Esping-Andersen, G., 1990. *The Three Worlds of Welfare Capitalism*, Princeton, NJ: Princeton University Press.

Esping-Andersen, G., (ed.), 1996. *Welfare States in Transition. Social Security in the New Global Economy*. London: Sage.

Ferrera, M., 2005. *The Boundaries of Welfare: European Integration and the New Spatial Politics of Social Protection*. Oxford: Oxford University Press.

Gallotti, M. 2009. *The Gender Dimension of Domestic Work in Western Europe*. Geneva: ILO.

Graziano, P.R., Jaquot, S. and Palier, B. (eds), 2011. *The EU and the Domestic Politics of Welfare State Reforms: Europa, Europae*. Basingstoke: Palgrave Macmillan.

Gregson, N. and Lowe, M., 1994. *Servicing the Middle Classes*. London: Routledge.

Gutierrez-Rodriguez, E., 2010. *Migration, Domestic Work and Affect: A Decolonial Approach on Value and the Feminization of Labor*. New York: Routledge.

Hochschild, A., 2012. *The Outsourced Self: Intimate Life in Market Times*. New York: Henry Holt and Company.

Hoerder, D., 2014. Historical Perspectives on Domestic and Caregiving Work: A Global Approach. In: D. Hoerder, S. Neunsinger and E. van Nederveen Meerkerk (eds), 2014. *A Global History of Domestic and Caregiving Work*. Leiden: Brill, in press.

Hondagneu-Sotelo, P., 2001. *Doméstica: Immigrant Workers Cleaning and Caring in the Shadows of Affluence*. Berkley, CA: University of California Press.

ILO, 2011. *Convention Concerning Decent Work for Domestic Workers n. C189.* Geneva: ILO.

Isaksen, L.W. (ed.), 2010. *Global Care Work. Gender and Migration in Nordic Societies.* Lund: Nordic Academic Press.

Kofman, E. 2012. Gendered labour migrations in Europe and emblematic migratory figures. *Journal of Ethnic and Migration Studies*, 39(4), pp. 579–600.

Kofman, E. and Raghuram, P., 2009. *The Implications of Migration for Gender and Care Regimes in the South.* Social Policy and Development Programme Paper Number 41, Geneva: United Nations Research Institute for Social Development.

Kristeva, J., 1980. *Pouvoirs de l'horreur: essai sur l'abjection.* Paris: Edition du Seuil.

Lan, P-C., 2006. *Global Cinderellas: Migrant Domestic Workers and Newly Rich Employers in Taiwan.* Durham and London: Duke University Press.

Leslie, D.A., 1993. Femininity, Post-Fordism and New Traditionalism. In: L. McDowell (ed.), 1993. *Space, Gender, Knowledge: Feminist Readings.* London: Arnold, pp. 171–97.

Lundstrom, C., 2012. 'Mistresses' and 'maids' in transnational 'contact zones': Expatriate wives and the intersection of difference and intimacy in Swedish domestic spaces in Singapore. *Women's Studies International Forum*, 36(1), pp. 44–53.

Lutz, H., 2011. *The New Maids: Transnational Women and the Care Economy.* London: Zed Books.

Marchetti, S., 2006. 'We had different fortunes': relationships between Filipina domestic workers and their employers in Rome and in Amsterdam. Master's Thesis, Universiteit Utrecht.

Massey, D., 1994. *Space, Place and Gender.* Cambridge: Polity Press.

Metz-Gockel, S. et al. (eds), 2008. *Migration and Mobility in an Enlarged Europe: a Gender Perspective.* Opladen: Barbara Budrich Publishers.

Momsen, J., 1999. Maids on the move. In: J. Momsen (ed.), 1999. *Gender, Migration and Domestic Service.* London: Routledge, pp. 1–21.

Mosse, G., 1985. *Nationalism and Sexuality. Respectability and Abnormal Sexuality in Modern Europe.* New York: Howard Fertig.

Nare, L., 2013. Migrancy, gender and social class in domestic labour and social care in Italy – an intersectional analysis of demand. *Journal of Ethnic and Migration Studies*, 39(4), pp. 601–23.

Näre, L., 2012. Moral encounters: Drawing boundaries of class, sexuality and migrancy in paid domestic work. *Ethnic and Racial Studies*, 37(2), pp. 1–18.

Palmer, P., 1989. *Domesticity and Dirt: Housewives and Domestic Servants in the United States, 1920–1945.* Philadelphia, PA: Temple University Press.

Parreñas, R.S., 2008. *The Force of Domesticity: Filipina Migrants and Globalization.* New York: NYU Press.

Parreñas, R.S., 2001. *Servants of Globalization: Women, Migration and Domestic Work.* Stanford, CA: Stanford University Press.

Ray, R. and Qayum, S., 2009. *Cultures of Servitude: Modernity, Domesticity, and Class in India*. Palo Alto, CA: Stanford University Press.

Repetto, Margherita, 2004. Donne e lavoro. In M. Ombra (ed.) *Donne manifeste*. Milano: Il Saggiatore.

Rollins, J., 1985. *Between Women: Domestics and Their Employers*. Philadelphia, PA: Temple University Press.

Ruhs, M. and Anderson, B. (eds), 2010. *Who Needs Migrant Workers?: Labour Shortages, Immigration, and Public Policy*. Oxford: Oxford University Press.

Sarti, R. 2007. The Globalisation of Domestic Service in a Historical Perspective. In: Lutz, H. (ed.), 2007. *Migration and Domestic Work: a European Perspective on a Global Theme*. Aldershot: Ashgate, pp. 77–98.

Triandafyllidou, A. (ed.), 2013. *Irregular Migrant Domestic Workers in Europe: Who Cares?* Aldershot: Ashgate Publishing.

Van Walsum, S., 2011. Regulating Migrant Domestic Work in the Netherlands: Opportunities and Pitfalls. *Canadian Journal of Women and the Law/Revue Femmes et Droit*, 23(1), pp. 141–65.

Vega Solis, C., 2009. *Culturas del cuidado en transición: Espacios, sujetos e imaginarios en una sociedad de migración*. Barcelona: Editorial UOC.

Williams, F., 2012. Converging variations in migrant care work in Europe. *Journal of European Social Policy*, 22(4), pp. 363–76.

Yeates, N., 2009. *Globalizing Care Economies and Migrant Workers: Explorations in Global Care Chains*. New York: Palgrave Macmillan.

Yeoh, B. and S. Huang, 1999. Singapore Women and Foreign Domestic Workers. Negotiating Domestic Work and Motherhood. In: J. Momsen (ed.), 1999. *Gender, Migration and Domestic Service*. London/New York: Routledge, pp. 273–96.

Zelizer, V.A., 2009. *The Purchase of Intimacy*. Princeton, NJ: Princeton University Press.

PART I
Everyday Negotiations through the Employers' Eyes

Chapter 2

Employers as 'Care Managers': Contracts, Emotions and Mutual Obligations within Italy's Invisible Welfare System

Maurizio Ambrosini

This chapter focuses on the perspective of employers within what I call 'invisible welfare': a system of elderly assistance operating in parallel with the official welfare system, managed by families and based on the work of migrants, mainly women, and often irregular (Ambrosini 2013; Triandafyllidou 2013). In Italy, according to various estimates, this distinctive care regime involves between 500,000 and 1,600,000 workers (Censis-Fondazione Ismu 2012); this is certainly a number higher than that of the workers employed by the National Health Service (about 400,000). But other Southern European countries, like Spain (León 2010) and Greece (Lyberaki 2008), share the same 'curoscape' (Lopez 2012); and in central Europe, Austria and Germany are moving in the same direction (Gendera 2011; Lutz and Palenga- Möllenbeck 2010). Fiona Williams has talked of 'converging variations in migrant care work in Europe' (Williams 2012, p. 363).

In Italy, the evolution of the role of traditional care providers (previously the women of the family) is of foremost importance in the advent of this parallel welfare system, which is often subsidised by the state through *cash for care* allowances. Thus Italian families today have shifted from direct care provision to the management of a care system centred around the figure of a paid care worker (Bettio, Simonazzi and Villa 2006; Da Roit 2007; Tognetti Bordogna and Ornaghi 2012; Van Hooren 2010). This solution has enabled numerous adult women, culturally loaded with the burden of care for fragile members of the family, to combine participation in the labour market, care of the family and looking after elderly parents (Catanzaro and Colombo 2009).

I call this new role the 'care manager' (see also Degiuli 2010). Yet, these care managers often struggle to see themselves as employers. They know they have to manage an employment relationship, but they actually experience it as a much denser and more multifaceted interpersonal relationship, with all the ambiguities that may arise (Triandafyllidou and Kosic 2006).

I shall explore this issue on the basis of qualitative data gathered in the northern Italian regions of Lombardy, Liguria and Trentino-Alto Adige.

Sources

The results presented in this chapter come mainly from two research studies conducted in Northern Italy some years ago, where employers of immigrant care workers were directly interviewed. The first one was an inquiry into the regularisation process of 2002–03, based on 420 structured interviews with migrant workers. Both men and women were involved in the procedure carried out in Milan in 2003 in various centres (Caritas, trade unions and others) offering advice and support for the submission of regularisation applications (116 domestic workers, 159 company employees, 131 unemployed at the time of the interview); 14 qualitative interviews with Italian care managers; and 13 qualitative interviews with company employees (Ambrosini and Salati 2004).

The second study drew on qualitative research conducted in 2004 on the work of immigrant women in the 'live-in' home-care of elderly Italians in the areas of Milan and Brescia (Lombardy region). The following people were interviewed: 11 members of staff at agencies matching labour supply and demand (mainly NGOs, voluntary associations, services related to trade unions); 17 foreign workers, aged between 24 and 50, mainly from Eastern Europe and Latin America; 5 elderly people with carers; and 14 Italian care managers (mainly sons and daughters of elderly people requiring care) (Ambrosini and Cominelli 2005).

In other research studies that I have conducted in various regions of Northern Italy (Lombardia, Liguria and Trentino) in subsequent years, the attitudes of care managers was studied through the voices of immigrant care workers (Ambrosini and Boccagni 2007; Ambrosini and Abbatecola 2010; Ambrosini, Bonizzoni and Caneva 2010; Boccagni and Ambrosini 2012). Also these results will be used in the analysis presented in this chapter.

How Care Givers Become Care Managers

The employment relationship around which invisible welfare rotates is a triangular one. Formally, the employer is the elderly person receiving the care. Besides him/her, a large part of the practical management of the employment relationship is undertaken by another family member, usually a daughter; or if not, by a son, a daughter-in-law or another relative. This person is the 'care manager'.

Entrusting care to a person external to the family enables the children to avoid part of the emotional labour of a relationship that has entirely reversed the role of parent and child, making the child become the main care-giver of their parent:

> The problem is that the children or the reference kinship figures are so exhausted by the work that the relationship [with the elderly] requires around the clock … because they are out or exasperated … So people like G. [the immigrant care worker] make it possible that the relationship is delegated [to somebody else] for some hours during the day so when relationship is again in your hands, you can

handle it with a bit more serenity and lucidity [because you were released for some hours], because otherwise you get so resentful … (Care Manager [C.M.], interview no. 5, daughter, 59 years old, cit. in Antonioli and Cominelli, 2005, p.127).

The switch from the role of care-giver to that of care manager entails a psychological and organisational recodification of the relationship with the elderly person. It means opening the doors of the home, the intimate space *par excellence*, to a stranger who will live in the home as long as she/he is needed. This is a difficult decision, which is taken with hesitancy and apprehension. Consequently of importance are what we may call 'trust intermediaries': people or institutions endowed with moral or professional authority that help with putting the future care manager in contact with the care worker to be hired. The following case is interesting because it evokes the figure of the family doctor as an authority who guarantees the reliability of an ethnic stereotype, but at the same time persuades a hesitant family to accept an immigrant live-in care worker:

The doctor told us: 'Look, you can't force her to keep on someone she doesn't like. And it's damaging to her health if she doesn't like a person. If she is so negative towards this person, then change her. I recommend a Peruvian, because Peruvians are particularly suited to the care of the elderly. They have traditions of great reverence and respect for the elderly, so they have a lot of patience' (Care manager, cit. in Corrias, 2004, pp. 82–3).

Even when prospective Italian employers make use of external services, they tend to go to religious institutions, parishes or congregations. These are viewed, on the one hand, as guarantors of the worker's morality and reliability, and on the other, as witnesses to the fact that hiring an irregular immigrant can be justified as a humanitarian gesture. From this derives the importance of Catholic organisations in the domestic sector in Italy (Andall 2000) – although probably more so in the early stages of the phenomenon than thereafter, when the migrant networks became more autonomous and self-fuelling.

These networks have become the main channels of recruitment used by employers. For them, trust relationships, brokerage by people known to them and accredited and word of mouth are the factors that determine hiring choices, especially when they involve letting strangers into the intimate space of the home and entrusting frail and dependent persons to them. Typically, the worker introduces and guarantees a relative or co-national who will substitute her if necessary:

Last Christmas she went away for three weeks, she returned to Romania and one of her relatives substituted for her, an aunt I think, who came from Piedmont to take her place for those weeks. The other girl found one for Easter … I mean, she promised not to go on holiday until she'd found a substitute, and that's what she did (Interview with Care Manager, son about 45 years old, cit. in Cominelli 2005, p.184).

Perhaps in Italy more than in other countries, personal links are worth more than formal certifications and credits, and they are preferred to the use of intermediary agencies and professional services, even when these exist as is recounted by an interviewee:

> So, what I would distrust is going to an agency. ... [An] agency makes me a bit wary. I'd say, 'Why am I in an agency, when there is this word of mouth that I have never been without, never ... a friend, that friend, I've got a Filipino man, I've got a Filipino woman, my cousin, my grandmother' ... so the idea of going to an agency to find someone, this is what makes me a bit wary ... If I was on my own because R. had left, I'd go to M., I'd go to the Filipino, I'd go to the doctor to ask if there was a Romanian girl ... right? Rather than going to an agency (Interview no. 12, with Care Manager, cit. in Corrias, 2004, pp. 79–80).

Due to reliance on networks as the main channels for the recruitment of workers, one observes the formation of stereotypes in Italian families, as in many other countries. In the following excerpt, the collectivising stereotype operates ambivalently: on the one hand, with generalised praise for the professional skill of immigrants; while on the other, with censure for their 'mercenary' attitude to care work. This reveals that many employers do not want to buy labour services alone, but also genuine affective commitment:

> The Eastern [European] countries are countries where this type of work is done, maybe they're very good, but they do it because they have to ... those countries are devastated, so where there is no family, where everything has fallen apart, they're here for work purposes, and that's it. So they're purely economic, and it's very noticeable (Interview with Care Manager, daughter about 40 years old, cit. in Davi, 2005, p. 116).

The highly informal configuration of this care regime and the fact that immigrants (above all: female immigrants) are the main providers of labour concur in the devaluation of the occupation of domestic care worker. The term *badante* commonly used in Italian to denote the carers for elderly people[1] is indicative of this devaluation: literally, *badare* means 'to supervise' or 'watch over'. In fifteenth-century Italian it denoted a minder of livestock. Today, the term has been transposed to the 'surveillance' of elderly people in need. On the one hand, it belittles the various activities of housekeeping, personal care and emotional support that workers actually perform; while on the other hand, it emphasises only one aspect, perceived as the most critical and necessary one: the continuous monitoring of the person being cared for, independently solving simple problems and raising the alarm in the case of more serious crises.

---

1   For a discussion see: Sarti, 2011.

In regard to the work of home-carers, many of the employers interviewed by Asher Colombo (2007) commented that there were not many things to do, that they did not require much effort and that they gave the carer a great deal of free time. The work consisted substantially in 'keeping an eye' on the elderly person and 'being present' in the house for any need that might arise. In fact, the tasks performed, although varying from one situation to another, are much more complex and delicate than this. They range among household chores, feeding tasks, cleaning the person and nursing care (administering medications, giving injections, treating bedsores).

Striking in the following passage is the description of a work-day with an elderly person as 'very normal', and the use of the plural to describe the sharing of household chores, although the respondent admits in passing that his mother is no longer able to do the housework:

> A typical day is the day of an ordinary woman who has to run a household: she gets up, makes breakfast, they do the housework, or she does the housework ... because my mother doesn't do those [tasks] any more[;] they do the shopping, cook, in short, a normal day, very normal (Interview with Care Manager, son about 45 years old, cit. in Antonioli and Cominelli, 2005, p. 129).

When care is provided to old men, employers are less likely to describe the work of live-in carers as some sort of joint cooperation. But many descriptions still tended to give a reductive interpretation of their work as this daughter describes: 'He doesn't need much, he doesn't need help with either washing or getting up. He just needs someone to be with him, do the shopping, prepare food, keep the house' (Interview with Care Manager, interview no. 5, daughter, 59 years old, cit. in Antonioli and Cominelli, 2005, p. 135).

Actually, even though the work is described in such dismissive terms, the expectations of elderly care recipients, care managers and families as a whole are very different. They need someone to perform complex and delicate functions in nurturing, listening and providing emotional support, not to mention bodily hygiene and health care, tasks traditionally undertaken by family members – more precisely, by adult women in the family. Many families purchase labour, but what they actually want is affection. In the following excerpt, the care manager complains that the worker, although irreproachable in terms of her professional services, does not give what the mother needs: empathic communication, companionship and moral support. The son describes the care and emotional needs below:

> Then, the judgment is very positive, because, I repeat, for us it was a great relief. Of course, she also has some faults, but ... Her main fault is that she is very shy, very reserved, not very talkative, so my mother is at home as if she has nobody there. It's a bit because she speaks the language badly, but in any case she can now speak Italian quite well, but she is a very reserved person, you know, shy. Instead, the first one that we had ... the first care worker was energetic, a sunny

person in the sense that … she gave my mama a shock (Interview with Care Manager, son about 45 years old, cit. in Antonioli and Cominelli, 2005, p. 149).

Another care manager, in this case a middle-aged son, lucidly described the care worker's central importance for management of balances in the family, the emotional dependence of the elderly parents on her, and the fear of losing her:

> We soon saw her human qualities and, after some time, now, she is like a daughter. It's clear that I'm the only family member, and then also all our relatives came to appreciate her and care about her. Even all the relatives that have met her greatly respect her. … Ah, yes, she's become like a member of the family, but because we need her, because one of the dramas that I've seen, and it is a dramatic situation, is when after an emotional attachment has formed, after a year, for example, the foreign lady has to leave, and then it becomes a real tragedy, because she's become a point of reference. Before, I was the point of reference, but now … In fact, when I come here to my parents, they do nothing but ask 'Where's E.?' If they need something, they want her (Interview with Care Manager, son about 50 years old, cit. in Cominelli, 2005, p. 171).

Care Managers' Functions

Once the employment relationship has been established, a first function performed by the care manager is to mediate between the care worker and the elderly person, balancing their needs and expectations. As long as the health of the care recipients permits it, they can make their voices heard: they are not the passive patients of a care system, but can express preferences, pleasure or dissatisfaction in regard to the care that they receive. They can decide to maintain distances, to assume a despotic stance, or they may choose to become emotionally involved in a relationship of confidence and affection with the care worker. Care managers must supervise care recipients in their relationships with care workers, moderating their demands in order to reduce strains and conflicts. At other times, the mediation concerns relationships with other relatives, who want to intervene and often criticise the care worker. Care managers usually defend care workers: they do not want to upset the balances that have been established as we can see below:

> … they all have something to say. I've got three sisters, one lives in Rwanda but when she comes here she always has something to say, then she goes back to Rwanda. But certain things that N. [the immigrant care worker] does or doesn't do, are never right. And also the other two sisters say the usual things: things are not clean enough, it's untidy … but they should also try to understand (Interview with Care Manager, son, 40 years old, cit. in Cominelli, 2005, p. 168).

Apparent in yet other cases are forms of mediation among the needs of the various persons involved in the care delivery: for instance, use of the cared-for person's home by the care worker to enjoy social meetings. In these cases, with the tacit consent of the elderly persons and their care managers, family assistants take turns to socialise with friends and colleagues in the homes of those they care for by organising small parties. They thus meet their twofold need to stay close to the elderly person and to meet other care workers in sheltered places (especially in winter). These agreements sometimes give also the elderly person opportunities to socialise (Cominelli 2005, p. 179).

A second function of care managers is managing the employment relationship. It is usually the care manager who pays the care worker's wages. It is with him or her that the care worker discusses contractual conditions: wages, working hours, time off and holidays. It is him or her that the care worker asks to be regularised when the opportunity arises. It is from him or her that the care worker receives instructions on aspects such as schedules and the ingredients of meals, rest times and outings with the elderly person, the administering of medicine or other medical treatment. Moreover, the care manager is the reference point in cases of emergency and for all needs that go beyond ordinary administration. It is to the care manager that the care worker reports the elderly person's health problems, asks about what should be done and implements the decisions taken. The care manager fulfils his/her care obligations by interposing the care worker between him/herself and the elderly person. S/he remains involved but defends his/her private life by being responsible and active but not in the front line, so to speak. The care manager delegates the more strenuous activities and tasks of constant supervision of the elderly person cared for, but he/she has to manage the caring relationship at a distance, to provide support and fill the gaps. Here one finds a gender difference: male care managers tend to delegate more and distance themselves more from the care worker and her needs. Female care managers more often remain at the forefront in taking charge of replacing the worker on her days or hours of rest, doing activities together with the elderly person and interacting with the care worker.

Thirdly, the care manager attends to administrative and economic matters. The care worker leaves it to the care manager to deal with every task of this kind: making necessary purchases, paying bills and so on. The care manager also handles relations with the public services, principally the care recipient's doctor(s) and the health service. S/he is the principal link between the elderly, the care worker and external society with its institutions as this care manager describes:

> Specific duties are those of the type ... you know, bureaucratic ... you know, going to the bank, paying bills, getting the documents for her tax returns, things like that ... All that part of the home management, the service charges, everything else, that is, day-to-day and current expenses are her job. My mother now has regular medical examinations, so all these things are my responsibility, all the rest, the normal management of the house is M's [the care worker] (Interview with Care Manager, son about 45 years old, cit. in Antonioli and Cominelli, 2005, p. 138).

The care manager is then responsible for supervision and control of the care worker as this interview illustrates:

> I previously had a lady who came to look after my dad, and it was fine with me. I liked her. She'd already looked after two ladies in our village until they passed away. She was good, alert, she went around on her bike. But then she got herself a boyfriend here in the village and, unfortunately, there were some minor episodes ... She was very nice, good, bright, but she went off at one o'clock in the afternoon and didn't come back till evening. I couldn't put up with that! I couldn't keep on checking whether or not she was there (Interview with Care Manager, daughter, 59 years old, cit. in Cominelli, 2005, p. 179).

The Care Manager as Gate-keeper

What makes care managers of key importance for immigration policy is the fact that they very often play a crucial role at a decisive point in the migratory careers of care workers: the acquisition of the status of legal resident. In repeated regularisation campaigns (seven in 25 years), the Italian state has granted employers the faculty to regularise the positions of the irregular immigrants working for them. It is therefore the employer who decides whether an immigrant worker will acquire legal status and that of a lawful worker. In the case of domestic and care work – the sector in which most regularisations have occurred in recent years – this decision is substantially taken by the care manager.

The following example illustrates the widespread and almost banal nature of irregularity, the ability of employer families to move without too many problems between the legal and informal domestic-care markets (Bonizzoni 2013) and the coverage provided by Italian NGOs, in this case a religious congregation:

> That first one, yes, she was hired regularly, this one, no, because the regularizing process is blocked. So she's here illegally ... Can I say that? I talked to the nuns, and they told me that now it's not possible, and I asked them how to act if somebody stops us. They told me to answer that C. is under their protection, and when the time comes [to be regularised] they will let me know. Then we'll put everything in order. ... It's important to put them in order, for them but also for us, if they get hurt ... well, it's always a risk. But the nun told me so, and I'm pretty calm. But I hope to regularise her soon (Interview with Care Manager, daughter-in-law, about 55 years old, cit. in Antonioli and Cominelli, 2005, p. 143).

The idea of a deliberate endeavour to keep the worker in illegality so as to protract a situation of asymmetric power relations and severe exploitation is contradicted by the willingness – as confirmed by the data on regularisations – of numerous families to regularise the employment relationship. It is relationally and psychologically difficult to maintain such a particular relationship based on cohabitation in the restricted space of the home, to entrust loved ones to a person external to the family, to grant her full responsibility and great autonomy in everyday management and then deny her the right to acquire the dignity of regular immigrant status and a formal work contract.

This step is sometimes taken with a certain enthusiasm, with a sense of fulfilling an ethical obligation, or at least relief at resolving a situation perceived as threatening and potentially embarrassing as seen in the two interviews below:

> We were waiting for the amnesty just like manna from heaven, and as soon as the regularisation was announced, we applied for it (Interview no. 10, cit. in Corrias, 2004, p. 96).

> Because I find it absolutely fair! Because they have rights, because there are rights and duties[. T]hey perform their duties, why shouldn't they have rights? And it also sets my mind at rest, it seems right after all! (Interview no. 12, cit. in Corrias, 2004, p. 96).

In other cases, use of the regularisation procedure is less spontaneous and induced by fear of sanctions. It is felt to be an unnecessary burden, almost an injustice, but it still occurs – as in the following testimony:

> It's the law; we must do it … If we don't, they can cause you problems because they're always right. I've always paid, I've always left her free, and she's lived in the family … but, unfortunately, you don't know who you are dealing with. Because I have friends who've had foreign domestic workers [and] they gave them everything, they had their children come here, helped them, and then one complained, and the unions say that the worker is always right, and so, you understand? But I wanted to be regular in these things anyway. Apart from that, it costs, but what can I do? (Interview no. 13, in Corrias, 2004, p. 96).

Note that in this case, as in many others, regularisation is depicted as a concession, a 'favour' done by employers for their employees. Indeed, it is common in Italy to saddle workers with the costs of a procedure[2] and bureaucracy which, until recently, was long and difficult, with hours of queuing, even at night, and repeated returns to the designated offices. The practice of declaring the minimum number of hours worked necessary to obtain permission to stay – lower than the actual number – is widespread. Sometimes, the employment relationship is subsequently dissolved, and the employment relationship returns to the black economy. In other

---

2   The Italian state, on the occasion of the regularization, requires employers to pay a lump sum in compensation for the social security contributions evaded. In the last but one amnesty (September 2009), the amount was 500 euros per worker regularized; in the latest regularisation (September–October 2012), the amount was doubled to 1,000 euros per worker.

words, the care worker maintains a regular status of residence, but becomes an informal worker. This care manager describes the relationship as follows:

> No, I don't feel like her employer, even if, alas, I must be, in the sense that every month I have to pay her wages, I have to show her that I pay the contributions, and so on, but I don't feel like an employer[;] I feel more like a person who pays because I have need of her, not her of me, that is, we don't feel ourselves to be employers. But also because the relationship that has developed is a quite relaxed one ... we ask her to stay in for weekend and she asks us if she can leave maybe a day early, because she has to go somewhere. If we can do it, why not? But an employer, no, anything but. The real problem is that in reality we have to act as employers, because with the regularisation of these people there is a whole bureaucratic part that needs to be kept under control (Interview with Care Manager, son about 45 years, cit. in Antonioli and Cominelli, 2005, p. 142).

A Working Relationship without Borders

Perhaps the most peculiar and controversial aspect of domestic care is its mix of work and private life, of the professional, personal and emotional spheres. As regards care managers, especially when they are women dealing with other women (the care workers), this situation translates into a tendency to become involved in the problems and needs of the worker, and sometimes of her family network. Whether the elderly care worker has health issues, needs economic help, has love problems or wants to promote the arrival and employment of any relative, the care manager tends to become enmeshed in the private and family life of the immigrant woman. This results in interest and involvement in the life of care workers and forms of support unthinkable in other labour relations, as well as invasions of space, feelings and relationships pertaining to the private sphere. Sometimes these conflicting relationships occur at the same time.

Many care managers assume roles not formally pertaining to them in order to support care workers in very serious difficulties, as when they provide aid that goes well beyond their contractual obligations (Tognetti Bordogna 2009). Hence, as Lutz (2011, p. 110) points out, the relationship between the parties involved is framed by mutual uncertainty regarding modes of address and designations, lacking in rule systems and established behavioural conventions. On the one hand, they cannot be seen as simple exploiter-exploited relationships; on the other, they are clearly characterised by multiple interlocking asymmetries. Family designations, involvement in the personal and family problems of care workers and various other forms of help can be seen as attempts to mask the differences in status and power. In these two interview excerpts, for example, the care managers claim that they 'know everything' about the lives and family affairs of the care workers:

Yes, I know everything about her family … everything about her mother … we know everything. Then I've met two of her brothers, who are also here in Italy, them as well … and now there's another brother here with his wife, and we know him too. Yes, by now I know everything about her family (Interview with Care Manager, daughter-in-law, 72 years old, cit. in Cominelli, 2005, p. 163).

… she tells me everything, that she's now got a house in Ukraine, she has a son and a grandson who wants to get married, but she's not very happy about it. When she goes out with her friends on Sundays, she always tells me where they've been and what they've done. No, she tells me everything (Interview with Care Manager, daughter, 59 years old, cit. in Cominelli, 2005, p. 163).

But care workers can turn this involvement into a resource useful for their needs and projects. In the following testimony, it is interesting to note the expression 'the social worker of the lady', that is, her care manager. In the perception of the immigrant care worker, the care manager had created a contact so direct and effective that she presented the Italian social worker as if she were at the disposal of the 'lady'. The woman had no clear understanding of procedures, but she knew how to get clear information and the help that she needed:

The person who helped me was the social worker of the lady. But she is a very dear person, if I ask her she helps me. She gave me a hand for the renewal of residence permit. Not anymore, because now you have to go to the post office. I do not understand anything! But when I need her, she is there! She's s a very good person (Interview with Care Manager, Mabel, cit. in Abbatecola, 2010, p. 121).

Care managers very frequently give loans to care workers or advances on their wages as we see from what this care worker recounts:

Yes, she helped me when my dad was sick for a month and a half. I asked for economic help, a loan, and they gave it to me. They were helpful (Interview with Care Worker, Peruvian, 24 years old, cit. in Cominelli, 2005, p. 170).

In another case, the husband of the care manager acted as a financial advisor and did not hesitate to intervene in the economic relations between the care worker and her family in the homeland as this care worker states:

Mister M. opened a bank account for me, and he told me: 'Put some money in the bank, because it's not right that you give everything to others!' But it's not easy, in our country they don't pay from month to month, so I send money to my son (Interview with Care Worker, Moldovan, about 50 years old, cit. in Cominelli, 2005, p. 170).

Another important aspect is intervention by care managers to enable care workers to access public services, especially health care. At times they circumvent the rules that restrict access by irregular immigrants. In the relationships with public services, where interpretative and discretionary margins can be found, employers mediate, insist and protest, bringing into play their knowledge and their ability to influence civil servants, social workers and decision-makers. The care manager below explains of his assistance:

> She has also had, poor thing ... she also went into depression and luckily we came out of it ... but I have seen bad moments, because I did not know what to do, because I know that if I sent her to hospital with these diseases here, the hospital may find the right treatment, but most of the time with these problems ... and if you are sent to the department of psychiatry and they begin to bomb you with psychiatric drugs ... I had my father who is perpetually depressed and I had met at the Centre for Public Health (CPS) a physician ... and I called her and told her: 'Look, I have this problem here ...' and she told me: 'Take her to me and let's see ...' and thankfully now she has come out well, but she had reached a point where she said that she did not want to live anymore (Interview with Care Manager, son, about 50 years old, cit. in Cominelli, 2005, p. 170).

The other side of the coin is the expectation of the availability of the care worker that goes beyond the terms of the contract. Although arrangements concerning days off and holidays have been regulated more closely, cases of abuse persist even in formal employment relationships. This care worker describes her situation where she had no free time:

> What can I do? He's on his own. There's nobody who can substitute me and give me a hand. The lady [the care manager] can come when I have to go into town, to the post office to send a parcel home, or when I go to buy something that I really need. Otherwise I'm here. I don't have anybody to substitute me, and the lady says that she wouldn't trust another person to look after him. Also because he can't see, and there's nobody to keep check on things here. I said to the lady: 'Look, on Sunday ... during the week I can be here all day, but on Sunday I have my life, a friend I can talk to'. Now he doesn't sleep any more, not even at night. He talks the whole night, I can't get to sleep. I told the lady: 'Look, on Sunday I'll get the gentleman dressed, I'll give him something to eat, I'll clean him up, and then I'll go out'. But it didn't last long, because I had to feed him at twelve o'clock, and I went out at four ... but it was too late to go and see my friends, and if I went, I had to return immediately (Interview with Care Worker, Chilean, 54 years old, cit. in Cominelli, 2005, p. 177).

It should be emphasised that the mix of work and emotions, of family relationships and contractual ones is not just a strategy of employers-care managers to obtain greater effort from the care workers, or even to exploit them. This type of relationship may also be solicited by the care workers themselves. Ironically, part of the dissatisfaction expressed by some care workers that came to the fore in the last survey conducted in Trentino (Boccagni and Ambrosini 2012) concerned attempts by employers to compress the emotional component of the relationship. Sometimes, the negative judgment of live-in care work arises from the aloofness manifested by the elderly person or, perhaps more often, by the care manager. This is exacerbated by the fact that this environment – the household – demands human warmth, flexibility and a personal relationship which is very difficult to define by a contract. The literal application of the provisions of a contract is unlikely to give rise to a relationship that is satisfactory to both parties. For instance, an experience of dissatisfaction, notwithstanding formal observance of the rights of workers, emerged repeatedly in the interview with T, a Ukrainian care worker. Striking in her narrative was the desire to express her care for the elderly person also in terms of dialogue and relationship. When the attempt to establish a meaningful bond meets resistance, and the experience of care work is reduced to the mechanical provision of a sequence of material aids, this may prove even more difficult to bear. It was on the basis of the quality of the relationship with the elderly person and the family that T distinguished among the families with which she had worked for several years and those which she had left after a few months:

> She [the elderly care recipient] told me very often: 'Your chit-chat is absolutely no use to me. I need your work'. So work was like, 'This curtain must be so, five centimetres here five centimetres can't be here. With these saucepans you must only cook this food and not that ...' So, everything was regulated. [Since] I'm a pretty creative person, for me it was a disaster ... In families where I worked for a long time, they always told me ... there was a dialogue between us, they always asked how things were going, what the situation was, how my mama was ... There was close contact ... I consider myself an open person and I want ... how to say ... to dialogue with people. For example, I assisted an elderly couple, they also told me how the work had to be done. As for their personalities I was ... for them I was like a useful thing in the house, like a vacuum cleaner, like a washing machine, something like that. As a person, as a personality, for them I did not exist. This is something absolutely unacceptable for me. But maybe some people would accept it (Interview with Ukrainian care worker, 59 years old, in Italy for 12 years, cit. in Boccagni and Ambrosini, 2012, p. 83).

The idea often proposed of tying domestic work to the general scheme of any employment relationship clashes with the inevitable proximity between the parties that cohabitation entails. Neither care managers, nor care workers, or elderly care-recipients express any great enthusiasm for the idea of cooling relationships by adopting the impersonal codes of a standard employer/employee relationship. Certainly, care managers are very peculiar, and often involuntarily, employers.

Concluding Remarks: Care Managers and the Social Order

The invisible welfare system of elderly care in Italy and southern Europe was brought about by the contradictions amongst the welfare regime, care regime and immigration regime. The southern European welfare system is skewed towards families as the suppliers of services for the elderly (Ferrera 2009). The socially approved conventions on appropriate care require adult women to provide it within the household. In principle, immigration policies do not envisage – or do so to only a very limited extent – admission into the country of female immigrants for work in the care sector. Especially in Italy, a series of restrictive provisions, allegedly introduced for the purposes of security, have been intended to combat irregular immigration and those who encourage or use it.

The political will to defend borders and the central importance given to households as providers of personal services have a common origin which we can identify as the desire to preserve the social order. Both instances refer to the vision of a stable, cohesive society able with its own resources to satisfy its needs for labour and care. In times of great turbulence and uncertainty about the future, the need for stability increases and results in political demands: governments seek to meet these demands by claiming that they have closed the borders and by calling on families to perform their traditional tasks, possibly subsidising those that must cope with increased care loads.

The two instances, closure of borders and commitment of families in care duties, however, are conflicting. This is demonstrated everyday by families that resort to the underground market for irregular immigrant labour so that they can continue to provide home-care for elderly relatives who depend on them. Confirmation of the centrality of the family as the locus of care and response to fragility contradicts immigration rules, and effective compliance with the restrictive provisions would upset the 'curoscape' (Lopez 2012) which is based on the family. This would require a much greater deployment of public services of various kinds, as well as a change of cultural paradigms regarding the most appropriate sites and methods for meeting social needs, especially for elderly care.

As a consequence, the care managers become key actors in the restructuring of the care regime from the bottom up. They are the main actors responsible for the transformation of dreaded irregular immigrants into deserving care workers. They act as employers in the informal labour market to solve the contradiction between restrictions to economic immigration on the one hand, and the expectation that families continue to provide the basic services for the frail and elderly on the other.

This silent and particularistic arrangement struggles to generate cultural awareness and political change. Italian society – of which families and care managers are an important part – continues to prefer policies of closure towards irregular immigrants and their punishment. But Italians then breach privately the rules that they have approved in the public arena.

One of the consequences of this ambiguity is the difficulty of introducing measures for the better management of invisible welfare, to the advantage of the employed and employers. Such measures could include the creation of an external agency as the employer of care workers, so that elderly persons and their families assume the role of service beneficiaries; the sharing of a care worker's labour among two or three elderly persons, at least during the day; improving the linkage between formal services and informal welfare; strengthening systems midway between home care and sheltered housing (Ambrosini 2013). Informality apparently gives more power to care managers and more flexibility to service management, but in the end it proves an unsatisfactory solution to the huge social challenge of caring for the elderly.

References

Abbatecola, E., 2010. Essere madri e padri a distanza In: M. Ambrosini and E. Abbatecola (eds), 2010. *Famiglie in movimento. Separazioni, legami, ritrovamenti nelle famiglie migranti*. Genova: Il melangolo. pp. 91–130.

Ambrosini, M., 2013. *Irregular Migration and Invisible Welfare*. Basingstoke: Palgrave-MacMillan.

Ambrosini, M. and Abbatecola, E. (eds), 2010. *Famiglie in movimento. Separazioni, legami, ritrovamenti nelle famiglie migranti*. Genova: Il melangolo.

Ambrosini, M. and Boccagni, P., 2007. *Il cuore in patria. Madri migranti e affetti lontani: le famiglie transnazionali in Trentino*. Trento: CINFORMI (Centro informativo per l'immigrazione), Provincia di Trento.

Ambrosini, M. and Cominelli, C. (eds), 2005. *Un'assistenza senza confini. Welfare 'leggero', famiglie in affanno, aiutanti domiciliari immigrate*. Milano: Osservatorio regionale per l'integrazione e la multietnicità, Regione Lombardia.

Ambrosini, M. and Salati, M. (eds), 2004. *Uscendo dall'ombra. Il processo di regolarizzazione degli immigrati e i suoi limiti*. Milano: FrancoAngeli.

Ambrosini, M., Bonizzoni, P. and Caneva, E., 2010. *Ritrovarsi altrove. Famiglie ricongiunte e adolescenti di origine immigrata*. Milano: Osservatorio regionale per l'integrazione e la multietnicità, Regione Lombardia.

Andall, J., 2000. *Gender, Migration and Domestic Service. The Politics of Black Women in Italy*. Aldershot: Ashgate.

Antonioli L. and Cominelli C., 2005. La dimensione del rapporto di lavoro: ruoli e vissuti a confronto. In: M. Ambrosini and C. Cominelli (eds), 2005. *Un'assistenza senza confini. Welfare 'leggero', famiglie in affanno, aiutanti domiciliari immigrate*. Milano: Osservatorio regionale per l'integrazione e la multietnicità, Regione Lombardia, pp. 125–58.

Bettio, F., Simonazzi, A. and Villa, P., 2006. Change in Care Regimes and Female Migration: The 'Care Drain' in the Mediterranean. *Journal of European Social Policy*, 16(3), pp. 271–85.

Boccagni, P. and Ambrosini, M., 2012. *Cercando il benessere nelle migrazioni. L'esperienza delle assistenti familiari straniere in Trentino*. Milano: FrancoAngeli.

Bonizzoni, P., 2013. Undocumented Domestic Workers in Italy: Surviving and Regularizing Strategies. In: A. Triandafyllidou (ed.), 2013. *Irregular Domestic Workers in Europe: Who Cares?* Aldershot: Ashgate, pp. 135–60.

Catanzaro, R. and Colombo, A. (eds), 2009. *Badanti & Co. Il lavoro domestico straniero in Italia*. Bologna: Il Mulino.

Censis-Fondazione Ismu, 2012. *Elaborazione di un modello previsionale del fabbisogno di servizi assistenziali alla persona nel mercato del lavoro italiano con particolare riferimento al contributo della popolazione straniera*, Final Report. Roma: Ministero del lavoro e delle politiche sociali.

Colombo, E., 2007. L'estranea di casa: la relazione quotidiana tra datori di lavoro e badanti. In: E. Colombo and G. Semi (eds), 2007. *Multiculturalismo quotidiano. Le pratiche della differenza*. Milano: FrancoAngeli, pp. 99–127.

Cominelli, C., 2005. Obbligazioni extracontrattuali: le attese e i comportamenti. In: M. Ambrosini and C. Cominelli (eds), 2005. *Un'assistenza senza confini. Welfare 'leggero', famiglie in affanno, aiutanti domiciliari immigrate.* Milano: Osservatorio regionale per l'integrazione e la multietnicità, Regione Lombardia, pp. 159–88.

Corrias, R., 2004. Tra prestazioni di servizio e legami personali. Rapporti di lavoro e processo di regolarizzazione nel settore domestico-assistenziale. In: M. Ambrosini and M. Salati (eds), 2004. *Uscendo dall'ombra. Il processo di regolarizzazione degli immigrati e i suoi limiti*. Milano: FrancoAngeli, pp. 78–99.

Da Roit, B., 2007. Changing Internal Solidarities Within Families in a Mediterranean Welfare State: Elderly Care in Italy. *Current Sociology*, 55, (2), pp. 251–69.

Davi, M., 2005. Donna e migrante. Il genere tra vincolo e risorsa. In: M. Ambrosini and C. Cominelli (eds), 2005. *Un'assistenza senza confini. Welfare 'leggero', famiglie in affanno, aiutanti domiciliari immigrate*. Milano: Osservatorio regionale per l'integrazione e la multietnicità, Regione Lombardia, pp. 103–23.

Degiuli, Francesca, 2010. The burden of long-term care: How Italian family care-givers become employers. *Ageing and Society*, 30, (5), pp. 755–77.

Ferrera, M., 2009. The South European Countries. In: S. Leibfried (ed.)., 2009. *The Oxford Handbook of Comparative Welfare States*. Oxford: Oxford University Press.

Gendera, S., 2011. Gaining an Insight into Central European Transnational Care Spaces: Migrant Live-in Care Workers in Austria. In: M. Bommes and G. Sciortino (eds), 2011. *Irregular Migration, European Labour Markets and the Welfare State*. Amsterdam: Amsterdam University Press, pp. 91–115.

León, M., 2010. Migration and Care Work in Spain: The Domestic Sector Revisited. *Social Policy & Society*, 9(3), pp. 409–18.

Lopez, M., 2012. Reconstituting the Affective Labour of Filipinos as Care Workers in Japan. *Global Networks*, 12(2), pp. 252–68.

Lutz, H., 2011. *The New Maids: Transnational Women and the Care Economy*. London: Zed Books.

Lutz, H. and Palenga-Möllenbeck, E., 2010. Care Work Migration in Germany: Semi-Compliance and Complicity. *Social Policy & Society*, 9(3), pp. 419–30.

Lyberaki, A., 2008. *Deae Ex Machina: Gender, Migration and Care in Contemporary Greece. GreeSE paper* n. 20. London: The Hellenic Observatory, London School of Economics.

Marchetti, S. and Venturini, A., 2014. Mothers and Grandmothers on the Move: Labour Mobility and the Household Strategies of Moldovan and Ukrainian Migrant Women in Italy. *International Migration*, 52, pp. 111–126.

Sarti, R. (ed.), 2011. *Lavoro domestico e di cura: quali diritti?* Roma: Ediesse.

Tognetti Bordogna, M., 2009. Lavoro di cura e sistema di welfare. In: R. Catanzaro and C. Colombo (eds), 2009. *Badanti & Co. Il lavoro domestico straniero in Italia*. Bologna: Il Mulino, pp. 279–98.

Tognetti Bordogna, M. and Ornaghi, A., 2012. The 'Badanti' (Informal Carers) Phenomenon in Italy: Characteristics and Peculiarities of Access to the Health Care System. *Journal of Intercultural Studies*, 33(1), pp. 9–22.

Triandafyllidou, A. (ed.), 2013. *Irregular Domestic Workers in Europe: Who Cares?* Aldershot: Ashgate.

Triandafyllidou, A. and Kosic, A., 2006. Polish and Albanian Workers in Italy: Between Legality and Undocumented Status. In: F. Düvell (ed.), 2006. *Illegal Immigration in Europe: Beyond Control*. Basingstoke: Palgrave, pp. 106–37.

Van Hooren, F., 2010. When Families Need Immigrants: The Exceptional Position of Migrant Domestic Workers and Care Assistants in Italian Immigration Policy. *Bulletin of Italian Politics*, 2(2), pp. 21–38.

Williams F., 2012. Converging variations in migrant care work in Europe. *Journal of European Social Policy*, 22(4), pp. 363–76.

Chapter 3

Modern Domesticity: Why Professional Women Hire Domestic Workers in Spain

Pilar Goñalons-Pons

Introduction

The prevailing public discourse in Spain says that domestic workers are being hired to reconcile work and family demands. The Spanish labour market offers limited part-time or flexible employment opportunities and, unlike other European countries, work-days easily extend until after 8pm (Salido 2011). Women who want to work and have children, so the story goes, require substitutes at home. Politicians and other public representatives often make causal claims that relate the expansion of the paid domestic work sector to women's employment rates. A similar rationale underlies much of the scholarly literature about paid domestic work. Researchers have documented that the paid domestic work sector is expanding in a number of Western countries. This change is often described as a natural response to women's growing incorporation into formal employment (Anderson 2007; Hondagneu-Sotelo 2007; Lutz 2011). Scholars also mention other factors like welfare regimes or migration flows, which are seen as shaping the contours of this trend (Williams 2012). Considerations about the gendered and classed dimensions of the division of labour sit in the background, and so does men's persisting resistance to do housework (Orozco 2012). Other researchers who deviate from this framework emphasise class inequality and elitist privileges to characterise the paid domestic work sector (Ehrenreich and Hochschild 2002; Peterson 2010; Ray and Qayum 2009).

This prevalent narrative – that women need to hire substitutes to work – contrasts with the fact that only a small fraction of working women do in fact hire domestic work. Estimates from the Spanish Time Use Survey 2009–10 indicate that 12 per cent of the households report hiring domestic workers, and 25 per cent among dual-earner households. These households that employ domestic workers concentrate, unsurprisingly, in the top quartile of the income distribution. Why is then the assumption that working women require domestic workers so common? This chapter turns to professional women's explanations for hiring domestic workers to examine this puzzle.

The literature on domestic work has yet to closely examine the reasons that motivate the hiring of domestic labour. Studies either presume that households hire because 'they can afford it' or, alternatively, because they 'need it'. The data for this research suggests, however, that the motivations are more complex. Choices to outsource domestic and care work are not simply expressions of necessity or comfort. Instead, these choices constitute a specific move among middle-class women who navigate a constrained set of gendered and classed discursive and material structures. We argue that through hiring domestic workers professional women engage in a collective effort that modernises ideals of domesticity in ways that, on the one hand, fit a new image of professional femininity and, on the other hand, preserve the conventional gendered order at home and in the workplace. As a result, the spread and legitimacy of hiring domestic work limits the transformative potential that the growing rates of formal employment among women could have on gender relations.

Discourses about Domestic Workers

The world of paid domestic workers illuminates how social inequalities shape the intimate relationship between homes and markets. The very act of employing a domestic worker can be used to signify that a household belongs to the dominant group in a given society (Glenn 1992, 1999; Ray and Qayum 2009). Relations of subordination and hierarchy are deeply rooted in the routines, rituals and relations of domestic work (Rollins 1985; Romero 1992). Gendered and radicalised discourses are routinely mobilised to signify the status hierarchy between workers and employers.

Ideals of femininity claimed by employers often marginalise and devalue domestic workers' symbolic and material family relations. Evelyn Nakano Glenn (1992) found that at the turn of the twentieth century women of colour in the US were said to lack the appropriate skills for other jobs, or to require the discipline of domestic servitude to enforce proper family norms among the African American community. A number of studies found that similarly racialised and gendered images are being currently deployed to characterise and control domestic workers (Anderson 2000; Lutz 2011; Macdonald 2010; Parreñas 2008). Employers use maternal rhetoric to relate to and talk about their domestic workers, and refer to their domestic workers being 'inferior' as women and mothers. Such rhetorics help employers justify and navigate the relationship of subordination between themselves and their domestic workers (Glenn 1992; Rollins 1985). Ironically, however, employers often say that domestic workers are 'like one of the family'. This family rhetoric, which appears to express emotional closeness on the surface, is in fact a discursive strategy that demarcates, normalises and naturalises classed and racial hierarchies (Collins 1998).

No single ideal of femininity is fully hegemonic, different imaginaries of femininity compete with one another and are distinctively classed and racialised. Domestic workers might mobilise gendered discourses to position themselves as morally superior and confront the marginalisation from these dominant norms of femininity. Domestic workers also racialise and categorise employers

(Anderson 2007) and oftentimes challenge their female employers' performance as mothers. Researchers found that transnational mothers claim to have a stronger emotional attachment to their children living in their home countries than the busy professional mums who hire their services (Hondagneu-Sotelo and Avila 1997). Cameron Macdonald (2010) argued that in the US, mothers closely policed and micromanaged their nannies so as to decrease the perceived threat to their status as mothers.

The scholarly literature shows that ideals about femininity, motherhood and families feed the cultural fabric whereby the paid domestic work sector is thought, perceived and represented as part of the social structure of economies and families. These cultural codes vary at different times and places, and provide a fruitful standpoint to analyse the relations between women. The following chapter analyses the gendered and classed discourses that professional women in contemporary Spain deploy to explain their decisions to hire domestic workers.

Methodology

The women interviewed belong to a group of highly educated professionals living in urban areas. Fieldwork was conducted in Madrid from January to July 2012. Thirty-five professional women with children living in dual-earner heterosexual households and who employed domestic workers were recruited to be interviewed. Young professionals in their 30s and 40s who represent the first cohort of women to gain formally full and equal access to education after Franco's military dictatorship were purposely selected. This cohort entered the labour market in the 1990s. All interviewees held university degrees (and often Masters or PhDs) in a variety of fields, including but not limited to lawyers, engineers and economists.

The recruitment took place through announcements in professional women's networks. After initial contact, a snowball strategy that sought to expand the range and variation of interviewees' occupations and job characteristics was utilised. Interviews lasted between two and six hours, and were recorded and transcribed. The content of the interview focused on women's career trajectories and on the organisation of housework and care work; which included a comprehensive overview of women's motivations for hiring domestic work, their experiences as employers and their relationships with domestic workers.

Overall, interviewees' first experience hiring domestic work occurs upon marriage or cohabitation. Domestic workers are commonly recruited through family or friends. At this point, domestic workers typically enter the household for three or four hours a couple of days per week and they do general cleaning and laundry, among other tasks. Pregnancies constitute a point of inflexion in which the demand for domestic work changes; they shift from hiring hourly cleaning services to hiring full-time employees who do both housework and care work. Two of the interviewees hired live-in domestic workers and the rest hired live-out workers. All but three of the domestic workers were foreign-born; most of them had come from Latin America and a few from Eastern Europe. The Spanish-born domestic workers were considerably older than their foreign-born counterparts.

Professional Women in the Marketplace

Shaped by the prevailing narrative in Spain, this study began with the expectation to find that the majority of professional women were fully committed and devoted to their careers. It was presumed that these women wanted to once and for all, and legitimately so, fully pursue their professional ambitions. It was assumed that they would embody the image of the avant-garde woman moving forward, breaking barriers and cracking the glass ceiling. In 2011, working women in Spain earned 82 cents for every euro earned by men, an unadjusted gender wage gap of 16 per cent (Eurostat 2013), and women made up only 36 per cent of members of Parliament (World Economic Forum 2013, p. 371).

Research has repeatedly shown that women's wages are on average lower than men's partly because they do more housework, spend more time with their children or take time off after childbirth, among other things (for a review see England 2010). Discrimination also influences the gap, but most researchers frame it as residual or marginal (Gornick and Meyers 2003). In light of this research, one could hypothesise that the women interviewed, having delegated domestic and care demands onto other women, would not be much exposed to motherhood penalties and other barriers that curtail their incomes and mobility prospects.

Surprisingly so, however, only a small fraction of the interviewees had professional careers that resembled that of the idealised male worker or unencumbered worker (Acker 2006). Maternity and care demands from children and other relatives were leaving clear traces in their work trajectories. These interviews gathered stories about women requesting workday reductions, changing jobs or refraining from promotions. To some degree these marks responded to what they defined as personal preferences and values negotiated with their husbands and other family members; the interviewees were not all overachievers. For the most part, however, experiences of discrimination in the workplace centrally shaped women's earnings and often lead them to reconsider their professional careers.

Professional women were more likely to succeed in their careers whenever they found a supportive environment that valued their work and did not penalise their maternity. Regrettably these supportive environments were rare to come by. The women interviewed encountered co-workers and bosses who recurrently questioned their work and commitment ever since they became mothers. They also confronted organisational routines and barriers that made it harder for them to continue performing the same job, such as late evening meetings or unpredictable work-time demands. Interestingly enough, these work cultures often permitted adaptation in cases of illness or travel, but were much more rigid when applied to mothers.

The following two vignettes illustrate the ways in which the careers of these professional women intersected with their experiences in the workplace and their decision to hire domestic work. To highlight the influence of workplace discrimination, the interviews are classified according to answers about professional ambition and the work environment. The following two interviewees represent unexpected outcomes. Sonia succeeded and became a chief manager despite her relatively low ambition and conservative views about family and gender relations. Sandra, however, shifted to a mummy-track job despite her ambitions to move up the ladder and being married to an involved father.

Sonia, Nine to Six Manager

Sonia's interview was conducted in her office. The company she ran sold printing and paper-related equipment, she was in charge of the Spanish corporation and a set of subsidiary offices in Portugal, Italy and France. She used to travel a lot, she indicated, but not anymore. 'My children took it very badly when I travelled … When a father travels it feels ok, but a mother traveling feels different. My husband, who helps a lot at home, used to tell me that I should not leave when our kids got a fever' (Sonia). Eventually, she did cut back from travelling. This change was partly intentional and partly due to changes in the organisation of the company.

When Sonia got married, she looked for somebody to do weekly cleaning and ironing. She hired Nora who at the time was also working for her mother. After a couple of years, Sonia gave birth to her first child and took a standard four-month maternity leave. When she returned to the job, Nora became a full-time employee who worked every weekday from 9:00 to 18:00. In addition to doing household chores, she now also took care of the baby, only months old.

Sonia got pregnant for the second time when her first child was three. Because she had been recently promoted to chief manager, this time she took a shorter maternity leave that lasted a month and a few weeks. Nora took on caring for the second child. At the time of the interview, the youngest child was six years old and about to start elementary school later that year. Sonia was considering what to do with Nora: 'there's not enough work for her to be at home every day, but I still need somebody to pick up the kids after school till I get home' (Sonia), she assured. By the end of our meeting, she showed me a picture hanging on the wall. The picture featured her and four other women as Spanish women leaders in managerial positions.

Sonia was proud of her professional accomplishments. Her ideas about women's equal competency for high-profile careers, however, did not match with her views about a mothers' special role in child rearing. She believed that children felt the absence of a mother differently to how they felt the absence of a father, and so did her husband. She felt anxious when she was travelling a lot and these feelings of guilt haunted her for a while. When external conditions reduced her travel rhythm, however, she felt relieved and completely comfortable with her position as a manager mom.

At the company Sonia felt greatly valued and her promotion opportunities had been promising. She was never too ambitious, she assured that she did not pursue the job as a manager: 'I was very comfortable at my previous position'. But her father, who was the former manager, had sponsored and mentored her; she explained that she agreed to substitute her father only when it became obvious that the other candidates were not good enough. At home, Sonia described her husband as 'helping a lot' and considered their division of labour to be egalitarian. This statement about egalitarianism, very common among the interviewees, did not correspond with reality. Sonia spent much more time both doing housework and caring for the kids than her husband did (about two hours a day difference).

Sonia's career path followed a trajectory that resembled that of an idealised worker, an unencumbered worker. She rarely skipped work and agreed to shorten her maternity leave when she became a chief manager. The work environment was supportive and organised around a predictable work-day that she could easily adapt whenever necessary. Perhaps because her father was the former manager, her status as a mother did not weigh against her chances for promotion. To some extent, hiring Nora facilitated Sonia's availability and flexibility in the workplace. Most importantly, however, Nora allowed Sonia to feel that she was successfully fulfilling the ideals of modern domesticity.

Sandra, Forced to the Mummy Track

Sandra arrived at the site of the interview wearing non-professional clothes and telling me about how much she loved her work schedule. 'It makes such a huge difference to have three afternoons per week to do stuff', she affirmed, 'though I am rarely out there', noting that she normally dedicated these *free* afternoons at home and with the kids. When I met her, Sandra had been a lawyer for a multinational consulting firm for the past 12 years. She requested a work-day reduction when she gave birth to her second child. 'It is our right now, they could not deny it to me', she explained in reference to recently passed legislation about work-day reduction for parents with children under eight.

When she started working at this company she experienced rapid upward mobility. She had been highly regarded by her colleagues, who used to call her 'a machine'. She won recognition prizes and large productivity bonuses. At the time of her first pregnancy she was supervising several teams and in charge of a number of projects. She took a standard four-month maternity leave and hired Ana to stay at home while she returned to her job. Ana was, she assured, 'the centre of the family'.

Sandra's bosses did not object to the maternity leave but they demanded the same yearly productivity goals as if she had been working 12 months instead of eight. She was unable to meet the goal and, as a result, that year she did not qualify for any recognition prizes or productivity bonuses. She felt unfairly treated and complained to her bosses, who did not rectify their policy. This experience was highly frustrating and became a point of inflexion that shifted how Sandra related to her career. She felt undervalued and discriminated against; she decided to make no more 'sacrifices' for the company.

With her second child on the way she requested to move to a different department with no supervision or managerial duties, 'where all moms go', she said. She also requested the work-day reduction mentioned above. Ana continued to care for the children at home, but now Sandra was able to pick up her kids from school three times a week. For the past five years she felt satisfied with this arrangement. At the time of the interview, however, Sandra explained that she desired to expand her professional profile again; she wanted to become involved in new projects but felt that she had 'missed the train'.

Like Sonia, Sandra hired a care-giver soon after her first pregnancy. Ana, like Nora, had been a reliable, trustworthy, loving and efficient domestic worker. Unlike Sonia, however, Sandra's husband was more involved. Sandra and Brian were one of the few cases among the interviewees that actually had an egalitarian division of labour. Despite having it all to her advantage, Sandra's professional career looked much more like one on a mummy-track.

Sandra had not originally planned to be on this path, but she felt pushed into it. She also strongly criticised her company for benefiting from her work-day reduction. Working fewer hours meant getting paid less, but she often found herself catching up on work during the weekend: 'I work for free', she said. Her devotion to the job seemed justified when she got bonuses and had upward mobility prospects, but not after she felt disregarded and penalised for being a mother. She justified these decisions in a way that boosted her status as a mother: 'the stuff about quality time is bullshit', she said, 'It is the quantity of time that matters and being there when your kids need it, like at the school exit'.

Regardless of her efforts to persist as a devoted worker, Sandra faced a highly hostile environment at work and was penalised for becoming a mother. Hiring Ana full time to take care of the children and do the housework did not offer any protection against this form of discrimination. This example illustrates how replacement for household services is clearly insufficient and inappropriate to address gender inequality in the labour market. Discrimination in the workplace is widespread in Spain and serves to isolate, dissuade and discourage working mothers to remain on the job and pursue their careers.

Despite the prevailing public discourse, hiring domestic workers cannot prevent discrimination in the labour market and yet this practice is widespread. Even though Sandra decided to shift to the mummy-track, she did not change her decision to employ Ana full time. Clearly, hiring was not simply to overwork or pursue professional ambitions as an unencumbered worker. Neither was it simply a matter of comfort and class distinction that little had to do with their gendered expectations at home and on the job. In the following section it is argued that professional women hire domestic workers partly to meet the ideals of modern domesticity that reconcile contemporary professional femininity with conventional values about families and homes.

Recasting Domesticity

Middle-class women embrace their roles as wage earners but find themselves within a set of cultural discourses that challenge their performance both at work and at home. It is well known that growing rates of formal employment among women and mothers tend to increase social anxieties about the transformation of families and gender relations. In Spain, two discourses are particularly relevant. One states that working mothers do not spend enough time with their children and the other argues that working mothers overburden their parents who are forced to take care of their grandchildren.[1]

The interviews demonstrate that hiring domestic work sits at the core of a collective effort to reclaim and actualise domesticity values. Beyond constituting a material arrangement to balance work and family, hiring domestic workers allows professional women to mobilise a discourse that presents their roles of wage earners as protecting these values. Unlike research in the US that emphasised concerns around motherhood (Macdonald 2010), this research in Spain highlights concerns about preserving the domestic space and its associated family and gender norms.

Modern domesticity relies on both conventional and new gender norms to govern the relationship between home and markets. It de-emphasises women's physical and exclusive presence in the home, while at the same time preserves core values of conventional domesticity. Women's femininity remains associated with securing a private home that is a space of peace, comfort, leisure, love, nurture and care. Simultaneously, modern domesticity adopts gender equality rhetoric to advance its own models of wifehood and motherhood as representing gender progress and modernity. The demands of this modern domesticity, however, are unreachable for other working women. Modern domesticity illuminates the gendered nature of class boundaries and the classed nature of gender relations in contemporary Spain.

Gender Modernity

The interviewees detached themselves from images associated with gender backwardness. This meant, generally, stating their own agency in refraining from the most daunting and undesirable housework tasks. They declared having

---

1   Two news stories can serve as an illustration of these discourses: 'Working women, your kids are fine' [Original title: 'Madres trabajadoras, vuestros hijos estan bien'] in *El Mundo* on 31 July 2011. Available online at: http://www.elmundo.es/elmundosalud/2011/07/29/mujer/1311950025.html [accessed: 13 March 2014].

'The enslaved grandparents phenomenon is growing' [Original title: 'Aumenta el fenomeno de los llamados abuelos esclavos'] in *La Vanguardia* on 14 October 2013. Available online at: http://www.lavanguardia.com/salud/20131014/54391927724/aumenta-fenomeno-abuelos-esclavos.html [accessed: 13 March 2014].

strategically distanced themselves from these burdens. 'I did not learn how to cook on purpose', said Sonia, 'and this is how I guaranteed I would have an egalitarian division of housework with my husband'. They also considered housework to be outdated, unimportant or banal. Some of the interviewees were notably bothered for having to answer questions about this subject and insisted that this topic was not relevant. This attitude resembled what other researchers found in relation to caregiving, that when women take on 'father roles' they also tend to undermine the value of care work (Nelson 1990; Rothman 1989).

Generally speaking, professional women seemed to refuse non-egalitarian relations at home. They were remarkably invested in claiming that they equally shared the housework with their husbands. These claims, however, only rarely reflected the actual division of labour in their homes. Like Sonia, the majority of interviewees made claims about egalitarianism that did not match their detailed description of the division of housework and care work. This mismatch between reported and actual housework arrangements reflected their efforts to align with dominant gender norms and social expectations. Just like working-class men who, under the housewife-breadwinner cultural norms, tended to underreport their time spent on housework (Ferree 1984; Hochschild 1989).

Besides, interviewees strongly emphasised their identities as wage earners. They agreed that being employed was fundamental for their own personal development and self-esteem. And they particularly emphasised the positive aspects of professional jobs, but not so much these of rudimentary jobs. They had all stepped out of their jobs for short periods of time after giving birth; the standard paid maternity leave in Spain lasts for four months. They considered the time spent at home to be important, but only because it was temporary. None of the interviewees ever considered quitting their jobs or taking longer unpaid leave. In reference to women in more rudimentary jobs, however, they expressed that staying at home was preferred, as the benefits of being employed in terms of wage and personal development did not match the sacrifice of leaving the home.

Embracing this identity as professional workers came at a cost, however, because they encountered a rigid and hostile environment in the job place as illustrated above. The interviewees were readily aware that appearing as an unencumbered worker was crucial for career advancement and promotion. They felt pressure for doing so and were penalised when failing to do so. Employing a domestic worker seemed to them an ideal strategy to avoid these penalties and take on the conventional 'father role'. Specifically one in which the parent does not run home when a child is sick or needs to call a family relative when working late. Like Carmen who proudly said, 'I told my boss he wouldn't even notice I was pregnant, and indeed he did not; he even congratulated me!'

Despite these obstacles, interviewees rarely raised critical views about the lack of policies or sexism in the workplace. Actually, they often displayed an arguably masculine pride for being able to overcome these barriers. Carmen, for instance, said: 'the easy thing to do would be to quit the job and stay at home, it is much harder to do both things at the same time!' The only common complaint they had was about rigid work-days and face-time. Only exceptionally did they express general dissatisfaction with the position of women in the labour market or demanded more governmental intervention (for example with childcare support).

In sum, professional women embraced a view of modern womanhood that was attached to professional jobs. Housewifery was associated with gender backwardness and boredom, and they sought to distance themselves from this spectre. Husbands' resistance to do housework constituted a recurrent obstacle to fulfil this movement, particularly because these women sought to simultaneously preserve a set of domesticity values. As illustrated in the following section, hiring domestic work appears *necessary* not to remain employed but to protect the domestic sphere as the exclusive space of peace, love, family and care.

Peace and Pleasure, No Politics at Home

The interviews showed that professional women hire domestic workers to turn their homes into peaceful and pleasurable spaces. This argument was commonly deployed to explain why they decided to hire weekly cleaning services, but less frequently in reference to hiring full-time care-givers who also did housework. The interviewees emphasised that domestic workers secured marital peace and comfort. For instance, when Olga was asked about how she and her husband divided the housework, she explained:

> Our strategy is fundamentally based on having a girl; otherwise we would have already divorced. My husband has very little consciousness of … household stuff, now a little bit more than before. But the fundamental condition for family peace is to hire someone to take care of housework, no question (Olga, lawyer).

Unlike conventional ideas that women should display mastery and interest in housework, as shown above, professional women saw themselves as members of a new generation of women who were not confined to the domestic sphere. While they rejected gendered expectations that associated them with housewives, they simultaneously held gendered expectations about being nice as opposed to being conflictive or demanding. The interviewees very actively avoided conflict with their husbands who often resisted sharing housework. Olga continued:

> Because I am not the kind of woman who is going to take the house by herself, I do not like cooking and in general housework tasks either. And there is no reason why I might have to do these things by myself to have family peace … if we have to divide the housework I become a fairly unfriendly person because I say all the time what needs to be done, I remind him of this or that … having another person avoids many of these choices and many of these annoying interactions, cause this is what it means at the end. For this reason, I'm telling you, our strategy is paying somebody else to do it (Olga, lawyer).

This quote illustrates how femininity is more closely held accountable towards being pleasant than having an interest in housework. Given husbands' resistance to become more involved, women's ideals of shared housework conflict with the ideal of peaceful homes. Many of the interviewees expressed their efforts to keep homes peaceful, by which they meant silencing themselves and not complaining. Hiring domestic workers, thus, became an arrangement whereby professional women resolved this incompatibility. Domestic workers allowed professional women to feel that the division of housework was fair. They could distance themselves both physically and discursively from what was seen as banal and irrelevant work.

Young Children at Home

Cameron MacDonald (2010) argued that the ideology of intensive mothering in the US involved a 'birth-to-three' fetish which posed that child's cognitive development depends on stimulation received during this period. In Spain, the 'birth-to-three' fetish had less to do with cognitive development and more to do with policing the boundaries between the public and private spaces. The interviewees reiterated that they hired domestic workers *because* children should not leave the home until the age of three.

The home was categorically presented as the *natural* environment for young children, and professional women avoided violating this norm. Only one interviewee, Patricia, took her child to day care by the end of her maternity leave (when the baby was four months old). The rest made very strategic use of day care, if at all. About half of the sample had children who went to day care at some point. As a general rule, children were only taken to day care well after their first birthday and, even then, for very limited periods of time – three to four hours per day or every other day.

Day care centres were described as heartless spaces where children do not receive appropriate care. These descriptions relied on analogies to the workplace. They insisted that young children require privacy and individual attention. Day care centres, they argued, force children to interact with other children before it is appropriate for their age. They claimed that these spaces impose strict rules and routines that violate a child's natural rhythm. Paradoxically, however, similar daily routines required by nannies, notably to monitor children's sleeping and feeding schedules, were not seen as disruptive when imposed to the child at home. Moreover, day care workers were depicted as not motherly enough, as if their position as professional staff was incompatible with sacrifice and devotion. According to Francis, an economist, she had the following to say about day care centres, 'they close and leave your kid there!'

Day care centres can, indeed, have rules that conflict with the demands of working parents. Two regulations stood out as particularly adverse: rigid or short opening hours and the policy to not accept sick children (for example children with a cold or mild fever). Professional women normally worked for long hours and, as unencumbered workers, they wanted to avoid unexpected events to interfere with their work-day and at young ages children get sick quite often. Ursula, a self-employed psychologist, expressed this idea in the following way, 'day care centres open from half past eight to six in the afternoon, if I am not wrong … but if he gets sick, what do I do with him?'

Patricia, a human resources consultant, was an outlier because she had decided to take her first son to day care. The decision was ideologically motivated, she said: she believed in public education and thought, at the time, that hiring domestic work was elitist. Her son, however, got sick very often and she recurrently needed to find alternative care for him and be late or even miss work. She felt lucky because her parents lived close by and they were able to take care of him. Nonetheless, she recalled the experience as being highly stressful and frustrating. She also felt highly indebted and uncomfortable for having relied so much on her parents. When her second child was born, she hired a full-time care-giver.

Interestingly enough, public childcare centres seemed to implement these rules more rigidly than private ones. This suggests that the public sector in Spain, supposedly an advocate and agent for gender equality, puts barriers on working parents. Celia Valiente (2003) argued that the Spanish day care system was developed to assist housewives and not working parents. Perhaps this feature unravelled a path-dependent course that makes the adaptation of public day care to the demands of working parents difficult.

Despite the limitations of childcare schools, it remains unclear that professional women would choose differently should day care be more flexible and comprehensive. Only exceptional cases, like Patricia, seemed to resent not being able to take their children to day care or advocated for extending and improving the public childcare system. For the majority, their preference for domesticity and privacy well surpassed the shortcomings of day care. Consequently, many interviewees stigmatised mothers who mostly relied on day care services. Carmen, for instance, and industrial engineer said:

> What those people [working class women] do is take their children to day care, but they have their children *parked* there, literally *parked* at the day care centre, they pick them up exhausted after work, and because they feel guilty they make their children stay up late, and mess up with their rhythm, so that they can spend some time with them (Carmen, industrial engineer).

Carmen implied here that when professional women spend the same amount of hours at work, just like her, they do not have the same sense of guilt because their children are at home. The domestic worker provides the care and attention that kids require, whereas at day care kids are being *parked* and parents need to compensate for that later at night.

Middle-class women's dismissal of day care and praise of the private household begs the question as to why do they do not turn to relatives. Like Patricia's testimony indicates, professional women react to the aforementioned social anxieties that accuse them of exploiting grandparents. Olga, for instance, who employed Gladys to take care of her two children explained:

We agreed that we did not want to take our daughter to childcare so early. And we did not want to take her to her grandmothers either, it wasn't practical, and we didn't want to *chain* our grandmothers to that. Thus, we reached the conclusion that for both the best solution was, if we found the right person, for her to stay at home (Olga, lawyer).

The interviews show that discourses criticising working mothers constrain the choices of professional women, but they themselves mobilise and adopt parts of these discourses to their advantage. Modern domesticity protects the domestic ideal of the nuclear family in a peaceful, private and self-sufficient space that constitutes the *natural* realm for young children. Under this framework, working-class women and mothers are bound to fail and be seen as insufficient or inferior. Modern domesticity thus legitimises the *need* for private caregivers and cleaning workers while obscuring the ways in which it polices gendered class relations.

Embodying the Family

For Spanish professional women the ideal domestic worker was in some ways similar to the *shadow mother* described in Cameron Macdonald's book. They sought somebody who would take over *mother* tasks when they were absent but move to the background when they were at home (MacDonald, 2010). Unlike US mothers, however, Spanish mothers did not exhibit a similar sense of threat towards their nannies despite living similar experiences (for example both MacDonald's and these interviewees reported that their children had sometimes called the domestic workers 'mum' but Spanish mothers did not report feeling threatened by these experiences as US mothers did). The cultural code in Spain more profoundly emphasised references to the family and the domestic space.

The interviews revealed that the ideal domestic worker should typically embody the maternal imaginary. In addition to physically female bodies, the employers wanted a domestic worker that behaved like a mother or grandmother (Souralova in Chapter 10 also finds that Czech families seek nannies that resemble grandmothers). In the most extreme cases, professional women wanted a duplicate of themselves to be at home while they were at work. Dolores, for instance, who works as a professor at a university in Madrid, expressed this feeling and summarised it in the following sentence: 'she is my hands and my feet, I could not live without her'.

What was meant by the (grand)mother role was a set of relations that stood in opposition to those described for day care. Professional women sought exclusivity; they wanted the care-giver to be solely focused on their children and not on a group of children. They also looked for privacy; they did not want babies to interact with other children at young ages. They demanded flexibility; they wanted domestic workers to adapt to children's natural rhythm. Dolores, for instance, preferred to let her baby sleep in his own cradle rather than waking him up and drive him to day care. Finally, they looked for personal 'sacrifice' from their care-givers who were expected to renounce to their own personal interests for the benefit of the children, which often meant being available on demand. Domestic workers rarely had regular or fixed work-days. Their work-days generally ended when the mothers returned from work.

Helma Lutz (2011) has argued that contemporary employer-employee relations in Germany entailed complex trust relations that could not simply be qualified as exploitative or reminiscent of the past. My findings corroborate her argument but also add that in Spain, references to the family govern the meanings and qualifications of these trust relations. The closest the resemblance between domestic workers and maternal roles, the better their arrangement is. Embodying the maternal role is a measure of domestic workers' quality and trustworthiness.

This association between family and trust is relevant in a number of ways. Depicting domestic workers like family members reinforced their closeness to conventional ideas of domesticity, and addressed a common critique that professional women faced from this angle, that which depicts domestic workers as 'strangers'. Interviews with professional women with a working-class background suggested that mothers were challenged for letting 'strangers' into their homes and with their children. This finding suggests that working-class women mobilise a different set of conventional ideals of domesticity to resist those that accuse them of overburdening family relatives. In both cases, the competing claims about domesticity reinforce much more rather than challenge gender relations that align femininity with domesticity.

Concluding Remarks

This chapter argued that professional women's explanations for hiring domestic workers represent a broader cultural effort to reclaim domesticity in ways that align with modern womanhood. Complementing the emphasis on motherhood found in other studies, in Spain these discourses invoked the domestic space and the family. Mobilising ideals associated with the domestic sphere is a powerful discursive tool in a familist country. Modern domesticity selectively takes and honours what are considered to be positive norms of the past, such as caring for children in the home, and presents working mothers as protecting rather than disturbing these social orders. Moreover, modern domesticity also recurs to references about gender equality to represent progress and modernity. In turn, hiring domestic work does not enhance professional women's success in the labour market, but it does legitimise their positions as working wives and mothers.

Modern domesticity provides a framework for understanding the configurations of gender and class relations among women in Spain. Modern domesticity does little to transform the gendered expectations related to the wife, the mother or the worker. The wife continues to be responsible for providing a peaceful and comfortable haven at home, the mother continues to be in charge of sorting out the best childcare arrangement and the worker continues to be an unencumbered one who can refrain from household responsibilities. By and large, professional women are not challenging the gendered expectations attached to the modern wife and mother, much like white upper-class women in the US went along with the rising standards of cleanliness at the turn of the twentieth century rather than challenge them (Glenn 1992).

Class inequalities are also importantly involved in the workings of modern domesticity. Professional women face a hostile marketplace and public discourses that criticise their performance at home. They use their position of privilege in at least two ways: monetarily to hire domestic work, and discursively to mobilise domesticity and gender equality to their advantage. This discursive framework manages to present hiring domestic work as a *necessity* rather than a privilege. And, more importantly, relies on depicting working-class women as less deserving workers and worse mothers and wives. Their positions are mutually dependent, modern domesticity allows professional women to achieve domesticity at the expenses of devaluing that of other women. Modern domesticity serves to demarcate class boundaries and puts the majority of working women in a very difficult position.

The prevailing political discourse mentioned in the introduction echoes professional women's reclaim of domesticity. Politicians and media are privileging the voices of these women to define gender progress. In so doing, politicians are contributing to the production and reproduction of cultural ideals that not only reproduce gendered inequalities at home and in the market, but also marginalise working-class women. Modern domesticity depicts these women as either gender backward if housewives or deficient mums and wives if working for pay. Class is not just income, but performance, and modern domesticity constitutes one of the ways in which Spanish women perform class. Hiring domestic workers is, more than a requisite for women's emancipation, a buffer that prevents broader transformations in gender and class relations.

References

Acker, J., 2006. Inequality Regimes. Gender, Class and Race in Organizations. *Gender and Society*, 20(4), pp. 441–64.

Anderson, B., 2007. A Very Private Business. Exploring the Demand for Migrant Domestic Workers. *European Journal of Women's Studies*, 14(3), pp. 247–64.

Anderson, B., 2000. *Doing the Dirty Work? The Global Politics of Domestic Labour*. London: Zed Books.

Collins, P.H., 1998. It's All in the Family: Intersections of Gender, Race and Nation. *Hypatia*, 13(3), pp. 62–82.

Ehrenreich, B. and Hochschild, A.R., 2002. *Global Woman: Nannies, Maids and Sex Workers in the New Economy*. New York: Metropolitan Books.

England, P., 2010. The Gender Revolution: Uneven and Stalled. *Gender and Society*, 24(2), pp. 149–66.

European Commission, 2013. Exchange of good practices on gender equality. *Discussion Paper – Spain*. In: Equal Pay Day, Estonia, 18–19 June 2013.

Available on-line at: http://ec.europa.eu/justice/gender-equality/files/exchange_of_good_practice_ee/es_discussion_paper_ee_2013_en.pdf [accessed: 21 April 2014].

Ferree, M., 1984. The view from below: Women's employment and gender inequality in working class families. In: B. Hess and M. Sussman (eds), 1984. *Women and the Family: Two Decades of Change*. New York: Haworth Press, pp. 57–75.

Glenn, E.N., 1999. The social construction and institutionalization of gender and race. In: M.M. Ferree, J. Lorber and B.B. Hess (eds), 1999. *The Social Construction and Institutionalization of Gender and Race*. Thousand Oaks, CA: Sage, pp. 3–43.

Glenn, E.N., 1992. *Unequal Freedom. How Race and Gender Shaped American Citizenship and Labor*. Cambridge, MA: Harvard University Press.

Gornick, J.C. and Meyers, M.K., 2003. *Families that Work. Policies for Reconciling Parenthood and Employment*. New York: Russell Sage Foundation.

Hondagneu-Sotelo, P., 2007. *Domestica: Immigrant Workers Cleaning and Caring in the Shadows of Affluence*. Berkeley, CA: University of California Press.

Hondagneu-Sotelo, P. and Avila, E., 1997. 'I'm here, but I'm there': The meanings of Latina transnational motherhood. *Gender and Society*, 11(5), pp. 548–71.

Hochschild, A. with Machung, A., 1989. *The Second Shift*. New York: Viking.

Instituto Nacional de Estadistica (2009–10). Spanish Time Use Survey. Results available on-line at: http://www.ine.es/en/daco/daco42/empleo/dacoempleo_en.htm [accessed: 21 April 2014].

Lutz, H., 2011. *The New Maids: Transnational Women and the Care Economy*. London: Zed Books.

Macdonald, C., 2010. *Shadow Mothers. Nannies, au pairs and the micropolitics of mothering*. Berkeley, CA: University of California Press.

Nelson, M.K., *1990. Negotiated Care: The experience of family day care providers*. Philadelphia, PA: *Temple University* Press.

Orozco, A.P., 2012. Crisis multidimensional y sostenibilidad de la vida. *Investigaciones Feministas*, 1, pp. 29–53.

Parreñas, R.S., 2008. *The Force of Domesticity: Filipina Migrants and Globalization*. New York: New York University Press.

Peterson, V.S., 2010. Global Householding amid Global Crisis. *Politics & Gender*, 6(2), pp. 271–81.

Ray, R. and Qayum, S., 2009. *Cultures of Servitude: Modernity, domesticity, and class in India*. Standford, CA: Standford University Press.

Rollins, J., 1985. *Between Women*. Philadelphia, PA: Temple University Press.

Romero, M., 1992. *Maid in the USA*. New York: Routledge.

Rothman, B., 1989. Women as Fathers: Motherhood and Childcare Under a Modified Patriarchy. *Gender and Society*, 3, pp. 89–104.

Salido, O., 2011. Female employment and policies for balancing work and family live in Spain. In: A.M. Guillén and M. León (eds), 2011. *The Spanish Welfare State in European Context*. Farnhan: Ashgate, pp. 187–208.

Valiente, C., 2003. Central State Child Care Policies in Postauthoritarian Spain. Implications for Gender and Carework Arrangements. *Gender & Society*, 17(2), pp. 287–92.

Williams, F., 2012. Converging variations in migrant care work in Europe. *Journal of European Social Policy*, 22(4), pp. 363–76.

World Economic Forum. 2013. The Global Gender Gap Report. Available online at: http://www3.weforum.org/docs/WEF_GenderGap_Report_2013.pdf [accessed: 21 April 2014].

Chapter 4

Class Guilt? Employers and Their Relationships with Domestic Workers in Poland[1]

Anna Kordasiewicz

Introduction

This chapter focuses on the complex relationships between employers and workers in domestic work (including both household and care work) in post-WWII Poland (1945–2011). These relationships are grounded in latent inter-class contact and are managed by employers with reference to superiority as well as intimacy frameworks in their narratives. The purpose of this chapter is to reveal and interpret the particularly problematic character of domestic work for Polish employers, which shows in the interviews where their accounting practices come to light and (Scott and Lyman 1968) take the form of extensive references to the biographies of domestic workers they hire. A range of discourses[2] from this study will be referred to and then the focus will centre on the 'discourse of biographical superiority', which is especially telling for contemporary social relationships in paid domestic work.

Personal relationships in paid domestic work can be problematic for several reasons. First of all, there is a stranger's entry into the intimate life of a family. Secondly, private (domestic) and public (work) spheres overlap creating an ambivalent situation, which is volatile at times (Anderson 2000; Marchetti 2006; Mariti 2003; Miranda 2002; Momsen 1999; Yeoh and Huang 1999; Aubert 1956). Thirdly, the contemporary Polish context lacks any clear social definitions of the role of a domestic worker. This is due, among other things, to the employment gap under the People's Republic of Poland (post-WWII to 1989) and during the early democratic transformation years (the 1990s), which were the years when other parts of Europe and the US also experienced a decrease in the popularity of

---

1   The earlier versions of this chapter were presented in the following conferences: Symbolic Interaction and Ethnographic Research: 26th Annual Qualitative Analysis Conference, University of Waterloo, Canada, 30 April to 5 May 2009, and in: Biographic Research in Social Sciences, University of Łódź, Poland, 23–24 September 2011.

2   We refer here to the understanding of 'discourse' proposed by the critical discourse analysis perspective, which defines a discourse as a semiotic practice representing a social one (Fairclough 1995, p. 131; Wodak 1996).

paid domestic work (Coser 1973; Gregson and Lowe 1993). That is why for most employers today, relations with domestic workers are a sort of a social puzzle to be solved in everyday interactions. Some potential employers refrain from or stop employing a domestic worker altogether since solving this social puzzle turns out to be too problematic for them (Kordasiewicz 2011).

It is argued that the relationships in paid domestic work are essentially inter-class contacts that are perceived as problematic (apparently more so by employers than by domestic workers themselves) and that the problematic nature of relationships in this microcosm stems from employers' lack of acceptance for the class gap that separates them from their domestic employees. This is due to a number of factors, such as the egalitarian ideology in previously communist Poland, where social stratification was decreed a relic from the oppressive past (Najdus 1976; see also memoirs of a former servant in Witowska 1951),[3] and the general democratic attitude of today's Polish society (Zaborowski 1988). We will return to the particularities of the problematic character of domestic work in Poland in the conclusion of this chapter.

Generally, in paid domestic work evident asymmetry enters the private or personal life, which creates a combination of closeness and hierarchy so peculiar to the history of domestic service and contemporary paid household work (Elias 1983; Ally 2013; Aubert 1956; Anderson 2000). According to a recent study (Kordasiewicz 2011), employers seek to neutralise the combination of asymmetry and closeness by dressing up the relationship in various guises, or more precisely, alternative frames of reference. This leads them to adopt one of the two main coping strategies to neutralise the tension between asymmetry and close contact within the private sphere, that is to say, either reducing the hierarchical distance or emphasising their superior status in the hierarchical scheme. In the 'reducing distance' approach we observe friendship and the 'one of the family' strategies (Kordasiewicz forthcoming). Contrary to the existing body of research into the 'fictive kinship' model where the domestic worker is presented as one of the family, the Polish case interestingly shows that these strategies do not always have to be oppressive for the workers, who sometimes reciprocate or even initiate these kinds of relations (Kindler 2011). There are three strategies of superiority, namely moral, biographical and cultural pedagogical ones. The first two, that is the moral one and the biographical one, are universal in a sense that they are applied both to foreign as well as to native workers. The particular 'cultural pedagogy' strategy is applied only to Ukrainian domestic workers in Poland. It pertains to a quasi-postcolonial construction of the Ukrainian domestic worker in the narrative, where these workers are seen as pedagogical objects coming from an inferior cultural context (Kordasiewicz 2009). The moral superiority strategy is connected with moral judgement of the domestic worker as being inferior. The biographical superiority strategy is a strategy particular for today's employers, who construct the domestic worker using extensive comments on her biography.

---

3   On the generally anti-servant ideology under communism see Trotsky, 1936.

The aim of this chapter is to address the question of the narrative function of these biographical comments and to interpret them within the context of the employer's identity (Kordasiewicz 2009). We will analyse what those biographical references reveal about the mutual relationships in contemporary paid household work and in particular how employers frame these relationships.

The subsequent parts of the chapter are as follows: firstly, the employers' narratives of their household workers' biographies will be analysed. Then, the employers' accounts will be compared with autobiographical comments made by the household workers themselves (seven cases), which will allow for the identification of some recurring narrative patterns within the entire domestic work milieu. They will be interpreted against the socio-cultural background as the discourse of biographical superiority, which is one of the discursive forms applied to depict the relationship between employers and employees in the domestic work sector, and one of the variants of managing the biographical gap between the parties in domestic work exchange.

Research Design and Methodological Approach

This chapter is based on an analysis of materials gathered for my PhD research project 'Domestic service/ants: Changing asymmetrical social relations' conducted in Poland between 2007–11.[4] The project concerns the employment of care and household workers in post-WWII Poland (between 1945 and 2011). Interviews were conducted with 58 individuals associated with the world of domestic services: employers, domestic workers and agents in Warsaw area. Hitherto, studies on domestic work focused exclusively or primarily on the workers' perspective, with few exceptions, as the Editors point out in the introduction. What is more, the studies tended to privilege the workers' perspective as they are seen as the oppressed ones who occupy the weaker position. The focus is on the employers' perspective as the one that is under-researched and we argue that to have a complete view of the world of domestic work it is necessary to listen to the party that is often not heard from or deemed dominant and oppressive. Even if that is the case, it is worth investigating their interpretations to understand the discourse of these relationships.

The interpretative frames applied to grasp the relationships are especially telling of what is happening in Polish society in terms of concurring social orders: the traditional pre-war memory, the egalitarian communist project and the contemporary rampant capitalism involving radical income polarities.

---

4 The research was partly financed by a Ministry of Science and Higher Education grant. 'Asymmetrical social relations in the field of domestic services on the basis of the example of Ukrainian women working as household workers in Poland' directed by Professor Antoni Sułek.

I sought to reconstruct the employers' perspective by interviewing 37 employers of different social backgrounds, age and gender and supplemented these with 21 interviews with workers, in seven cases achieving a double perspective.

Employers are defined as persons who employed or are currently employing domestic workers as well as those who come from families that employed servants/domestic workers and were able to reconstruct a narrative of their past relations with the domestic worker based on family stories. Interviews with 37 employers were conducted, of which 22 persons employed a nanny/housekeeper, four persons had the experience of employing a caretaker for an elderly person and 24 persons had the experience of employing a cleaner. Of the 37 employers, 22 had a family history of employing domestic workers, and 15 persons did not. Seven of the respondents were male and 30 were female. Three of the employers were born in the 1920s, one person in the 1930s, three in the 1940s, 11 in the 1950s, six in the 1960s, 12 in the 1970s and one person in the 1980s.

To understand the Polish case it is crucial to bear in mind that the so-called migratory transition has not occurred in Poland: we do not face mass immigration, on the contrary, we still emigrate (Okólski 2004). Thus Poland has not seen the ethnicisation of the domestic sector (Williams 2012; Momsen 1999), although migrant workers do play an important role in the Polish market, contributing to the supply side of the equation (Kordasiewicz 2011). That is why any study of paid domestic work in Poland must include both domestic and foreign workers.

Women of Ukrainian and Polish background were included in this study, 21 workers altogether were interviewed, of which 14 were Polish and seven were Ukrainian. The workers interviewed performed various types of housework and care work, sometimes changing the type of work performed in the course of their careers; they were women of different ages and educational status.

The main research method used included semi-structured, in-depth, face-to-face interviews. The interviews consisted of three parts, the first part being an uninterrupted narrative (Schütze 2008), the second included a more structured, in-depth interview and the third (applied only in a few cases) followed with a joint reconstruction of domestic life and positioning of events on a timeline. In other words, biographical objectifications with the research subjects were created (such as graphs) on which we have located milestones in their domestic biographies (such as birth of children, changing apartments, jobs, life-partners, countries of living, as well as hiring subsequent domestic workers). The aim of the research has been actually to reconstruct the stories of domestic life with special consideration for the people employed as domestic workers over the years.

Opening questions used in the interviews included: 'Can you to tell me about the ladies that come here to clean, how it happened that you decided to hire them, and what was the whole story', 'Can you to tell me how it started from the very beginning, as far as you can remember, what happened next, who the persons were, whether they changed', 'Can you to tell me what you remember about your home, since the earliest days, whether it was or was not related to those persons. How was domestic work organised in your home?'

Domestic Workers' Biographies in the Narratives of Their Employers: 'Sad Tales'

Domestic work is perceived as 'dirty work', one that requires no qualifications, brings very low prestige and is burdened with a significant social stigma. Socially stigmatised work often requires some form of stigma management. Household workers and even their employers resort to narrative practices of accounting to explain why a person has become a domestic worker. This means that they perceive this work as deviant and stigmatised; consequently, becoming involved in this kind of activity requires a justification. Accounting for being a household worker in most of the cases takes the form of telling a 'sad tale' of the household worker's life. Can we then assume that the parties classify the activity of doing domestic work as deviant, while they do not necessarily perceive as deviant the person who is engaged in this kind of activity? In the next section we will investigate this issue by looking at the way domestic workers' biographies are used in their employers' narratives.

Indeed, what drew our attention in the process of analysis was how often and in what particular way the employers refer to their workers' biographies. Let us take a look at an example of Marta, an employer who currently has a domestic worker who does housekeeping and at the same time cares for the employer's mother; the worker shares the household with the employer:

> Then came the child so we hired a girl who also came from around ... Eastern Poland, following the announcement in the paper, she was somehow very motivated to find any kind of work, because she had an alcoholic husband, who on top of all did some time in prison, since he also had something to do with car theft (Marta, approximately 60 years old).

A characteristic feature of this one, and many other interviews conducted during this research, was the fact that they included some dramatic events from the domestic workers' lives related by their employers. Surprisingly, these relations that appeared in the narrative interviews focused primarily on the history of hiring domestic workers. Bearing that in mind, the biographies of household workers as told by their employers were somehow out of the immediate topic of these interviews. The information was given spontaneously and was not requested. We refer here to the understanding of the interview as an interaction characteristic of the narrative approach towards biographical interviews. Marek Prawda says: 'When I invite someone to visit the world of my experiences, I accept the rules which make such a visit meaningful' (Prawda 1989, p. 89). It is assumed that the narrative uninterrupted by questions is an organised unit composed according to the narrative imperatives of condensation, detail and textual closure (Kaźmierska 1997, p. 40 Helling 1990, p. 26). The way the employers introduced their household workers' biographical information in the narratives drew our attention because there was a visible lack of connection to the core storyline.

Spontaneously emerging fragments of domestic workers' biographies inside their employers' narratives made us think about the function of these intrusions. The concept of 'accounting' practices was analytically useful as presented in the seminal work by Scott and Lyman (1968), and later developed by Nichols (1990). Both employers and household workers accounted for hiring/entering domestic labour with reference to biographical arguments. In portraying this aspect of the interviews it will be helpful to make reference to the studies within the area of sociology of deviation and consider such problems as either stigmas (Goffman 2005[1963]), social labelling or interactionist approaches to deviations (Becker 1966), and 'sad tales' as one form of social accounting (Goffman 1961). Scott and Lyman adapted Goffman's concept of the 'sad tale' as a form of social accounting with respect to justifying one's actions: 'The sad tale is a selected (often distorted) arrangement of facts that highlight an extremely dismal past, and thus "explain" the individual's present state' (Scott and Lyman 1968, p. 52).

Accounting practice is closely connected with socially constructed deviation. Here we refer to the interactionist perspective on deviation, which shifts the analytical interest from deviation itself (that is the violation of a group's rules) towards 'potential deviation'. Becker describes this: 'The deviant is the one to whom that label has successfully been applied; deviant behaviour is behaviour that people so label' (Becker 1966, p. 9). In fact, only behaviours or facts perceived as deviant require accounting according to Scott and Lyman who explain: '[I]t is with respect to deviant behaviour that we call for accounts, the study of deviance and the study of accounts are intrinsically related' (Scott and Lyman 1968, p. 62).

In the case of accounting we deal with the management of deviations oriented towards someone's protection from being declared as deviant. Following this logic, where we see social accounting, we should be able to trace down a socially constructed definition of deviation.

The main narrative pattern in the interviews with domestic workers included the information about biographical troubles, while domestic work was presented as a solution to these hardships (irrelevant of how problematic it was itself). The deviant cases (that is the cases diverging from the general pattern) stressed the pleasure and satisfaction derived from performing domestic work, although such cases happened rather incidentally, mainly among professional nannies. We can thus draw the conclusion that the 'sad tales' in workers' narratives could be read as protection of the positive self-image of household workers, who try to justify the fact of entering domestic work, the kind of work they dislike and depreciate. These tales function as 'classical' social accounts (Kordasiewicz 2012).

The interviews began with the domestic workers' employers by asking them to tell a story of hiring household workers in their house and the tradition of domestic workers' employment in their families as far back as they can remember. The interviewees introduced their household workers into the stories, making frequent references to biographical elements. It was in these biographical remarks that accounting practices emerged.

The general pattern of the employers' narratives included a description of their domestic workers via enumeration of various facts from their lives, which revealed hardships, failures and biographical dramas. In the few deviant cases (those diverging from the prevalent framework) the employers did not bring forward any biographical information, but emphasised the quality of the employees' work or the quality of relationships with their household workers and those were the qualities that constituted the basic descriptive categories used to characterise their domestic workers.

Below are excerpts from interviews which describe the 'sad tales' (Goffman 1961, Scott and Lyman 1968):

Employer: 'the sad tale' 1

It was such a lady Joanna X, a little bit retarded, with a hump on her back. I guess her life was ill-settled because of this handicap, and she was such a well-qualified, true housekeeper (Krystyna, approximately 60 years old, hires a household worker for cleaning and caregiving of her mother).

In the fragment quoted above as well as in the one quoted previously, from the interview with Marta, we observe the employers' tendency to bring forward some biographical facts about their domestic workers, thus departing from the general instruction for the interview, which asked them to tell the history of hiring household workers. Krystyna's interview reveals the reasoning which implies that a physical handicap makes domestic labour a reasonable occupational choice for the handicapped person. The fragments quoted include a moral judgement of the household worker's life course ('her life was ill-settled'). Using the same line of reasoning we could ask the following question: if there were no handicapped persons in the society who would perform domestic labour?[5]

Marta's interview shows an ironic picture of the household worker's family situation ('because he also had something to do with car theft'). Again, private hardship (family problems) becomes a factor pushing the protagonist towards entering domestic labour ('she was somehow very motivated to find some work, because ...').

---

5 When the biographical background of domestic labour was analysed, it was revealed that out-of-norm biographies were one of the paths that led into domestic labour (Kordasiewicz 2011). To some extent we believe in the interpretation of domestic work as the biographical 'emergency solution', which is chosen when other options have failed. It is not our intention to put in doubt these parts of employers' interviews, we only want to draw attention to the following facts: firstly, that the employers feel obliged to account for household workers' professional choices; secondly, that they use biographical circumstances to justify those choices; thirdly, that they tend to link biography and domestic labour in an unquestionable causal way, while the correlation in fact may be only mildly influential; and finally, that they attribute the determinant power to one's biography which means that they portray the household worker as an individual totally determined by external factors.

Employer: 'sad tale' 2

Kasia comes from Masuria [north-eastern Poland], she came here to stay with her uncle. He lives here in Warsaw, she lived with her uncle and searched for a job, she wanted to work and earn money, in Masuria she had no job. She had finished a secondary medical school, post-secondary medical school, occupational therapy, that kind of course, and here she searched for a job, the only one she could find was to clean or babysit. She liked kids, she was very good with children and she got on very well with kids. And Kasia worked for us for five years (Olga, approximately 50 years old, hires a nanny-housekeeper).

In the story quoted above, the employer tries to convince us of the 'no other way out' type of situation in Kasia's life, while her educational achievements would have suggested that at least there was potential for an alternative type of employment. The time when she stayed with the family, babysitting a child (for five years), was also a time when she graduated from the university with a Master's Degree. Once she graduated, she moved to a job more suited to her qualifications. The employer's account, based on an implicit 'no other way out' story, provides a convenient excuse for keeping the girl in the family during her university studies. One could suspect that the 'no other way out' story became recreated in the narrative for the purpose of reinforcing the logical course of the past state of affairs.

Employer: 'the sad tale' 3

An old lady, already a pensioner, wife of a pre-war army major. A person with an okay level of education. With tough experience, since her husband died in Katyń, and she was deported to Kazakhstan along with her two children. She came back after the war, but these really are fortunes, such as, the picture of human fortunes, Polish fortunes. Her son went to the army when 17, when the war was to end, and there he went, that is, he wanted to go to the army to make it easier, you know, and to fight Germans, then he died in Kołobrzeg, which was virtually at the end of the war. So everything at once, so she was heavily experienced by the fortune, while before the war she was well situated, very very beautiful, and she lived without preoccupations, she had an easy life, had many abortions, poor little thing, as it seems it was more common before the war than you would have thought, and she didn't want any more children, and that's how she was punished by the fortune for that (Honorata, approximately 70 years old, hires a cleaner).

In the quote above we find a moral history, where domestic work and related humiliations are explained as a 'punishment/penance for sins committed' (for moral aspects of domestic work see Kordasiewicz 2011).

As we see, a general pattern emerged in the employers' narratives: making references to household workers' biography. In order to conclude whether and what exactly is particular for the employers or perhaps they just echo workers' own narratives, it is necessary to compare how the biographical elements function in narratives of employers and workers, which will be done in the following section.

Domestic Workers' Biographies in the Narratives of their Employers and in Their Own Narratives: Case of Beata and Gabriela

As mentioned previously, interviews (seven cases) were conducted with both the employer and the household worker he or she hired. This allowed for the comparison of the construction of biographies of these seven household workers reconstructed in the employer's as well as the employee's narrative.

Table 4.1 was formulated to illustrate the comparison and includes the story of entering domestic labour by Gabriela as told by Beata (her employer) and by Gabriela herself.

Table 4.1   Element of domestic worker's biography mentioned by the employer and by the worker

Employer: Beata, born in the 1950s, hires a live-in housekeeper and cleaning service*	Domestic worker: Gabriela, Polish, born in the 1960s, works as live-in housekeeper
Positive assessment of Gabriela as a domestic worker	Previous working experience – managerial position
Gabriela's character traits: a friendly, orderly human being	Macroeconomic changes made her close her business
Age: 40 years old	Unemployment
Gabriela's assessment as a domestic worker	Started university studies during previous employment
Gabriela's problems: exaggerated ambitions, university degree, place of origin (small town in South-Eastern Poland)	Another temporary job before entering domestic work
'That's how her life got settled'	Financial needs of her family
No work	Daughter at university, bank loans
Pensioner husband	No work
Husband got into debts, she needs to pay them, court case to divide their properties	Husband's health situation, husband's pension, problems in marriage
Daughter at university	Decision to enter domestic work

Source: Author compilation as a result of interviews with Beata (interviewed on the 12.11.08), and Gabriela (interviewed on the 3.12.08).
* Information underlined in one account does not appear in the account of another narrator.

Gabriela, a live-in housekeeper, stresses the professional aspects of her biography, contrasting these with her present work. Beata, the employer, openly presents the household worker's problems with her husband, while the household worker herself seems much more discreet in telling this part of the story.

Similarly to Beata and Gabriela's case, the biographical narratives of other household workers reconstructed from their own and their employers' perspective do provide an overlap of the majority of the information quoted. However, it should be noted that the employers in general appear to be more eager to talk about household workers' biographies than household workers themselves (such as the husband's debts) and tend to tell stories in a more open and emotionless way (like, 'she married a drunkard', 'she left her child in Ukraine').

Recursive ardour in quoting troubled parts of their household workers' biographies suggests the employers' sensationalist attitudes. Similarly to the migrant household workers in USA who are interpreted as 'windows to exotica' for their employers (Rollins 1985), domestic workers in Poland seem more of 'windows to trauma' for their respective employers. The histories of domestic workers appear to constitute a point of encounter with dramatic stories, bad fortune, trajectories and human suffering for their employers. We can interpret them as the incarnation of the employers' subconscious or their fears. The situation reminds us of the Victorian opposition between the lady and the servant, that is, the opposition between the pure, spiritual and angelic on the one hand (the lady), and the sensual, dirty and sinful on the other (the servant) (Atkinson 2003).

This creates an impression that information about the difficult facts is somehow useful in the employers' narratives: on occasion they decide to further dramatise some facts from the household workers' lives where even when a plain version would seem dramatic and troublesome enough. This way of presenting the biographical content appears to highlight the absence of similar experience among employers; in other words, it communicates a profound biographical gap.

The fragments of the employers' interviews that contain biographical information about domestic workers appear to echo the respective narratives of the workers themselves. Nevertheless, these parallels selectively expose and amplify some elements, in particular those related to the difficult facts from the household workers' biographies. The function of biographical information does not seem to be limited to the protection of a positive self-image of domestic workers. We believe that there are different meanings in the same biographical arguments, dependent on whether they are used in an autobiography, or by an external commentator.

On the one hand, the employers' intention could be to justify the household workers' decision to engage in domestic labour by attributing their miserable state of professional affairs to external conditions, and simultaneously reinforcing the positive image of household work as a way out of personal hardships. On the other hand, many of the accounts recorded could be analysed as a secondary inculcation of persons who were simply employed in the household with the preponderant domestic worker's role. It is expressed by the acceptance of the state of affairs in the household workers' lives manifested in such expressions as: 'That's life',

'That's how life got settled', 'Poor one', 'She didn't have a choice'. They contain an assessment of the household workers' lives and imply a deterministic vision of human fate. The employers' remarks could be read as elements of their 'identity work' (Snow and Anderson 1987) or attempts to establish their self-image. With these comments the employers seek to justify the fact a person becomes a domestic worker, while in fact they seem more interested in justifying the fact they hire one. So we may say the employers commonly use biographical references relating to past or present hardships of their domestic workers in search for excuses (justifications) for the very fact of hiring domestic labour.

The Problematic Character of Domestic Work in Poland

In the introduction to this chapter, the problematic character of domestic work was touched upon. The focus will now shift to what is particularly disturbing for Polish employers and explain the reasons behind it. The first thing to note is that in the course of this research we encountered people who actually could afford and wanted to hire a household worker, but refrained from it or stopped employing because of a projected or felt sense of uneasiness. Below is an excerpt from email correspondence with Marzena, one of the employers, who was asked to gather the opinions about hiring domestic workers in a closed parents' forum, and one of the answers reveals precisely the sort of resistance. It begins by referring to financial issues:

> I haven't got much to write. I don't use [domestic worker's help] because I simply can't afford it. When I had enough money to pay for it, I partially used the help, for example for cleaning windows. When I have financial liquidity again and sufficient means, I'm sure I will sometimes hire a worker (Message in closed on-line forum for parents, November 2009).

It seems that the financial aspect prevails in this case. However, the next fragment testifies to a puzzling sense of resistance:

> On the whole I am not opposed to the idea, but I'm not sure if I could handle the mental pressure if I had somebody take care of all the chores. Things like cleaning, hoovering, washing the windows, the doors, kitchen or bathroom are okay, but I prefer to wash and iron myself, for example (Message in closed on-line forum for parents, November 2009).

It is very puzzling why one needs to 'handle the mental pressure' if one 'has somebody take care of all the chores'. The second sentence reveals the issue of 'circles of intimacy' for Marzena's forum member, washing and ironing are more intimate in character than cleaning. Among the research sample, there were persons who had been accustomed to having domestic workers around the house since their childhood as well as those who were pioneers of sorts in terms of introducing domestic workers into their respective families. One could expect that dealing with a domestic worker would come naturally to persons who have inherited a long family experience of hiring domestic workers (experience going back one or two generations), whereas the same situation would give rise to many doubts among those who have had no earlier socialising experiences. Thus the novelty of the situation might seem to be the most straightforward explanation of the embarrassment felt. However, there is no overlap between the two divisions, that is, one with the employers who find relations with a domestic worker (or, more generally, employing a domestic worker) problematic and those who find it unproblematic and the second division of persons with and without a similar family experience in that respect. Persons 'without a tradition' do not develop a homogenous pattern: some of them find it problematic to employ and maintain relations with a domestic worker (such as Aleksandra, cit. also in Kordasiewicz 2009), and some find it unproblematic. The attitudes towards domestic workers may also vary among persons who have been accustomed to domestic workers at home.

In the interview with Aleksandra, a new employer, the narrator's fundamental problem was learning to perform a superordinate function in her relation with the domestic worker. Aleksandra was brought up in a home where there were no domestic workers, and so the lack of relevant experience could be seen as the source of difficulty she has with these relations. However, not all persons without family experience describe the domestic worker as problematic (Kordasiewicz 2009). Another case is Jan, whose family have been hiring domestic workers at least since the inter-war times (between WWI and WWII) and who was brought up in the presence of domestic workers. This is how he describes his attitude towards domestic labour:

> The biggest problem I would have, luckily, I haven't got it 'cause the lady who does the cleaning in our place is just ideal, but I've had two cases like this, where the cleaning lady was not the best in the world. I just couldn't tell her and I don't think I could do it now, just couldn't tell her to do something else. Whether it was to tell her to do something in a different way or she left something unclean. I am messy myself, but I can quite clearly see if the place has been properly cleaned, I know I could do it better myself and I can't, if I see it, I can't put it in words. So, at one point I didn't tell this Ukrainian woman, 'cause she was pretending she was cleaning, we just went away on a holiday, and after the holiday she never turned up. I find it tough even to say, although I do manage after all, but I have to force myself, to tell her what she is supposed to do on that day. I'm not sure I'm not asking for too much, whether it isn't, I don't say, please do this or do that, but I say, if you find the time, so maybe instead of other things, maybe you will see how much time you will have left (Jan, approximately 40 years old, hires a cleaner).

What is striking in the fragment above is the close similarity to what we found in Aleksandra's interview: unwillingness to give orders and perform a superordinate role in relation with the domestic worker (Kordasiewicz 2009).

One could expect that this attitude is motivated by the shared generational experience: Jan and Aleksandra are of similar age and they were both born in the 1970s. It could be that members of this generation display a high intensity of the tendencies we noted, but it certainly does not explain all the cases. Marta, born in the 1950s, faces a similar difficulty in giving orders and performing a superordinate role in her relations with the domestic worker. Below is a fragment of the notes taken after the interview with Marta:

> Marta wanted to tell me something she didn't say during the interview and she did not want to say it in front of the domestic worker, who was present at the time of interview. It is her observation that people who find it easiest to get on with domestic workers are those who 'have few scruples' and that does not mean that they take advantage of these workers. These are the people who have no problem 'calling them with their first names', who 'keep a distance' and, from what I understood they do not have the kind of problems giving orders but they seem to clearly delineate the social difference. And, paradoxically, the domestic workers (I asked whether she meant today's or 'yesterday's'? the answer was: 'all of them') find it more comfortable, the well-defined boundaries, it is very clear. Marta has a problem giving such orders, although she was brought up in a home where there were domestic workers, she is used to having a domestic worker since she was little, she was brought up in the spirit of equality, 'in a socialist way' and it is a problem for her (Marta, approximately 60 years old, hires a domestic worker who at the same time cares for her mother. They all live in the same house).

Besides the lack of family experiences with domestic labour of the past generations, it is the egalitarian attitude that seems to matter (in this case the value was instilled by Marta's socialist grandmother). So what is the source of problems in dealing with domestic workers among people with such diverse characteristics?

Let us now have a look at the way relations with domestic workers are presented by those who see it as something obvious and unproblematic. The first group who find the employment of a domestic worker as unproblematic are those employers who equate domestic workers with the network of meanings typical of the corporate world. They have a managerial approach to the domestic workers they employ: they talk of 'recruiting', 'motivating' and 'managing' the workers. Let us take a look at the quotation from the interview with Ewa: 'It's just a regular labour market' (Ewa, approximately 40 years old, hires a nanny-housekeeper). Ewa tries to convince us this is a regular labour market. We could take this statement at its face value. The unquestionable fact of existence of domestic workers is explained by the logic of market inequalities: some people are poor and some are rich, so the poor work for the rich. Ewa's statement is clearly quite emphatic: the use of the adjective 'regular' underlines the message of the sentence. It seems to oppose some unspoken argument to the effect that this is not the case. The emergence of this statement could also be considered a sign of 'accounting' referring to the relation with the domestic worker as an ordinary work relationship. It could be that if it was, there would be no need to stress and normalise it.

The second category of persons whose narratives about domestic workers present them as tamed are those descended from landed gentry, who have developed a 'good spirit' interpretive frame (a traditionalist framework of a domestic worker as a good spirit of the house, indispensable both physically and emotionally). They see domestic workers as a natural and obvious figure, indeed, a transparent one, for their descriptions contain no references to the various interpretive frames such as family or work. The domestic worker constitutes a particular aspect of the social reality and as such does not require any further explanation. In this case, the naturalness of domestic workers stems from tradition, from the deeply rooted social experiences of ancestors of the contemporary employers referring to the presence of persons who serve and those who are served.

Thus the unproblematic attitude manifests itself in two varieties. Persons using different frames normalise and 'account' for their relation with the domestic worker by resorting to phraseology belonging to different symbolic worlds: they speak about class hierarchy and about closeness to the worker. In either case, the worker requires supervision in order to perform well. Persons who find relations with the domestic worker unproblematic (in one way or another) accept that closeness and asymmetry in this case are intertwined. In other words, they accept the hybrid nature of relations with the domestic worker. To resort to a metaphor, they operate with a white light. The white light may be split into the different spectral colours in a prism and so in the case of domestic workers there is room for familial intimacy, contractual relations, education and morality, and these elements constitute a whole that is greater than the sum of its parts.

There are two more sources of egalitarian attitudes we can employ to explain this problem. The first one is the condemnation of 'exploitation of one man by another' going back to the times of the People's Republic of Poland (this could pertain more to Aleksandra's case). The second source is found in the egalitarian elements of the ethos of intelligentsia clearly represented by Jan's family (this information was collected in a different part of the interview). In the case of Jan and Aleksandra, and also Marta, we find the characteristic sense of guilt connected with employing a domestic worker.

The employers seek to minimise their sense of guilt connected with hiring domestic workers via references to biographical conditioning of the employee's entrance into domestic labour. These references take the form of dramatic 'sad tales' and their purpose is to legitimise the emerging social inequality as previously noted. When the responsibility is transferred to fate and switched to the individual level, attention is turned away from systemic aspects of the observed inequality between domestic workers and their employers and the inequality itself is hidden or legitimised. We call this tendency 'the discourse of biographical superiority'. It involves narrating dramatic circumstances from the employee's biography, which is hardly justified from the narrative point of view, as these interviewees were not queried to provide this information, and their narrative was complete without this information. The discourse constructs a justified biographical distance between the employer and the employee, interpreted as a sign of the employer's superiority and the employee's inferiority.

Concluding Remarks

In analysing the employers' narratives, including biographical stories of their domestic workers, an interesting case of social accounting practices was discovered. A Polish proverb says: 'it is the guilty one who looks for an excuse', which, in other terms, means that every justification implies the conception of deviation to be accounted for. Tracing the accounting practices in the narratives of the employers allowed for the identification of the doubly problematic nature of labour relationships in the domestic sector: for both employers and employees. It turned out that biographical data are often used to ease the sense of ambiguity of the situation. In the course of analysis, we discovered the deterministic vision of social order lying at the heart of the employers' comments about the household workers which was referred to as biographical superiority discourse. The reference to biographical elements of the household workers' lives in their employers' narratives was a way of justifying the social inequality in the relations within domestic work milieu.

What does the way to include biographical information on household employees tell us about the general features of contemporary domestic relationships in Poland? The class gap and class guilt perspectives will be used as guidance for our interpretation.

Within this research there are radically different biographies of domestic workers and their employers (biographical class gap), which may be interpreted as the expressions of class inequality perceived by both parties engaged in the interaction. The elements that are especially illustrative of class inequality in the observed relations regard the narratives of professional careers of the employers and household workers' children. Let us consider the example of Jadwiga's house. Maria, a household worker in Jadwiga's family, had three children. The difference between professional careers of her biological family members and the ones of her employers' family seems especially profound. All Jadwiga's children became medical doctors, while Maria's own children 'only' graduated from a railway vocational school. In fact, one of her sons was 50 at the time of the interview and still remained financially dependent on his mother, while another was an ex-alcoholic.

Research into the issues of domestic labour conducted in the years 2007–11 indicates that Polish employers are eager to become friends with domestic workers or welcome them as 'family members' despite the existing class gap between the two groups. Alternatively, they use the strategies of expressing superiority and push their employees into the unambiguous role of a domestic worker with the accompanying low social position. The third model identified in Poland seems inspired by the corporate order and involves constructing the domestic worker as a quasi 'corporate subordinate'.

The existence of various relationship strategies in the domestic labour sector could be seen as an answer to the problematic nature of domestic work in contemporary Poland. Maciej Gdula and Przemysław Sadura observed that this problem is to be found mostly among the members of the middle class. Other social classes display a more straightforward attitude to paid domestic labour: upper classes see it as a purchased service embedded in their status, while the working class treats it as a usual form of physical work which they cannot afford (2012, pp. 50–51).

In the research the problematic nature of domestic labour among people with diverse characteristics (those representing younger and older generations as well as those with and without a family tradition of domestic work) was identified. The problematic nature of these relationships manifests itself in the observed compulsion to justify hiring household workers. One of the possible interpretations of this phenomenon is to read it as a sign of the sense of guilt among the employers who are confronted with the situation of considerable social inequality between themselves and the household workers, while simultaneously sharing egalitarian beliefs and the egalitarian sub-conscious rooted in the socialist Poland's mentality.

Gul Ozyegin, a researcher of domestic labour in Turkey, claims that contacts with domestic workers provoke a sense of class guilt and require domestic work employers to do some form of 'class work' (akin to identity work) to reach a subjective sense of having closed the class gap between them and their employees (Ozyegin 2001).[6] Is it the *collective* class guilt that we observe in the case of Polish household workers' employers? Presently, relations between household workers and their employers in Poland are private and individual. In the interviews, remarks about the problematic nature of the relationship in collective categories were not encountered. We may thus assume that individual experience of guilt has not yet translated into the collective sense of guilt. Employers do not perceive themselves as the oppressors: they live their problem individually and experience it interpersonally. Referring to the biography of the workers as a source for accounting, the employers again confirm this hypothesis: they interpret the situation on an individual level, for instance they seem to believe there has to be something in the life of a given woman that forces her into domestic work. By so doing they overlook the systemic, structural and collective dimensions of the processes of social polarisation behind it. This attitude is a 'personal sense of class guilt', which points to the individual experience of systemic factors.

The discourse of biographical superiority belongs to the class of 'superiority discourses'. Superiority discourse is a discursive type based on the communication of advantage: be it moral, biographical or cognitive. Statements within superiority

---

6   It is worth noting that a few researchers claim there are cases where household workers intentionally generate a sense of guilt in their employers to obtain benefits (Ozyegin 2001; Lan 2006: pp. 217, 222, 200, 246; Parreñas 2001, pp. 190–191).

discourse show, confirm and legitimise the superiority of one side of the communication. Surprisingly, the superior status may also be perceived by some as an obstacle in the relationship (Kordasiewicz 2009). All the three forms of superiority discourse, the biographical, pedagogical and moral, intertwine. The moral assessment is often related to the biography of the domestic worker, and the biographical situation often influences pedagogical practices.

The superiority discourses were a recurring yet not universal framing found in the research. Fourteen out of all 37 employers used them, as did seven out of 21 employees. Biographical discourse occurred in all the three historical epochs which were identified in the course of the research (that is to say the decades of 1940s, 1960s, 1970s–1990s, and the 2000s) and across all occupational groups in the domestic sector, except for specialised nannies. This last finding may be explained by a relatively egalitarian and professional character of the occupation. These characteristics make it unnecessary to account for paid babysitting and for those reasons employers do not feel a personal sense of class guilt in relation to this type of domestic workers.

This chapter analysed several distinct uses of biographical data by each partner of the interaction in the special case of domestic labour relations. The analysis shows that biographical data are used to conceal the problematic nature of the social gap which exists between the interacting partners in the domestic labour milieu. It may be argued that the biographies of the household workers offer an important resource for the employers to construct justification for their employees becoming domestic workers, for them hiring such a worker and, more generally, for the existence of social inequalities.

References

Ally, S., 2013. Slavery, Servility, Service: The Cape of Good Hope, the Natal Colony, and the Witwatersrand, 1652–1914. In: *Towards a Global History of Domestic and Caregiving Work 49th Linz Conference*. Linz, Austria. 12–15 September 2013.

Anderson B., 2000. *Doing the Dirty Work? The Global Politics of Domestic Labour*. London: Zed Books.

Atkinson, D., 2003. *Love and Dirt. The Marriage of Arthur Munby and Hannah Cullwick*. London: Macmillan.

Aubert, V., 1955/56. The Housemaid- an occupational role in crisis. *Acta Sociologica*, 1, pp. 149–58.

Becker, H., 1966. *Outsiders. Studies in the Sociology of Deviance*. New York: The Free Press.

Coser, L.A., 1973. Servants: The Obsolescence of an Occupational Role. *Social Forces*, 52(1), pp. 31–40.

Elias, N., 1983. *The Court Society*. Oxford: Basil Blackwell.

Fairclough, N., 1995. *Media Discourse*. London: Edward Arnold.

Gdula, M. and Sadura, P. (eds), 2012. *Style życia i porządek klasowy w Polsce [Lifestyles and Class Order in Poland]*. Warszawa: Wydawnictwo Naukowe Scholar.

Goffman, E., 1961. *Asylums: Essays on the social situation of mental patients and other inmates*. Garden City, NY: Anchor Books.

Goffman, E., 2005. *Piętno. Rozważania o zranionej tożsamości [Stigma. Notes on the Management of Spoiled Identity]*. Gdańsk: Gdańskie Wydawnictwo Psychologiczne.

Gregson, N. and Lowe, M., 1994. *Servicing the Middle classes. Class, Gender and Waged Domestic Labour in Contemporary Britain*. London: Routledge.

Helling, I., 1990. Metoda badań biograficznych [The biographic research method]. In: J.Włodarek and M.Ziółkowski (eds), 1990. *Metoda biograficzna w socjologii [Biographic method in sociology]*. Warsaw-Poznań: PWN. pp. 13–37.

Hoerder, D., 2013. Historical Perspectives on Domestic and Caregiving Work: A Global Approach. In: *Towards a Global History of Domestic Workers and Caregivers, 49th International Conference of Labour and Social History*. Linz, Austria, 12–15 September 2013.

Kaźmierska, K., 1997. Analiza procesu wykorzenienia w narracjach wojennych mieszkańców kresów wschodnich [De-rooting process's analysis in wartime narratives of Poles from 'Eastern borderland']. *Studia socjologiczne*, 144(1), pp. 57–84.

Kindler, M., 2011. *A 'Risky' Business?: Ukrainian migrant women in Warsaw's domestic work sector*. Amsterdam: Amsterdam University Press.

Kindler, M. and Kordasiewicz A., forthcoming. Maid-of-all-Work or Professional Nanny? The Changing Character of Domestic Work in Polish Households, XVIII-XXI c. In: E. van Nederveen et al. (eds), *Towards a Global History of Domestic and Caregiving Workers*. Leiden: Brill.

Kordasiewicz, A., forthcoming. What does 'being part of the family' mean? A systematic analysis of family discourse in narratives of care and household workers and their employers. *Journal of Families, Relationships and Societies*.

Kordasiewicz, A., 2012. Biografie pomocy domowych jako tworzywo tożsamościowe ich pracodawców [Alter-biography. Biography of care and domestic workers as identity substance of their employers]. *Acta Universitatis Lodzensis. Folia Sociologica*, 41, pp. 23–46.

Kordasiewicz, A., 2011. *(U)sługi domowe. Przemiany asymetrycznej relacji społecznej. [Domestic Service. The Transformations of an Asymmetrical Social Relatioship]*. PhD University of Warsaw.

Kordasiewicz, A., 2009. La relation à l'employé vue du côté employeur: le travail domestique des migrantes ukrainiennes en Pologne. *Cahiers de l'URMIS*. Available on-line at: http://urmis.revues.org/index863.html [accessed: 6 April 2014].

Kordasiewicz, A., 2008. Służąca, pracownik, domownik. Polki jako pomoce domowe w Neapolu w kontekście retradycjonalizacji instytucji [Servant, worker, household member. Polish women as domestic workers in Naples in the context of re-traditionalization of the institution]. *Kultura i społeczeństwo*, 52(2), pp. 80–109.

Lan, P-C., 2006. *Global Cinderellas. Migrant Domestics and Newly Rich Employers in Taiwan*. Durham, NC: Duke University Press.

Lofland, J. et al., 2005. *Analyzing Social Settings: A Guide to Qualitative Observation and Analysis*. New York: Barnes and Noble.

Marchetti, S., 2006. *'We had different fortunes': Relationships between Filipina domestic workers and their employers in Rome and in Amsterdam*. Master's Thesis. Utrecht University.

Mariti, C., 2003. *Donna migrante, il tempo della solitudine e dell'attesa*. Milano: Francoangeli.

Miranda, A., 2002. Domestiche straniere e datrici di lavoro autoctone. Un incontro culturale asimmetrico. *Studi Emigrazione*, 39 (148), pp. 859–79.

Momsen, J.H. (ed.), 1999. *Gender, Migration and Domestic Service in Global Context*. London and New York: Routledge.

Najdus W., 1976. Wyrobnicy i służba w Galicji, ze szczególnym uwzględnieniem Krakowa w latach 1772–1870 [Dayworkers and servants in Galicia, with special focus on Cracow in years 1772–1870]. In: *Polska klasa robotnicza [Polish Working Class]*. Warsaw: IH PAN.

Nichols, L., 1990. Reconceptualizing social accounts: An agenda for theory building and empirical research. *Current Perspectives in Social Theory*, 10, pp. 113–44.

Ozyegin, G., 2001. *Untidy Gender: Domestic Service in Turkey*. Philadelphia, PA: Temple University Press.

Okólski, M. 2004. The effects of Political and Economic Transition on International Migration in Central and Eastern Europe. In D.S. Massey and J.E. Taylor (eds), 2004. *International Migration: Prospects and policies in a global market*. New York: Oxford University Press, pp. 35–58.

Parreñas, R.S., 2001. *Servants of Globalization: Women, Migration and Domestic Work*. Stanford, CA: Stanford University Press.

Prawda, M., 1989. Biograficzne odtwarzanie rzeczywistości [Biographic reconstruction of reality]. *Studia Socjologiczne*, 4, pp. 81–99.

Rollins, J., 1985. *Between Women: Domestics and their Employers*. Philadelphia, PA: Temple University Press.

Schütze, F., 2008. Biography Analysis on the Empirical Base of Autobiographical Narratives: How to Analyse Autobiographical Narrative Interviews. *European Studies on Inequalities and Social Cohesion*, 1(2), pp. 153–242.

Scott, M. and Lyman, S., 1968. Accounts. *American Sociological Review*, 33(1), pp. 46–62.

Snow, D. and Anderson, L. 1987. Identity work among the homeless. The verbal construction and avowal of personal identities. *American Journal of Sociology*, 92(6), pp. 131–371.

Trotskyi, L., 1936. Thermidor w rodzinie [Thermidor in the family]. In: *Zdradzona rewolucja. Czym jest ZSRR i dokąd zmierza? [The Revolution Betrayed.*

What is the Soviet Union and Where is it Going?] Translated by: Aleksander Achmatowicz, 1991. Warsaw: Oficyna WIBET.

Williams, F., 2012. Converging variations in migrant care work in Europe. *Journal of European Social Policy*, 22(4), pp. 363–76.

Willis K. and Yeoh, B. (eds), 2000. *Gender and Migration.* Cheltenham/ Northampton: Edward Elgar Publishing.

Witowska, J., 1951. *Ludzie i nieludzie. Pamiętnik służącej [Humans and Non-Humans. Servant's Memoire].* Kraków: PIW.

Wodak, R., 1996. *Disorders of Discourse.* London: Longman.

Yeoh, B. and S. Huang, 1999. Singapore Women and Foreign Domestic Workers. Negotiating Domestic Work and Motherhood. In: J. Momsen (ed.), 1999. *Gender, Migration and Domestic Service.* London/New York: Routledge, pp. 273–96.

Zaborowski, W., 1988. *Postrzeganie społecznych nierówności. Z badań nad świadomością*

społeczności wielkomiejskiej. [The Perception of Social Inequalities. Research on Social Consciousness in the Big Cities]. Warsaw: PWN.

Chapter 5

Dilemmas of Paid
Home-care for the Elderly in Spain:
Daughters, Elderly and Domestic Employees

Cristina Vega Solís

Introduction

There is little research on the perspectives of those who employ private home-care. In recent years studies on care have proliferated, generally focusing on analysing the work carried out by domestic employees. In Spain, as in other European countries, these studies have highlighted migrant women's employment and how their work is undervalued within intensely segmented and ethnicised labour markets in which restrictive migratory policies compound the feminisation and irregularity which have traditionally characterised the sectors of domestic work and home care (Escrivá 1999; Catarino and Oso 2000; Colectivo IOE 2001; Parella 2003; IMSERSO 2005; Mestre 20056; Díaz 2008; Vega 2009; Martínez 2010; Orozco and Gil 2011).

These studies explore the asymmetrical bond formed between the employer and the employee. Frequently, this bond is coloured by racial hierarchies (Caixeta et al. 2004; Gutiérrez 2010). The employer, often a white middle-class woman, transfers care work without necessarily compensating this emotionally engaging work with fair pay or – in the case of migrant women – with a formal employment contract (a legal contract or the regularisation of migratory status) (Parella 2003; Martínez 2010). The literature has also frequently pointed to the ways in which mothers with small children hire caretakers to do the 'dirty work' of child-rearing, saving for themselves the emotional rewards of parenting (Anderson 2000). Employers maintain a structure of unequal gender relations in the management of their households; the hiring and overseeing of the domestic employee is part of that structure. The relationship between employer and employee may be affectionate and respectful, but it seems beyond doubt that one of the two parties – the employee – is in a more vulnerable position. This vulnerability has as much to do with access to rights as it does with remuneration, recognition and the clear definition of tasks and work conditions.

Regulatory regimes that apply to domestic work – despite changes in some countries' adoption of the International Labour Organisation's (ILO) Convention 189 on decent work for domestic workers and Spanish legal modifications in the

Special System for Domestic Employees – still do not overcome the inequality at the core of these relationships. Furthermore, the ambiguity which characterises care work, in which affective involvement is interwoven with tasks that are unrestricted in terms of time and intensity, assures the perpetuation of a 'culture of care' based on (often racialised) servility (Vega 2009).

Feminist approaches to the study of the unequal implications of care work for employees show their commitment to uncovering those contemporary locations in which gender domination continues to operate. Care work – to the extent that it absorbs the tensions of an unjust distribution of labour between middle-class men and women, transferring them to poor women – is a clear example of inequality in a globalised world (Hochschild and Ehrenreich 2002). Women in the Global North have not achieved a new distribution of care work, and states – especially in the south of Europe – have not decommodified or deprivatised care or are in fact re-commodifying it. Employment in caregiving thus continues to be undervalued, contributing to the invisible reproduction of the workforce in a period in which capitalism has definitively discarded the 'family salary' and has widely incorporated first-world women into the labour market on subaltern terms (that is, in worse jobs with worse conditions and worse salaries) (Carrasco 1999; Maruani et al. 2000; Carrasquer and Torns 2007). The need for double salaries in order to survive, the intensified exploitation of work through flexible work hours and cut-backs in services and assistance all contribute to the increased demand of families for workers that perform cleaning and caring tasks in households.

These themes are approached in two ways. To begin with, the subjective processes that are produced in care work are addressed. Such an analysis displaces the study of the unequal conditions of work towards the subjective elaboration of these conditions. Secondly, I propose to understand not only the subjective effects of the asymmetries of care work, but also situate these in a framework of wider inter-relationships in which those who employ or manage, those who are cared for, those who are employees and even other potential intermediary agents take part.

The text focuses on the triangular relationships that are established between daughter-employers, the elderly and domestic employees in the practices of care. The interplay between these actors expresses the anxieties and dilemmas that traverse these relationships in a period of change. Therefore, these relationships must be viewed through an analytic lens that foregrounds the dimensions of gender, class, generation and migratory condition.

As will be illustrated below, the inter-subjectivity that is articulated in care work practices is linked to several factors. One being the difficulties that the elderly have in assimilating their new condition of vulnerability; or the external pressures and internal pressures that daughter-employers experience with regards to their responsibility in caring for those who once cared for them. And finally, the affective projection that paid workers feel towards the elderly, as well as their role as witnesses, intermediaries and 'translators' between the elderly and their daughters. I argue that in order to understand the dilemmas that the employers experience, it is necessary that we comprehend the complex dynamics that unite these participants in care, that separate them and confront them as they come to grips with the very links that care work establishes.

These inter-subjective dilemmas that constitute the triangular relationships of care will be illustrated based on my work from two different studies. The first of these was a study of care and domestic work carried out in Spain between 2002 and 2004 in the context of a comparative European project (Caixeta et al. 2004). In-depth interviews were conducted with employees and employers in Madrid, with different household structures and from different social strata. In this research project, we found that the variables of household type, gender and social class were key to understanding the ways that care was emotionally managed. While solitary elders were more willing to accept caretakers who showed a strong affective demand (and were occasionally prone to servility), elderly couples, with pronounced gender differences, were more resistant to the caretakers' presence, which intensified the daughters' roles of intermediation and management.

The second study was conducted in 2006, and was more specifically focused on the care of elderly people in the province of Barcelona. Interviews with employees were complemented by interviews with the elderly and their family members, mostly daughters as managers of the care workers. This study focused on the ways that the different participants dealt with new care arrangements through contracting care workers, and the manner in which this was linked to an acceptance of aging or of sickness. It also focused on the affective and work commitments that these arrangements represented for the different participants with regards to their own ideas regarding reciprocity and good care.

Since the time that the studies were conducted, there have been some significant changes in care work in Spain. A move towards protection of care workers' rights was part of the 2013 Spanish legislation regarding domestic work. These changes, that involve putting more pressure on employers to pay the social security of care workers, have been reverted by the economic crisis. The crisis has also had an important effect in curbing the processes of regularisation in this labour sector (Martinez forthcoming). In this sense, legal transformations towards a framework that might better protect domestic workers has been limited in the last few years, with informality continuing to be a characteristic feature of this migrant labour sector. It is also for this reason, in comparison to other migrant labour sectors, that migrant care workers have experienced fewer dismissals and subsequent migratory returns to their countries of origin. Despite these changes in the legal and economic frameworks for care work, the cultural and subjective dimensions of this work transform far more slowly. Therefore, many of the dilemmas explored below have remained constant or have even worsened given the tendencies towards informality and precarity accentuated in the context of the economic crisis.

The text is organised as follows: in the next section theoretical shifts that have led to greater attention to the subjective dimensions of care will be reviewed. In the third section the theoretical point of departure which has influenced the study of elderly care will be illustrated, detailing an analysis of the relationships of elderly care with a focus on Span.

The Production of Subjectivity in Care: Towards an Intersectional Approach

In recent decades, the shift in feminist analyses in how to approach work carried out by women in homes is significant. Although debates in the 1970s sought to make domestic work visible, as well as to explore its contribution to processes of capitalist accumulation, since the end of the 1980s, discussion has been increasingly directed towards care, not only in its labour dimensions, but also a central aspect in the production of subjectivities. The emergence of care, and a subsequent move towards the sustainability of life, is not simply a semantic change, however this issue will not be elaborated on further in this chapter. Rather, the change implies a shift in focus and in theoretical underpinnings. From a perspective that highlights intersectionality, care does not configure a single gender subjectivity, but rather multiple subjectivities depending on the social realities in which it unfolds. Among these, the social reality of paid care work in homes is central. In this section, key points and moments in the transformation of this analytic focus will be reviewed.

The analysis of exploitation which underlies the debate on domestic work had the virtue of confronting the blind spots of Marxism (Rodríguez and Cooper 2005). It addressed what Friedrich Engels (2008) considered the second aspect of production, that is, the 'production of immediate life': the production of people, of life itself in the family. However, the vision of the 'work' involved in this kind of production was on occasion rather simplistic. Producing was seen as a collection of discrete, routinised mechanical and evidently alienating tasks which did nothing but, as Simone de Beauvoir (1999) said, 'repeat life'. In any case, rather than being considered a natural prolongation of biological instinct (Marx 2000), reproduction came to be considered work, and therefore a social activity traversed by power relations and susceptible to generating political subjectivity as well as a process of struggle within the working class (Dalla Costa and James 1975; Dalla Costa 2009; Molyneux 2005; Federici 2013; Galcerán 2006).

A further turn in the analysis of domestic work towards the reproduction of the workforce in Marxist feminism emphasised the determining role of domestic work in the process of capitalist accumulation. This work was not marginal, nor was it limited to producing use-value. Rather, it was directly productive yet hidden to the extent that it was not linked to an individual salary but rather to the family salary borne by the male. Making this work visible, and later calculating its value, became part of the feminist economy research agenda (Borderías et al. 1994; Folbre 2011; Carrasco 2013).

The central figure of this analysis was the working-class housewife who, in many cases, might occasionally be employed in industry. Capitalists and male family members alike exploited and enjoyed the fruits of her work. This class-based approach arose from an excessive generalisation of the housewife figure, and while it served as a counterpoint to the attention Marx and others had shown to the exploitation of women in the factory, it paid little attention to the peculiarities of the home as a work place, or to service workers in bourgeois households nor certainly to their employers.

Influenced by a series of studies on feminine identity, maternity and socialisation published throughout the 1980s, the importance of the subjective dimension of reproduction and its role in the development of gender as such emerged. *Care*, in psychoanalysis-inspired approaches, principally focused upon women of the middle class and was assumed to be part of a process of identification with the mother. The important contributions of Carole Gilligan (1982) and of Nancy Chodorow (1984) on the reproduction of mothering serve as point of departure for this trend.

As these works show, the daughter's identification with her mother through care can prevent a process of individuation. According to Maria Jesús Izquierdo (2003), the character of merging that can mark relationships of care in the process of the formation of feminine subjectivity can produce a 'damaged subject' who perpetuates domination on a subjective level, potentially harming others through an attachment that fails to recognise individual boundaries. For these authors, the alternative to this subjective formation depends on the distribution and diversification of daily care in order to strengthen women's differentiation and autonomy while developing the men's ability to bond. Yet despite the important reflections on the process of subject construction through care that these works prompt – reflections that the Marxist feminism of the 1970s had not taken into account – they have been widely criticised.

Criticism of these approaches has hinged on the lack of an intersectional analysis which allows for an equal consideration of the dimensions of race, class and sexuality in the analysis of subjectivity (Hill Collins 1990; Hooks 2004). The excessively binary character of gender in such approaches was also questioned (Butler 2001). If the domestic work debate presupposed housewives as the subject of analysis, approaches to subjectivity in the 1980s implied that subjects' production through care was necessarily taking place in a mother-daughter/son relationship that could hardly hide its class, sexuality and/or race filiations.

The progressive attention to care, not only from the point of view of the care-giver, but rather simultaneously from the point of view of the person receiving care in interdependent relationships has opened and given further specificity to the analysis of care and the attention given to adults, children, the elderly, the functionally diverse, the chronically ill and so on. It is impossible to speak of a single gendered care relationship in which identity is established simply between women and men. Instead, one must think about the gendered relations within and between diverse men and women. The following questions arise: What happens in the practices of care when those who care and/or are cared for are not the ones these theories suppose? When, in the different spaces, environments and relations of care are the subjects who are produced singular and not necessarily equivalent? What happens with the subjects implicated in care are multiple and linked through emotions mediated by salaries? We will return to these questions further below.

Sociological studies, to the extent that they address global transitions in the social organisation of care, situate the analysis of gender identities in care within a more complex context. The explorations of social care come up against the limits imposed by their own excessive focus on unpaid care within the family (Thomas 1993; Daly and Lewis 2003). Studies on domestic employment, the commodification of care and global chains of care in the context of migration diversify the modalities of attention (Hochschild 1983; Parreñas 2001; Hondagneu-Sotelo 2001; Anderson 2011). The emotional burden which crosses through care, making this kind of work notably ambiguous, does not disappear. As Silvia Federici reminds us (2013), it takes place outside the limits of capitalism but takes on different meanings depending upon the relations within which it unfolds. It is no longer possible to theorise, if ever it was, on the basis of a social category or a homogenous kind of bond. While there are still 'primary care-givers', they operate together with other figures, among them the household employee. A reordering of social positions within care is taking place, as well as an important mutation in what different actors understand 'good care' to be.

Elements for Considering Subjectivity in Elderly Care in Spain

Until recently, in Spain as in other countries, studies on paid and unpaid care work carried out by migrant women have focused on child-rearing and the role of this work in the implementation of public policies as well as its role in the transformation of motherhood (Tobío 2005), including that of the employers and of employees who take care of their own children from a distance (Oso 1998; Caixeta et al. 2004; Gutiérrez 2010; Herrera 2013).

Less attention has been paid to the care of the elderly. Nevertheless, in the Spanish case, the phenomenon of an aging population (Abellán and Pujol 2013; IMSERSO 2010) and its impact on migrant female employment, and intergenerational gender relations has sparked interest in its own right (Parella 2003; Vega 2009; Martínez 2010). As such, the lack of services for the elderly has provoked research in public policy, partly inspired by the expectations generated by the Law of the Promotion of Personal Autonomy and Attention to Persons in Situations of Dependence.[1]

In the context of the theoretical developments outlined above, an approach to daughters-employers' perspectives implies examining the specificities of elderly care from an intersectional and dynamic perspective in the social contexts and arrangements in which this care transpires. The care of the elderly carries with it specific questions regarding subjectivity that must be understood as an ensemble of ideals and practices interwoven in the inter-relationships among the distinct actors involved. In this sense, taking the studies described above as a point of departure, I propose to address three axes of tension in these inter-subjective dynamics, with a particular focus on the Spanish case.

---

1   Given the weak implementation of the system of attention to persons in situations of dependency (with a budget cut-back of 283 million euros), a large part of elderly care is carried out by spouses: 39 per cent of the care of men, 12 per cent of the care of women (IMSERSO, Report no. 131).

The Fragility of Intergenerational Gender Reciprocity in Care

The obligation to care is placed upon the women in the family under a notion of intergenerational reciprocity. This notion has been highly valued by elderly people of the Mediterranean region over generations (Narotzky 1990; del Valle 2002). Spanish women who are currently confronted with their ageing parents' need for care belong to the generation that led a major change in Spanish society. These women were around 20 years old in 1975, the year Franco died. Now they are about 60 years old. They lived through political struggles, or at least witnessed the climate of socio-cultural change, women's widespread entry into the labour market, the extension of discourses of sexual emancipation and the changes in the family brought about by the legalisation of birth control and of divorce. All of this seriously undermined the 'ideology of the successor's obligation to care for their predecessors in the property until their death' as described by Narotzky (1990) in the rural communities which formerly had prevailed throughout Spain.

According to that ideology, in Spain social reproduction was guaranteed by a stable system of access to two fundamental resources: property and care. The elderly were provided for thanks to the maximisation of the gendered division of work (agriculture and care) amongst young couples who inherited the land. Despite the stability of this system, there was an element of strategic flexibility which allowed the elderly to manoeuvre the order of inheritance according to emotional/affective criteria rather than strict legal regulation. Care was therefore an element that couples could utilise to legitimately access assets. Affection, which is nevertheless genuine, seems to be 'encrusted' in the economic relations as a specifically feminine contribution.

Processes of migration and urbanisation, the rise of the nuclear family, the ascent of the society of mass consumption, the generalisation of education, the development of a (nuclear family-based) welfare state and increasing individualisation as a way of life would all modify female subjectivity and contribute to a questioning of the unjust distribution of care work between genders and generations (Vega 2009). The discourse justifying the strategic division of labour between genders and the emotional-affective ideology behind it is becoming less influential today, especially among women.

It is against this background that, until recently, the profile of most primary care-givers in Spain was female, within the family, unpaid, on a live-in, full-time basis (92 per cent, average 52 years of age, married, with primary education and no paid occupation) and with very little public support, but the continuity of this model is collapsing. In fact, this was never totally stable and was always subject to conflict, negotiation and impositions. Daughters interviewed in both research projects call into question the notion of reciprocity as a form of redistribution (not necessarily a fair or better one) as well as the material, moral and cultural order which sustained this notion.

The elderly that were interviewed have not experienced social transformations in the same way. Today's elderly are educated. As we have seen, their life expectancy grew thanks to the universal extension of health care, and they have witnessed the (inadequate) development of services for the elderly, first through the creation of residences and then through day centres and home-care.[2] However their understanding of care continues to be based upon the sacrificial culture of feminine care promoted by National Catholicism (a key ideology of the Franco era).

Thus, while the daughters interviewed questioned the mandate of care that weighed on their mothers and had come to rest on themselves, the elderly – both men and women – expected to be cared for directly by those daughters. In the situation of elderly couples, when new care needs arose, the elderly woman had difficulties in giving up (to an employee) what she felt to be her exclusive burden, or in any case her daughters' burden.

As the following interviewee explains with regards to the care of her father, many daughters justify partially assuming this care in order to relieve their mothers of that work:

> My relationship with my father has never been good, so now you wonder, 'Why do I have to worry now about someone who has never worried about me?' And we always come to the same conclusion: it's not for him, it's for my mother, because she's been his victim her whole life, so it's to help her (daughter/employer).

In this sense the system of intergenerational reciprocity is often interpreted by daughters as a form of solidarity between women. As we can see, an important axis of tension emerges between genders and between generations.

Paid Care as Deferred Reciprocity. The Employee as an Ally

In this scenario, hiring becomes – for the daughters who are themselves employees and at the same time become employers – an intermediary form in which they may simultaneously assume the obligation to care, escape the daily responsibility that this implies and offer a solution 'in their name'.

Normally, the hiring of an employee is undertaken by the daughters. They are the ones charged with finding the right person, managing the work by negotiating tasks, hours, salaries and other conditions in agreement with the other siblings, and ultimately being available for the parents and for the employee, if not everyday then certainly on a regular basis. It is understood that the employee, for better or for worse, serves as a partial replacement for the daughter. One daughter searching for someone to take care of her mother explains:

---

2   According to the Survey of Elderly Persons (IMSERSO) in 2010, a large majority of those who require care would wish to live in the home of one of their children or of a family member (46 per cent), a preference followed by the option to live in their own home albeit alone (15.4 per cent). If they were to require home care, 63.5 per cent would prefer that a family member provide it.

The conclusion I came to is that she didn't want any help, she said no and no and no, and I was getting desperate because I could see that she was getting worse, all that arthritis. I know exactly what they want: that I will tell them, 'I've thought it through and I've decided to take a leave from work and come here to take care of you'. I mentioned it to friends and they said, 'Of course!' And I say, 'Then when they aren't there anymore, who is going to hire me back?' One day I talked about it with my cousin and she said, 'You can't and shouldn't do that, because they don't want help, they want you' (daughter/employer).

As some studies show (Vega 2008; Martínez Buján 2010), in this triangular relationship, an alliance often arises between daughters and care-givers, through which the daughters manage to buffer some of the difficulties of the constant emotional demands which parents place upon them.

Hiring someone in the home is a strategy which serves to preserve one's own autonomy and that of the family/marriage, thus reducing the physical and emotional burden which care implies even in the first phases of aging. Not all the daughters express this clearly, but some allude to a sort of 'right to not provide care' which takes on special relevance when we see that some women – those who did not marry, those who do not have children or those who were widowed – are called upon to assume this responsibility more than other members of the family. A daughter-employer expresses this in the following way:

Don't oblige, don't pressure our children, which is what our parents did with us. Children don't have any obligation to take care of their parents, first of all. We didn't chose our parents, they were assigned to us, we never asked them to bring us here to then have to take care of them. I've always seen this clearly, and I've said as much to my parents: whatever we do we do because we want to. It isn't a moral obligation nor a personal obligation … I'm helping and doing all I can but I don't want to feel responsible or guilty (daughter/employer).

Obviously this attitude is only held by a minority, but even so it redefines relations between parents and children, as well as what is expected of a paid care-giver. *Double presence* as a subjective condition is embodied in two different women. While the daughters take on the management and attention to greater or lesser extents, the presence of the employee permits them to shift and redefine not only the tasks to be executed but also the relationship with the parents itself.

As Hondagneu-Sotelo (2001) explains, employers have ceased to fit into either the sacrificial maternal or filial model or the micro-managing one. They avoid giving overly specific orders to the domestic workers, and allow them a high level of autonomy in their work. This 'let them be' attitude is not without contradictions (Arango 2010). When employment consists of providing care in the home of the parents, this question becomes especially complex inasmuch as the employer, who in this case is not the direct beneficiary of the care, cannot supervise all the interactions which arise in caring for other people in another household. She (the employer) might not agree with some of these interactions, and may have conflicted feelings about them. Conflicts regarding how to do things are often buffered, and the employee becomes an 'accomplice' for the daughter, providing wellbeing to the elderly person while taking the side of the woman responsible for hiring her. At least this is the scenario the daughters hope for and seek out, although there are situations in which the employee becomes, as well as an accomplice, an awkward witness or, as Sabrina Marchetti also highlights (in this volume), a key factor in the regression of the elderly person.

We hear about conflicts that are almost always related to the lack of comprehension or of patience of the family members, from the employees or other intermediaries who are less involved in the emotions that are stirred up from a long, shared life together (like social workers, employment agencies, home care services, health care workers). This is what we can see in the following care worker's testimony:

> You can't take in this sickness. I think that as their children they can't take it in … we were just leaving and she said, 'The keys! The wallet!' and I explained [to the daughter], 'Don't contradict her'. The keys, I say, 'I have them right here' and so on. But the daughter doesn't have that patience, one day she said, 'Let her take the wallet! Don't you see you don't have to use the wallet?' One day she pushed her and nearly knocked her down. 'You and the keys and the wallet, I'm sick of it!' And when she pushed her I grabbed her by her dress from behind so she wouldn't fall. She looked back and saw me and thought it was me that had pushed her. 'You pushed me, but you won't get away with it!' And I said, 'I'm sorry Antonia, I didn't mean to, you stumbled and I caught you like this so you wouldn't fall'. The daughter didn't say anything. But then the lady realised it was her daughter that had pushed her and said, 'It was you that pushed me! Right, Isabel?' 'No, Antonia, you stumbled and didn't realise it'. Later we went to have a coffee and the daughter said to me, 'Isabel, thank you. I don't understand why she reacts like that'. 'How can you not understand, your mother has dementia, that is, she's crazy. It's hard to take it in. Don't treat her like that. Later you'll be sorry. Have patience with her' (employee, elderly care worker).

On the other hand, caring for the elderly implies a labour of inter-subjective, biographical re-elaboration which involves a lifetime of experiences and feelings, and which the paid care-giver may not know about and cannot confront unless others who have shared those experiences are committed to helping. Crisis moments for elderly people, which may seem inexplicable, are often directly related to life experiences (the moment the husband arrived from work, the time at which the daughter usually calls and so on). Over time, proximity generates a shared sensibility between the aging person and the care-giver, but as many professionals explain, attending to a person's needs is only part of the job; the worker must also provide company to the elderly person.

The balance between recognising the subjectivity of the elderly person and comprehending the exhaustion of age is difficult for daughters and hard for employees. Psychological wear and stress are part of the daily life for those who take part in relational activities.

The employee serves as a mediator and interpreter for the daughter, as they have a strong emotional and work commitment to the person being cared for ('I'm here for him' some workers say). The daughters provide support for the employees as they face emotional exhaustion usually experienced even when the elderly appreciate their care work.

Added to this is that domestic workers tend to project on the elderly they care for emotions that have to do with their own parents left in their countries of origin. This has been extensively described in the literature on affective transfers in the global care chains (Hochschild and Ehrenreich 2002). Many of these workers describe the care that they provide to these 'old folk' as that which they would 'give to their own parents'.

Thus, the relationship between daughters and employees tends to be based on complicity, which entails a fair amount of recognition and appreciation for the employees, leading to their greater negotiating capacity. Daughters, due to their emotional proximity, describe situations of desperation and lack of patience when faced with their parents' obstinacy or frailty, and attribute a more understanding and serene attitude to their employees. Thus care-givers' emotional and subjective work is clearly appreciated by their employers, even though it is seldom considered to be part of the care-givers' professional activity. In contrast to health care services or home nursing, the non-specialised paid employee continues to be an ambivalent figure. She is sometimes a worker, yet often plays a role closer to that expected from a loving daughter.

In summary, in the daughter-elderly axis, tension is linked to the different expectations each has regarding reciprocity in care; in the employer-domestic worker axis, the tension emerges from the ambivalence that exists between the care workers' (expected) patience and the desperation and stress felt by the daughters. This tension can generate an asymmetric complicity in which the daughter obtains not only relief from care work but also a sort of intermediation. In the daughter, the domestic worker can achieve recognition for her work as well as someone to share the emotional fatigue of caring and the anxiety produced by her distance from her own family. Yet in addition to this mediating attitude, the domestic worker can also become an uncomfortable witness that questions, although not openly, the terms in which the system of familial care responsibilities is developed.

Aging and (In)Dependent Life

Attending to the elderly means witnessing physical and often mental decline, preparing emotionally and practically for living through this, and ultimately for saying goodbye. Accepting these conditions and the social organisation of care that this implies represents an important subjective change for the elderly and those who take care of them or who manage their care. In a cultural and socio-economic context in which individualism, productivity and independence increasingly determine the characteristics of what is considered an appropriate existence (Fraser and Gordon 1997), attentiveness to those regarded as unproductive becomes a key element in the ethics of reproduction. The 'invalidating' way in which people requiring care are treated especially if they are aging or functionally handicapped does not make the processes of care provision any easier (Foro de Vida Independiente 2011).

Many elderly people resist hiring someone to take care of them. Men especially often reject their new condition of requiring care. Their vision of masculinity as invulnerability makes it hard for them to accept fragility and the passing of time. They often project an extension of sexual relations in care. The bodily intimacy imposed by care sometimes generates sexual excitement or the memory of it. They seek to affirm their lost sense of manliness with insinuations or groping, to the discomfort of the employee. The sexualisation of women's bodies in the context of a servile relationship, in this case a paid one, leads to a perpetuation of the body as a commodity.

In the case of women it is more often a matter of not wanting 'a stranger in the house'. They describe feeling invaded and do not trust this person they consider an intruder, a foreigner who tries to take over their control of the domestic sphere. This female rejection equates with elderly women seeing themselves displaced from what they see as their own prerogative. Whether this has to do with their husbands' physical or emotional attention, these women see the employee as a threat (She's the boss around here now!). They are frequently jealous, especially in situations in which the employee, a younger woman, has to have physical contact with their husband in the course of moving or bathing him. The daughters frequently describe how they have had to overcome these resistances: the fathers' demands for their privileges and the mothers' resistance to changing their possessive attitude towards the people and things in the house. The following excerpt is telling of those intra-family tensions:

> After a long struggle and a lot of wearing her down we convinced her to let an immigrant, a Romanian lady, go help her do the housework. Just the housework because she believes, she is convinced that taking care of my father is entirely her job, whether she's capable or not. … I argued with my mother, we even stopped talking to each other for a month which has never happened before, she was a very peaceful person, never raised her voice or argued or anything … But there came a time when I felt so helpless and she needed more help (daughter/ employer).

The alliance between employee and employer helps to make the new situation work. In this sense the new person is introduced bit by bit in order to overcome suspicions. Perhaps the care-giver starts working by the hour, principally in housekeeping, and then her work days are later extended. Or, as often occurs, a different person is sought to cover more hours until the elderly person has up to 24 hours of attention. In some cases the elderly person's decline is abrupt and hiring of help occurs from one day to the next, though in these cases families more often opt for old people's homes. If it is not too serious, both the elderly people and their children usually prefer that they continue living in their own home. The sense of uprooting and intensely de-personalising institutionalisation is one of the elements which prompts the depression that often accompanies aging. This concern is eloquently expressed by a daughter/employer below:

> What is true is that it makes you feel terrible, though I don't like to say it. For example, with my mother, she has to be there, but with the situations I've seen in the center [residence], there are situations which make you think, to live like that ... I wouldn't want to. But if it comes, what can we do? (daughter/employer).

The resistance to hiring a care-giver, in both cases and in their various gendered dimensions, often takes on a racist character. While Latina women are imagined to be more 'affectionate', they are also considered as having a dark skin complexion compared to natives. The exchanges between mothers, daughters, employers and other possible intermediaries are saturated with these perceptions. Daughters as well as other intermediaries play an important role in these cases, as we can see in the following testimony:

> So the daughter comes in and I can see that she's very much her mommy's girl, mommy this and mommy that. I sent her a lovely girl from El Salvador. Two months later the mother calls and tells me she wants to come talk to me personally. 'Look, the thing is that the girl you sent me, first of all I'm an artist and this girl is ugly, really ugly. And one day she told me that she never takes off her knickers, her husband had never seen her without her knickers, how do you think she washes? And I never see her wash her hair'. I tell her that the girl is very clean and tidy. 'But how does she wash her hair?' continues the lady. I tell her that its none of her business, that the girl is clean and that is all. Then the lady goes on, 'But she also follows me everywhere'. I say, 'She isn't following you, your daughter sent her so she would look out for you and that is what she's doing, looking out. Or is it that she talks too much?' 'No, no, no, she just leaves her room to see what I'm doing'. And when she saw that I wasn't impressed with what she was saying, she says, 'And I can't pay her 620 euros, find me another one'. And I tell her, 'We don't place anyone for less than 620 euros, plus two bonuses and vacations'. And she insists that she can't pay and that her daughter is paying the difference, and that she doesn't want her daughter to be paying anything. I tell her that she should talk to her daughter but that this is not our problem, maybe they could give her the mornings off and pay her less, and she can find another job in the mornings. She says that seems alright and that they'll talk about it. ... Then the daughter calls me and says that she's worried

about her mother because her mother says she's afraid of the girl, that her face scares her. I tell her, 'Might it not be that your mother is telling you things she's imagined, and that maybe she's telling a few lies? Talk to your mother and tell her not to worry because I'm going to find another job for M'. Then I talked to M. and she told me she was going back to her country, that she had spoken to her husband and her children and they had asked her to go home. ... The thing with the mother is that she didn't want to have anybody there at all. I have tons of cases like that (intermediary, hiring agency).

Elderly persons' refusal of their new condition and of this care relationship may have many aspects. They are clearly aware that once the first step is taken, their needs will only increase. As one social worker commented, 'The moment they have someone working in their house they know it is forever ... elderly people consciously or unconsciously don't want this process to begin'. With greater or lesser difficulty, the daughters attempt to overcome this resistance directly or through the employee.

Once these resistances are overcome, the elderly may develop closer ties to the care worker than their own daughters and sons. The employee is more patient, she shows more affection because she often demonstrates the servile attitude expected from a consoling presence, and she may be a confidante in their complaints about their children. For many elderly women, the employee becomes their loyal witness, while the employees themselves – especially immigrants – project their own anxieties about the care of their own families in their country of origin upon the elderly woman.

Women who live alone deserve special mention, for them loneliness is one of the key factors that pushes them to accept employing someone as long as they have the means to do so and the capacity to recognise the value of their work, like an elderly informant testifies below:

> Me, I have four taking care of me. In the morning I have a girl who has been with me for 14 years. ... In the afternoon another one comes, Lucía, then she goes at 1:30 and until 6 I'm alone and I'm afraid ... I get nervous when I'm alone, that's why this one comes. Lourdes comes at night, when she goes. And then on Saturdays and Sundays another one comes because the others don't want to. Of course, Lucy's obligation is from Monday to Friday, and Saturday and Sunday she doesn't work. It was different 13 years ago ... I had a full-time girl in the house, and she only went out Sunday afternoons after lunch, just for four hours ... It was a different kind of job ... She, that is Lourdes, is the only foreigner, and she talks to me the most. I enjoy talking to her more than to the others. They're good girls, but they have no education (elderly woman).

Because of the physical and mental decline which age implies, the elderly often require intensive care in which nursing, attention and company are interwoven in particularly complex ways. The care of senile people, those with Alzheimer's or other psychosocial problems requires professional care in order to avoid 'burn-out' on the part of the care-giver.

The confusion between the 'all-purpose girl' and caregiving personnel is common with elderly employers, especially with those from the middle or lower-middle class sectors who see domestic service as a necessarily servile relation that they observed among the privileged sectors, and to which they never had access before this point. The separation between attending to a person and to his or her household is not clear, just as the separation between service and the bonds of family obligation are also not clear. To distinguish these elements for analytical purposes does not mean that they can really be thought of as separate (Vega 2009; Anderson 2011). While home-care nurses try against all odds to safeguard their professional principles, domestic care-givers find it difficult to express these limits to others, and feel guilty when reminded of them.

The subjective dilemmas in the elderly-care worker axis are expressed as a strong initial rejection, since the elderly know that the entry of the care worker in the home begins a new phase in their lives. It is also an affirmation that their family members will not be in charge of their daily care. As we saw above, rejection takes on more accentuated gendered expressions when couples are cared for. Class and race are also significant elements insofar as servility and racism are ways of codifying particular visions of femininity that find a privileged place in the sectors of the most vulnerable family caretakers.

Concluding Remarks

Approaches to reproduction, both in theoretical and epistemological debates, have shifted towards an increasing recognition of the activity of care, including paid care in the home. Care has been exposed as a labour that is unjustly divided by gender, class, race and place of origin but is also a key element in the production of subjectivity. However this subjectivity cannot be thought of as a dichotomy (women vs. men). Rather, the different spaces, subjects and imaginaries in which caring is exercised and care is received must be taken into consideration.

In this sense, and taking into account the structural asymmetries between those who employ and those who are employed in care work, we find that the subjectivities and bonds established between the daughter/employers, the elderly beneficiaries and the employees represent one singularity as opposed to other kinds of paid and unpaid support systems. The decline of gendered filial reciprocity in the care of the elderly and the moral economy that sustains it, together with the transformation of female subjectivities in Spain since the mid-1970s, all in a context of an aging population, has brought about an intense reorientation towards hiring caregiving in the home. This has led to the emergence of new dilemmas produced in the triangular relationship between daughters, the elderly and care workers.

For the daughters, paid care is an ambivalent way of transferring some of the more difficult emotional aspects of their parents' care while still remaining involved. As we have seen, they rely upon the mediating role which the employees play. Managing daughters are confronted not only with the increase of care work concerning their elderly, but also with the emotional tensions that arise when seeing their parents' difficulties in accepting their new condition. This often means a lack of understanding and patience that only a collective arrangement with other family members or a third person might be able to relieve.

For the employees, the daughters provide a precarious yet available job. Domestic care-givers also find in the care-managing daughters a source of recognition in a form of work in which overload, solitude and psychological exhaustion are often extreme. This is accentuated in the case of immigrants. While emotional work is understood by care-givers as 'working on' the elderly in their particular ways of confronting age, health problems and depression, this work often also entails emotional work with the daughters.

For the elderly, whether they are direct employers or just beneficiaries, and taking into account differences in gender and class, the problem is principally a matter of accepting their new condition as 'dependents' in a society which rejects vulnerability and dependence. In many cases this puts them in direct conflict with the employees and, more often, with their daughters. Overcoming this resistance and elaborating a new sense of themselves is part of what elderly people must confront, and with them those who assist them and care for their wellbeing. Further research and attention should be devoted to the complex inter-subjective dynamics between employers, employees and the beneficiaries of care in the various stages of aging.

References

Abellán, A. and Pujol, R., 2013. Un perfil de las personas mayores en España, 2013. Indicadores estadísticos básicos. Madrid, *Informes Envejecimiento en Red*, no. 1.

Anderson, B., 2012. Who needs them? Care Work, migration and public policy. *Cuadernos de Relaciones Laborales*, 30(1), pp. 45–61.

Anderson, B., 2000. *Doing the Dirty Work? The global politics of domestic labour*. London: Zed Books.

Arango, L.G., 2010. Género e identidad en el trabajo de cuidado. In: E. De la Garza Toledo and J. Neffa (eds), 2010. *Trabajo, Identidad y Accion Colectiva*, pp. 81–107.

Beauvoir, S., 2005. *El segundo sexo*. Madrid: Cátedra.

Borderías, C., Carrasco, C. and Alemany, C. (eds), 1994. *Las mujeres y el trabajo. Rupturas conceptuales*. Madrid/Barcelona: Fuhem/Icaria.

Butler, J., 2001. *El género en disputa. El feminismo y la subversión de la identidad*. México: Paidós.

Caixeta, L. et al., 2004. *Hogares, cuidados y fronteras. Derechos de las mujeres inmigrantes y conciliación*. Madrid: Traficantes de Sueños.

Carrasco, C., (ed.), 1999. *Mujeres y economía. Nuevas perspectivas para viejos y nuevos problemas*. Barcelona: Icaria.

Carrasquer, P. and Torns, T., 2007. Cultura de la precariedad: conceptualización, pautas y dimensiones: una aproximación desde la perspectiva de género. *Sociedad y Utopía*, 29, pp. 139–56.

Catarino, C. and Oso, L., 2000. La inmigración femenina en Madrid y Lisboa. Hacia una etnización del servicio doméstico y de las empresas de limpieza. *Papers, Revista de Sociologia*, 60, pp. 183–207.

Chodorow, N., 1984. *El ejercicio de la maternidad*. Barcelona: Gedisa.

Colectivo IOÉ, 2001. *Mujer, inmigración y trabajo*. Instituto de Migraciones y Servicios Sociales, Madrid: Ministerio de Trabajo y Asuntos Sociales.

Dalla Costa, M., 2007. *Dinero, perlas y flores en la revolución feminista*. Madrid: Akal.

Dalla Costa, M., and James, S., 1975. *El poder de la mujer y la subversión de la comunidad*. Available on-line at: http://retoricasdaresistencia.blogaliza. org/files/2012/01/Las-mujeres-y-la-subversion-de-la-comunidad-1971.pdf [accessed: 23 April 2014].

Daly, M. and Lewis, J., 2000. The concept of social care and the analysis of contemporary welfare states. *British Journal of Sociology*, 1(2), pp. 281–98.

Davis, A., 2004. El trabajo doméstico toca su fin: una perspectiva de clase. *Mujeres, raza y clase*, Madrid: Akal, pp. 221–39.

Del Valle, T. (ed.), 2002. *Modelos Emergentes en los sistemas y las relaciones de género*. Madrid: Narcea.

Díaz, M., 2008. *Las dinámicas internacionales de cuidado: el caso de Madrid en la desnacionalización del cuidado de menores*. Ph.D. Thesis, Universidad Carlos III, Madrid.

Escrivá, M.A., 1999. *Mujeres peruanas del servicio doméstico en Barcelona: trayectorias sociolaborales*. Ph.D. Thesis, Universidad Autónoma de Barcelona.

Federici, S., 2013. *Revolución en punto cero: trabajo doméstico, reproducción y luchas feministas*. Madrid: Traficantes de Sueños.

Foro de Vida Independiente and Agencia de Asuntos Precarios Todas a Zien, 2011. *Cojos y Precarias Haciendo Vidas Que Importan: Cuaderno Sobre Una Alianza Imprescindible*. Madrid: Traficantes De Sueños.

Folbre, N., 2011. Medir los cuidados: género, empoderamiento y la economía de los cuidados. In: C. Carrasco, C. Borderías and T. Torns (eds), 2011. *El trabajo de los cuidados, historia, teoría y políticas*. Madrid: La Catarata, pp. 278–304.

Fraser, N. and Gordon, L., 1997. Una genealogía de la 'dependencia'. Rastreando una palabra clave del Estado benefactor en los Estados Unidos. In: N. Fraser, 1997. *Iustitia Interrupta*. Bogotá: Siglo del Hombre, pp. 163–200.

Galcerán, M., 2006. Introducción: Producción y reproducción en Marx. In: Laboratorio feminista. *Transformaciones del trabajo desde una perspectiva feminista, producción, reproducción, deseo, consumo*. Madrid: Laboratorio Feminista, pp. 13–27.

Gilligan, C., 1982. *In a Different Voice*. Cambridge, MA: Harvard University Press.

Gutiérrez, E., 2010. *Migration, Domestic Work and Affect*. London: Routledge.

Herrera, G., 2013. *'Lejos de tus pupilas': Familias transnacionales, cuidados y desigualdad social en Ecuador*. Quito: Flacso.

Hill Collins, P., 1990. *Black Feminist Thought*. New York: Harper Collins.

Hochschild, A., 1983. *The Managed Heart: Commercialization of Human Feeling*. Berkeley, CA: University of California Press.

Hochschild, A. and Ehrenreich, B., 2002. *Global Woman: Nannies, Maids and Sex Workers in the New Economy*. New York: Metropolitan Press.

Hondagneu-Sotelo, P., 2001. *Domestica: Immigrant Workers Cleaning and Caring in the Shadows of Affluence*. Berkley, CA: University of California Press.

Hooks, B., 2004. Mujeres negras. Dar forma a la teoría feminista. In: VVAA. *Otras inapropiables. Feminismos desde las fornteras*. Madrid: Traficantes de Sueños, pp. 33–50.

IMSERSO, 2005. *Cuidado a la Dependencia e Inmigración*. Madrid: IMSERSO.

Izquierdo, M.J., 2003. Del sexismo y la mercantilización del cuidado a su socialización: Hacia una política democrática del cuidado. In: SARE. *Cuidar cuesta: costes y beneficios del cuidado*.

Martínez Buján, R., 2010. *Bienestar y cuidados: el oficio del cariño. Mujeres inmigrantes y mayores nativos*. Madrid: CSIC.

Martínez Buján, R., (forthcoming). ¡El trabajo doméstico cuenta! Características y transformaciones del servicio doméstico en España. *Migraciones*.

Maruani, M., Rogerat C. and Torns, T., 2000. *Las nuevas fronteras de la desigualdad hombres y mujeres en el mercado del trabajo*. Barcelona: Icaria.

Marx, C., 2000. *El capital*. Madrid: Akal.

Mestre, R., 2005. Trabajadoras de cuidado. Las mujeres de la ley de extranjería. In: F. Checa and Olmos (eds), 2005. *Mujeres en el camino: el fenómeno de la migración femenina en España*. Barcelona: Icaria.

Molyneux, M., 2005. Debate sobre el trabajo doméstico. In: D. Rodríguez and J. Cooper (eds), 2005. *Más allá del debate sobre el trabajo doméstico: Antología*. UNAM, pp. 13–51.

Narotzky, S., 1990. La renta del afecto: ideología y reproducción social en el cuidado de los viejos. In: D. Comas d'Argemir and A. González Echevarría (eds), 1990. *Familia y relaciones de parentesco. Estudios desde la antropología social*. Valencia: Institut Valencià de la Dona, pp. 45–51.

Orozco, A. and Gil, S., 2011. *Desigualdades a flor de piel: Cadenas globales de cuidados. Concreciones en el empleo de hogar y articulaciones políticas (España)*. Onu Mujeres.

Oso, L., 1998. *La migración hacia España de mujeres jefas de hogar*. Madrid: Instituto de la Mujer.

Parella, S., 2003. *Mujer, inmigrante y trabajadora: la triple discriminación.* Barcelona: Anthropos.

Parreñas, R., 2001. *Servants of Globalization. Women, Migration and Domestic Work.* Stanford, CA: Stanford University Press.

Rodríguez, D. and Cooper, J. (eds), 2005. *El debate sobre el trabajo doméstico.* México: Unam.

Thomas, C., 1993. De-constructing concepts of care. *Sociology*, 27(4), pp. 649–69.

Tobío, C., 2005. *Madres que trabajan. Dilemas y estrategias.* Madrid: Cátedra.

Vega, C., 2009. *Culturas del cuidado en transición: Espacios, sujetos e imaginarios en una sociedad de migración.* Capítulo II. Barcelona: UOC.

Vega, C., 2008. Le soin des autres et le travail de l'affect. *Multitudes*, pp. 51–64.

Chapter 6

'Mum Seems Happy'. Relatives of Dependent Elders and the Difficult Task to Employ a Migrant Care-giver

Sabrina Marchetti

We were going out for dinner … I was driving when my mother felt sick … She
went in a coma, it seemed she would never wake up again but she did. Yet, a side
of her brain was seriously damaged, the one which is responsible for the limbs,
the movement, the speaking and all of that … I didn't like the idea of my mum
staying in the hospital 'cause I have a clear idea about what a family is … thus I
said: I want her at home … This is why I rebuilt this other side of my house, with
a room for my mum, a room for the caretaker and a bathroom especially made
for my mum's problems with the hips (Alice Melloni, 32 years old, unemployed,
married with children).

The story of Alice Melloni[1] contains in a nutshell some recurring elements in most
interviewees' stories: a sudden worsening of their relatives' health conditions;
their consequently becoming fully responsible for their relatives' health care and
living arrangements; the desire to avoid their institutionalisation; and thus the need
to hire a private home-care giver working in their homes.

Thirty-two people were interviewed who, like Alice Melloni, employ a migrant
woman to take care of elderly members of their family, being these their parents,
their partner or their in-laws, with the aim to keep them in their own homes. Although
they are not usually those who pay the care worker from their own money, we
will call these interviewees 'employers' because they are the ones who are mainly
in charge of selecting the care workers, organising their work and, eventually,
deciding to fire them if needs be. Despite the variety between these interviewees
in terms of class and educational backgrounds, their standpoints come together in
emphasising a novel perspective for the debate on migrant domestic and care work.

The aim of this chapter is to shed new light on the debate of migrant domestic
work that has concentrated on the question: is this job a job like any other? We

1   While thanking all interviewees for their participation in this project, I am preserving
their identity with the use of pseudonyms. I also would like to thank Savino Calabrese for
giving me all his support through this research experience. This has been carried out as part
of my wider project: Circular Care (2011–13) sponsored by a Marie Curie Intra European
Fellowship of the 7th European Community Framework Programme.

will return to this question offering, this time, the perspective of employers who are children and partners of dependant elders. It will be shown how, also from this perspective, this is not indeed 'just a normal job', in light of the tensions, expectations and needs which frame employers' attitudes toward paid migrant care-givers. In particular, a crucial feature is the ambiguity of the employers' involvement in assessing the service provided, which, in the specific case of elderly care, cannot rely any longer on the principle of customer-sovereignty.

This discussion will begin with a short overview of the debates on ageing, care giving and migrant domestic work; as well as an illustration of the contexts and the methodology of the research. Later, through analysis of the interview material, what challenges and emotions feature in the personal situation of the employers at the time when they decide to hire someone will be illustrated. Subsequently, we will discuss what is at stake in the commodification of elderly care. The emphasis will be on the way the desires of employers that their relatives will recover (although this is unlikely) enters into the expectations they put on the care workers. Then we will examine the opposite tendency, which is the fear that workers' behaviour might worsen the conditions of the elders which ultimately puts on the employers the responsibility for their wellbeing. Finally, in the last section, my focus will be on employers' narratives which construct a dichotomy between themselves, as those who care for the sick elders on the basis of love and moral commitment, and migrant care-givers who are negatively seen as pushed into it by economic necessity. This is the dimension in which, more than in the others, the fact that paid care-givers are migrants is shaping employers' views on their relationships.

Aging and Care

The rapid ageing of societies that, during the last decades, has taken place in several industrialised countries has fostered an intense academic debate amongst medical scholars as well as amongst economists and sociologists. The phenomenon that has probably triggered most of the discussions is what Olshansky et al. (1991) called the 'expansion of morbidity', meaning the increase in the presence of illness and disabilities due to the prolongation of life duration. The consequent preoccupation with ageing has made scholars talk of an 'anxiety of gerontification' (Posner 1995). This refers, first of all, to the urgency of improving the knowledge about old age, especially from the medical point of view, and to offer adequate support to ageing people through the provision of specific services. Moreover, it also refers to what Chris Phillipson sees as the tendency to depict ageing as a 'social problem' (Phillipson 2013, p. 31). Ageing is indeed seen as a threat to 'techno-muscular capitalism' (Chang and Ling 2000) where the emphasis is on productivity and autonomy, rather than on elders' dependency and sedentariness. The introversion and the detachment from everyday life of the elderly, although accepted in some cultural contexts, is indeed a reason of apprehension in the context being described (Phillipson 2013).

At the same time, the increase in the number of people aged 85 plus, otherwise called the Oldest Olds, has pushed towards a reconceptualisation of life in itself, inviting scholars to see ageing as an experience that involves all phases of the 'life course' (Passuth and Bengtson 1996). In this perspective, a 'solidarity' between generations becomes crucial: since the youngest are equally destined to ageing and illness. It is therefore essential that they take care of the elderly in order to be taken care of as well (in the economic, medical and emotional sense) when they will be old. Moreover, talking about ageing in terms of life course helps us to see it as a social phenomenon whose meaning is not intrinsic to biological and health conditions. In other words, the ageing of every generation will assume a different meaning depending on the cultural, political and social context in which every one of its stages takes place (Timonen and Ebray 2008).

Not only the condition of the ageing care-receivers, but also those caring for them will be greatly influenced by socio-economic and cultural conditions. In the aftermath of women's emancipation and the crisis of welfare states that occurred in the last decades, we observe conflicting tendencies within the political economy of care depending on the context (Mahon and Robinson 2011; Esping-Andersen 1999). In general, one could say that if, on the one side, a more culturally accepted defamilialisation of care encourages family members to discard caring responsibilities, on the other, states cannot come to terms with the promotion of a fully publicly financed and provided assistance, especially at times of economic recession. The implementation of a collective ethics of care remains so far a political ideal (Fraser 1989; Tronto 1993). What is rampant instead is the market commodification of care work, at the condition of using cheap and flexible labour that is predominantly found amongst working-class and (undocumented) migrant women (Triandafyllidou 2013; Folbre 2012; Glenn 2010).

It is of foremost importance to underline how both ageing and caregiving have strong gendered, ethnicised and class-based features. Scholars talk about a 'feminisation of care' with reference, first of all, to the fact that women generally outnumber men in the 85 plus age group, and they are thus the main recipients of elderly care. Secondly, this also refers to the fact that women are more frequently found amongst those that take care of the sick and the elderly: as paid nurses and care workers in hospitals, nursing homes and home-care; or as informal care-givers in their own households (Zelizer 2010). This second feature is strongly determined by the cultural and social norms that predominantly assign women – especially those who belong to economically and racially disadvantaged social groups – to such jobs. For instance, Beverly Skeggs (1997) shows how the specific socialisation of British working-class girls has a corresponding outcome in their willingness to engage in care-related occupations. Evelyn Nakano Glenn (2010) talks about how the system in the US is directly or indirectly 'forcing' many women to take up paid and unpaid caring jobs. Along the same lines, Nancy Folbre (2012) makes a distinction between the different kinds of motivations that push particularly women into care. Glenn's and Folbre's theories will be further discussed in the analysis of the empirical material that was gathered.

For now, let use conclude by linking this general debate on care and ageing to the more specific one on migrant women's paid employment within the 'international division of reproductive labour' (Parreñas 2001; Kofman 2012). The transnational commodification of care work has been at the centre of a debate that has remarkably explored the inequality characterising this scenario (Williams 2011; Yeates 2009). Great parts of this debate have focused on the uniqueness of this labour sector in comparison to others for the intimacy that it conveys, due to the physicality of the care work, the privacy of the domestic setting in which it takes place and the relevance of the interpersonal dimension it entails (Boris and Parreñas 2010; Wolkowitz 2006). Looking at this intimacy, some authors have thus concluded that this is 'not just another job' (Anderson 2001; Lutz 2008), and that 'love' is actually the matter of the commodification that it is at stake here (Hochschild 2002). As stated in the Introduction, our specific intervention will be exactly on this part of the debate. A transformative view on the issue of paid care work should also be adopted, by looking at the way the entrance of migrants into this sector has modified the traditional setting of family care provision in Europe. The increasing participation of migrants draws attention to the changes in the 'culture of care' (Vega Solís 2009), and to the gradual ethnicisation of caring skills and attitudes (Marchetti 2014; Marchetti and Scrinzi 2011; De Regt 2009). Whereas often these transformations are seen from the perspective of workers, this chapter makes the effort to look at them from the perspective of employers.

Context and Methodology

The empirical material that is used for this chapter is part of a wider project for which more than 70 people have been involved in semi-structured and in-depth interviews on the topic of paid elderly care and women's migration from Eastern Europe to Italy. The interviewees were almost equally distributed between migrant care-givers (from Ukraine, Poland and Georgia) and Italian relatives of elderly care-receivers. The narratives provided by this second group of interviewees will be the object of my analysis in this chapter.

The snow-balling of contacts allowed us to conduct interviews with 32 people who have a relative taken care of by an Eastern European woman. In four cases these interviews involved two people at the same time, usually two siblings who spoke together about their family experience. In three instances, two siblings were interviewed separately. There are thus a total of 14 interviewees who are related to other interviewees from the same 'care unit', meaning the same 'unit' of care-receivers which includes family members and paid care-givers. Most frequently, the care-recipients were the parents of the interviewees. More precisely, home-care was provided to one parent in 17 cases and to both parents in seven cases. There were also two cases in which the care-receivers were the husbands of the interviewees, and another six in which they were their in-laws. In nine cases the care-receivers had recently passed away.

All in all, the employers that were interviewed spoke about the care provided to 34 elderly people. The health conditions of 20 of them were characterised by dementia, due to Alzheimer's disease (six cases), or a mix of illnesses, for example Parkinson's, damage to the brain after a stroke and senility for the rest. Other care-receivers had a chronic illness as a consequence of cancer, heart disease, digestive problems and so forth. Several of these elderly had severely reduced mobility, spending their days in bed or a wheelchair, due to an injury (rupture of thigh-bone especially) or to their general condition. In six instances the care-recipient lived in the same apartment of the interviewee, while in another seven instances they lived in a separate apartment which was however in the same house or compound as their children.

This sample of employers was predominantly composed by women (26 out of 32), in line with the feminisation of caregiving that is illustrated above. This also corresponds to a feminisation in the group of care-receivers: 26 out of the 32 interviewees are responsible for the care of an elderly woman. It is also interesting that in the case of siblings, one may notice the tendency to a traditionally gendered distribution of tasks amongst them, with sisters doing everyday and physical tasks, and brothers the more detached organisational ones. This is however contradicted by a couple of cases in which the sisters were not participating at all in the care for their elderly relatives and left it in the hands of their brothers. Moreover, although the majority of interviewees are married and with children, several of them are also single, divorced, in an informal partnership or do not have children, thus testifying to the increasing variety of household composition in contemporary Italy.

From the point of view of class and educational backgrounds, interviewees showed a great variation especially in the case of women, going from university professors to housewives and factory workers. More limited is the profile of the six male interviewees who are all well-educated professionals. Looking at the care-receivers, their background is very heterogeneous in terms of their past professions: from former peasants or artisans, to teachers, bank clerks and professionals. This great variation suggests that, in today's Italy, the commodification of home-care is not a middle- or upper-class prerogative but it instead transverses all social groups.

The 'employers' could be very well be described as 'care managers', as Maurizio Ambrosini describes in Chapter 2. They are in charge of all decisions related to the provision of care for their relatives, for example about the choice between home-care and a nursing home, or about the kind of support to request from public rather than private services or finally about changes in accommodations or the reorganisation of their domestic spaces according to the specific care needs of the elderly care-recipient. Care managers are usually occupied with facilitating care-recipients in expressing their wishes, as well as with harmonising needs and expectations of all family members. They also gather information about the care services which are available from public or private sources, and their conditions (cost, modality, and the specific access procedures) in order to arrange what Da Roit calls a 'care package' (Da Roit 2012, p. 55).

It is important to notice that, in the Italian context, the actual make-up of these 'care packages' is very influenced by the region where people live. In fact, after the promulgation of the Law on Social Services (2000) and the Law on Federalism (2009), the provision of health and care services is differently financed and organised in each Italian region. For this reason, it is necessary to briefly mention that the interviews were held in a northern Italian province characterised by a dynamic industrial structure and a developed system of social services. Half of the interviews were done in the main administrative town, which has about 170,000 inhabitants, while the rest of them were conducted in smaller towns and villages in the surrounding area. The options available to care managers in this wealthy and well-administered region, to find the solutions that suit them best, are much greater than the rest of Italy. However, as Francesca Degiuli (2010) explains, the decision to recur to live-in home-care cannot be fully explained by the more or less availability of services and structures. It is rather based on shared cultural values and caring traditions. The private employment of a live-in care-giver is a predominant pattern in all Italian regions. The result is a figure of more than 800,000 workers for this sector, 70 per cent of which are migrants, providing assistance to about one million Italian elderly people (Pasquinelli and Rusmini 2013).

Employers and Care-giving

In this section, we will delve into the analysis of the ethnographic material by illustrating what emerged as the predominant response of employers in this sample to the care needs of the relatives of those interviewed. In so doing, this first section aims to present the dilemmas, the tensions and the emotions which are in the background of the employment of a migrant care-giver and upon which employers decide to hire someone.

The quote by Alice Melloni which opened this chapter has already shown the very common situation in which the dependent person had an unexpected loss of autonomy after an accident or a sudden illness. Different is the case when an elderly person gradually looses autonomy through the years. In a comparative study on elderly care in Italy and in the Netherlands, Barbara Da Roit argues this slow worsening of one's conditions could offer people the opportunity to choose the kind of care that they want to receive and make the corresponding arrangements (Da Roit 2010, p. 120). However, as Da Roit states, and we are in agreement, this 'gradualism' is a chance that is seldom taken by ageing people in Italy. This is the way Emma Donati describes the same problem in the case of her parents-in-law:

> We [me and my husband] encouraged them to deal with what, soon or later, would have happened. But it has been a fierce struggle. They never wanted to make any change in their house, to move to a new place, or to employ someone who could gradually take care of them, given that their health conditions were already precarious (Emma Donati, 54 years old, civil servant, married with children).

Just before the interview, the condition of Emma's father-in-law had utterly worsened with him having a double leg amputation due to diabetes. This required a care provision for which the whole family was fully unprepared; and forced Emma in a situation that Da Roit argues to be typical of the Italian context. Due to a mix of cultural and material reasons, Italian elderly are reluctant to make 'individual choices' about their imminent worsening, and therefore force their children, at one point or another, to make instead a 'family decision' in which gendered norms and caring traditions are likely to prevail.[2]

In general, urgent care needs of this kind find a solution in mobilising resources from inside the household and, in fact, more of the employers that were interviewed had been the direct care-giver at an early stage of the elderly person's deterioration. As an example, Giordana Carboni and Mauro Vicari slept at their mother's when she started to have the first signs of dementia and feared to be alone. In another case, Linda Santini has been sleeping on the sofa in her mother's bedroom for months. The personal mobilisation is stronger when the sick person is the interviewee's partner. Maria Fioramonti for example is personally taking care of her husband after he survived a stroke 22 years ago, and Graziella Minoli does the same with hers, who has had Parkinson's and reduced mobility for eight years now. A crucial form of direct engagement in caregiving is when a decision is made to let the sick person move-in – as Alice Melloni has done, restructuring a part of her apartment in order to accommodate her mother.

However, several interviewees also tell how the care needs of their relatives has threatened their spirit. In their own words, they describe what scholars call a 'subjective care-giver burden', that is when their perception about how the relative's sickness and the caregiving has worsened their lives by putting them under a strong psychological pressure (Stuckey et al. 1996). Renato Udeschini is a retired engineer whose mother's ageing is accompanied by reduced mobility and sight impairment. When asked to describe this period of his life, he says: '[It is] sad because you see the person that have you adored all your life, the person who gave you life, you see her slowly passing away' (Renato Udeschini, 64 years old, retired engineer, married with no children).

This burden becomes heavier to carry due to the fact that the actual moments in which the interviewees provide physical care to their loved one can be a real struggle. An example is offered by Giordana Carboni whose 84-year old mother is affected by Alzheimer's disease. Giordana tells me about her difficulty in handling her mother's situation by recounting the following episode:

> I realise that it's tough for me, with my mum. For example yesterday ... I bathe
> her and she was all the time pressing the shower-button: 'Mum, stop it! You are

---

2 This often exposes care managers to the burden of a 'substitute decision' for the elderly who can no longer express their fundamental wishes. These decisions involve complex ethical issues in relation to understanding what is the fine line between intervening and abstaining when caring for others (Botti 2000, p. 223).

opening the cold water!' ... I told to myself: keep calm. ... But at one point, yesterday, I got this impulsion to hit her on the hands. It occurs to me, sometimes, and that's scary. Then, I pretend to do as if everything it's ok, and I leave. ... It is not that I am bad, it's that it's difficult to accept seeing your parents in this condition (Giordana Carboni, 58 years old, secretary, divorced with children).

It must be noted that, as in the case of Caterina, seven of the 32 employers that were interviewed are caring for a relative with Alzheimer's disease. This is an extremely difficult illness to deal with, because of the stark change in the personality of the patients in comparison with the past (Atchley 2000). They appear fragile and locked in their thoughts and emotions which are difficult to deal with properly – especially for non-health care professionals. This exposes the 'othering' of portraying them as 'living deads' or as being in a 'second childhood' (Kitwood 1997; Douthit 2006). Along these lines, interviewees share an uneasiness regarding the 'new' identity of their parents, which further complicates the caregiving.

As a result, employers' need to delegate their commitment to caregiving, at least partially, comes to the fore. The employment of a paid worker is usually a relief for the interviewees as it prevents them from damaging their own physical and mental health. 'I could not take it any longer because I would become sick myself of sorrow and depression', said Graziella Minoli, a retired factory worker, who recently decided to employ a paid care-giver to help her in assisting her sick husband after eight years in which she did it all by herself.

The personal situation of the employers when they decide to hire someone has been described above. It is very important to underline how this is situated in a very specific moment of these people's lives during which they are sadly realising the passing away of their beloved, they are coping with their moral obligations to intergenerational care, as well as becoming aware of the distress that this situation is causing them. In addition, they have to find practical solutions that would allow their relatives to stay in their private homes while providing them the proper health and care assistance. The next section will examine the ways in which these tensions enter the employment relationship.

Expectations

The first dimension by which this happens has to do with the process that typically leads employers to formulate *what* is the care that they want to pay for. In general, interviewees tended to emphasise that they needed to find a 'nice' person that would assist their sick relatives in a 'caring' manner. They want their relatives to be in a 'quiet and calm' situation, with a paid care-giver that treats them with 'kindness'. They would like to find someone who is 'sweet', and able to 'reassure them' in moments in which they are anxious or feel lonely. In some cases they know that the diseases of their relatives require the care-giver's constant physical presence since only 'touching and hugging' gives them comfort. At the same time, this person should be able to bathe them, fix their toilet, dress them and comb their hair, as well as administer simple medications. In so doing, the employers acknowledge the profoundly emotional character of the work that there are paying for. It is a job very much based on what Carol Wolkowitz calls body-work; one that Rhacel Parreñas and Eileen Boris would list amongst the 'intimate labours' (Wolkowitz 2006; Boris and Parreñas 2010). The capacity of tending and being attentive to the care-recipient is of utmost importance in this realm.

However, when it comes to 'translate' all of that into working tasks, it is not so easy to say what is proper to expect from a paid care-giver. The interview with the sisters Paola and Marina Martini illustrates the complexity of this point. Their father recently fell sick and he had to have his stomach removed. He is also psychologically declining very fast. His daughters took care of him after he came back home from the hospital but also wanted to employ someone that could be with him while they work. Marina, who is herself employed in the elderly care sector, lives in the apartment above her father, in a village in the countryside. Laura, the other sister, lives in the big town a few kilometres away, but she comes to visit her father and sister every weekend. During the interview, these are the sorts of statements that they use in order to illustrate their disappointment with the first care-giver that they employed:

Paola: Our father needed someone next to him in order to allow us to go to work. A person that could motivate him … 'cause he was very down not only physically but also mentally.

Marina: She didn't speak much. She sat next to him and they would watch TV for hours and hours.

Paola: We told her to take care of the vegetable garden 'cause our dad has always loved gardening … But then she was doing it while dad was just sitting there.

Marina: Also with food: you have to tease him a bit, make something special … but she was not good at it … I tried to give her some tips … like: 'since dad needs to eat little but often, maybe you could prepare a cake'. But she: 'no, I never baked a cake in my life and I won't start now'. She was very rigid, in her mind (Paola Martini, 48 years old, secretary, married with children; and Marina Martini, 40 years old, care worker, married with children).

As stated, the two sisters are talking about a worker that did not satisfy them, and who they fired after a few weeks of employment. What it is interesting is the way Paola and Marina formulated the expectations they put on the shoulders of this worker. They would like someone that, while allowing them the time for their jobs, also provides their father what Nancy Folbre (2012) defines an 'interactive care', which is an active form of engagement in the physical and mental wellbeing of the care-recipient. In other words, they see their father's dementia as 'a disease that can be defeated' (George and Whitehouse 2010) and therefore are worried that if the care-giver does not properly engage in this 'struggle' to keep alive the resilient capacities, he will decline even faster. This confirms the character of home-care as a 'relational service' (Cranford and Miller 2013) where the personality of the worker puts her job in jeopardy, as her capacity to respond to the desires of the care-recipient and the daughters alike proved impossible. Laura and Paola are asking this woman to be witty and chatty in order to entertain and animate their declining father. This woman, however, does not seem to be able or to be willing to do so. Her refusal to bake cakes is perceived as the incapacity to adapt to the specific care needs of their father, and also as the proof that she is not honestly interested in his wellbeing.

In so doing, the interview with Laura and Paola suggests that the intimate character of this job lies not only in the care seen as body-work (Marchetti 2013), but also quite remarkably in the fact that the two sisters *expect* this woman to achieve to their desires. This form of intimacy takes place at an almost psychological level: they expect the care-giver to be able to put into practice what *they* wish could bring about a – yet unlikely – recovery of their father. It is a form of what Arlie Hochschild (2012) would call an 'outsourcing of the self' and which cannot go without repercussions on what is considered 'good care'.

This picture is further complicated when we consider the case in which care-receivers are affected by dementia. For Nancy Folbre, the fact that these people (care recipients) are not capable of expressing their own satisfaction subverts the assumptions on consumer sovereignty that dominate in customer services as well as in personal care (Folbre 2012, p. 3). Anna Yeatman (2000) argues that this unsettles the principles of contemporary welfare as far as this is based on the provision of 'services'. Likewise, in home-care, it becomes extremely hard to assess the output of paid elderly care. An illustration of how this has an impact on the employment of the paid care-givers can be found again in the interview with Alice Melloni. In making a comparison between the three women that she employed, at different times, for taking care of her mother, she explains:

> It is difficult to tell my mother's feelings. My mother doesn't talk. She communicates with her eyes. But her 'yes' or 'not' are not very clear. Yet, I'm sure that she got so used to Tanya. Because she was so sweet with my mum … My mum seemed happy … With the other two … she was often annoyed. And I'm not saying that because I didn't like them. With Tania my mother got sick only once in a whole winter. Afterwards, she was always sick (Alice Melloni, 32 years old, unemployed, married with children).

Alice is in the difficult position of having to judge, on behalf of her mother, the quality of the job done by different paid care-givers. Given the impossibility to fully rely on what her mother communicates with her glances, Alice is searching for other inputs to assess whether paid care-givers are improving or not her mother's wellbeing. A source of information was the changes in her mother's mood ('my mum seemed happy', 'she seemed annoyed'). Yet, given the vagueness of this criterion, Alice also refers to something more tangible: the fact that, with Tania, her mother was physically more healthy.

In concluding this section we must return to the initial question of what it is *really* at stake in the payment for elderly care. The expectations and judgements expressed by employers like Paola, Marina and Alice unsettle shared assumptions on service/work due to the intangible character of the satisfaction of the care-receivers. In addition, it is also impossible to measure precisely the correspondence between their wellbeing and the workers' performance. The object of commodification here is the capacity of the care-giver to embody the desires of their employers, meaning their wish that there could be a way to soften the hardship of their loved ones' illness.

Mistrust and Anxieties

At the very opposite side of these wishful expectations that paid care-givers could improve their elderly clients' condition is the fear that they could instead, in some ways, *hurt* them. Nancy Folbre, again, discusses how trust is a fundamental element in caring jobs, since the collaboration between *all* the people involved is what determines the quality of the service provided (Folbre 2012, pp. 35–6). Employers should find a balance between controlling workers and giving them freedom to accomplish their tasks as they wish, in a mutual spirit of collaboration and discretion. What happens instead is that employers are continuously checking on their employees in order to verify whether they are doing it right, and not, eventually, causing some damage. In fact, several interviewees talk about their anxiety for the possibility that care workers could damage the resilient mental and physical capacities of their relatives. When talking about their employees, they say statements like:

> [In the morning] she kept her in bed the longer she could … She had the tendency to give her tranquillizers (Anita Arrigoni, 55 years old, teacher, married with children).

> We told her thousands of times that she should not raise her voice and shout [to our mother] 'cause … it only makes it worse (Franco Casali, 52 years old, financial consultant, divorced with children).

> I gave her instructions to never leave my mother alone, not even for a second … but nothing: one day, it was exactly in this way in which she broke her thigh-bone (Loredana Basile, 65 years old, retired nutritionist, married without children).

Some interviewees mentioned the fear of finding bruises on their relatives' bodies, while others worried that the worker would give them the wrong medications.

The sisters Patrizia and Laura Micheli who, together with their brother Roberto, take care of their ageing parents, describe a worrying case. Roberto and Laura live, with their own families, in the same compound as their parents, although in different houses. Therefore, they always had the impression of being in control of what happened with the care-giver that they employed to take care of their parents until the moment they repeatedly heard loud voices coming from their parents' house, at night. This is how they found out that the care-giver was abusive:

> *Laura:* She was actually subjugating our mother. She forbade her to talk, to say certain things, and to do others. She was always at her back! *Patrizia:* In that period mum had strong difficulties in talking, she even stopped writing … *Laura:* We thought that it was our mother's fault, that she was declining. Until the moment we understood that the problem was this woman (Patrizia Micheli, 45 years old, teacher, married with children; and Laura Micheli, 55 years old, university professor, married with children).

After firing this worker, the conditions of their mother greatly improved which made them suspicious that she had secretly given her extra tranquilisers. The problem of physical and psychological abuse against dependent elderly is increasingly being investigated by international scholarship (Daichman 2005) and by NGOs (Ligabue 2010). These studies draw attention to the easy slippage into violent behaviour by all the subjects involved in home-care: the paid care-giver, the care-recipient and the employers. In the experience of Laura and Patrizia, this discovery was surely a reason for distress and caused them feelings of guilt and renewed anxieties.

These worries address the very important issue of training and competences for private care-givers. In Italy, the majority of persons employed in this sector are migrant women who might not have a specific professional background in assisting the mentally and physically ill or handicapped. However, this question of training tends to be undermined by the employers themselves who, during the course of the interviews, admitted that this was not one of their criteria for the selection of candidates. Some of them, however, were lucky enough to find workers who had specific knowledge about geriatric illnesses thanks to previous professional or personal experience. Some had participated in training courses that non-profit organisations are increasingly offering in Italian cities (Rusmini 2013).

It is important to underline, in conclusion, that the relationship between employers and employees in home-care is under pressure due to a series of dangers and conflicting expectations. The result is that most employers do not fully dismiss their role as care-givers, while they are taking on the role of care managers. What happens is rather a division between the role of the paid worker as the one in charge of everyday face-to-face interactions (the 'interactive care' that Folbre writes about), and that of the employer who cares more in a general sense for the physical and psychological wellbeing of the care-recipient. Similar worker-employer relationships have been observed in the field of private childcare where working mothers think of themselves as those in charge of the education and wellbeing of their children, although the everyday caring tasks are covered by a (migrant) woman that they employ (Anderson 2000).

This dichotomy, exacerbated by the usually poor health of the care recipients, demands the involvement of employers to assess the deteriorating health conditions of the care-recipient. Often this assessment, as illustrated previously, is based on very intangible signs which only those who 'love' or are very close to the care-recipient might be able to decipher. This is where the intimacy that employers describe in their taking care of their relatives is featured, despite the fact that they are employing someone else for day-to-day tasks.

The next section will show how, given these conditions, and the fact that the workers usually have a migrant background, their capacity to be fully responsible for the wellbeing of ill care-receivers is undermined.

Love and Money

The first urgent answer to the care needs of elderly relatives is usually found from inside the household. The availability of these resources is usually presented by interviewees as being based on their love and affection for their sick relatives. Also the decision to take their relatives inside their homes is presented in this same way. Licia Mannoia, for example, whose mother was diagnosed with cancer seven years ago, tells me 'I love my mother so much that I wanted her to be here, at home'. In a similar vein, the Martini sisters have said, 'We love very much our daddy, and this is why we are always here available for him'. This same view is shared by Giordana Carboni, 58 years old, divorced, who, in a self-reflective moment of our conversation, acknowledges, 'I never cut the umbilical cord'.

It is important to notice that seeing care provision as an expression of love is endorsed by those who delegated most of the care for their relatives to a paid worker. In other words, although these interviewees have become 'care managers' rather than direct 'care-givers', the hiring of a paid worker is not saving them from being mentally and physically devoted to their sick relatives. They fulfil this obligation through a mix of providing care directly and organising someone else who would do it on their behalf. This view on care work as an act of love is very much in line with what Nancy Folbre suggests in her book *For Love and Money* (2012). Folbre calls 'instrinsic motivations' the affection that pushes us to take care of needy friends and relatives (Folbre 2012, pp. 22–4): yet, while 'love' is seen as a proper 'intrinsic' motivation to perform caring tasks, 'money' is considered instead as a more suspicious 'extrinsic' reason to engage into it. Also Viviana Zelizer (2009) confirms such an understanding of care by arguing that, in the realm of intimacy, love and money have been constructed as two 'hostile worlds'. This distinction, I argue, affects the representation of migrant care-givers and therefore, in some instances, the relationship that employers have with them.

Engaging in paid care work with the purpose of earning money is something that it is clearly shared by those who migrate to Italy with the purpose of finding employment in this sector. 'Greedy' is the recurring attribute through which several employers described the women working for them. Below is an example from the interview with Renato Udeschini:

> I think that the goal of all of these women [from Eastern Europe] is to accumulate as much money as they can … It is obvious that working more, for example sacrificing their holidays to earn more money, is in their DNA … They have an attachment to money that is something be primordial, due to the fact that [in Eastern Europe] they live in great poverty (Renato Udeschini, 64 years old, retired engineer, married without children).

The quote from Renato introduces a specific form of ethnicisation of Eastern European women that is at play in narratives of this kind. They are portrayed as self-interested, money-eager and opportunist in an essentialist manner. Their willingness to work extra hours, renouncing their days off, is negatively interpreted as a self-deprivation aimed to accumulate more savings, and taken as proof that for Eastern Europeans 'the money is never enough'. Some employers are literally shocked when they find that the care workers are taking on small extra jobs in their free time, for example on weekends or during lunch-breaks.

The self-representation of employers as a 'loving family' that has been illustrated earlier in this chapter is in stark contrast with the image that some employers provide of migrant women, describing them as 'greedy' and as instrumentally taking up care jobs. The view of Evelyn Nakano-Glenn (2010) is illuminating in this respect. She sees care (for the elderly, the sick and disabled) as one of the most abject activities that some people are 'forced' to take up because of their specific condition and of the attributes that have been historically attached to it. Glenn distinguishes then between 'need' and 'status' as the main forms of coercion that push people belonging to specific categories to take up caring tasks. If traditionally daughters and wives are incited by moral obligations to do the care work, migrants and working-class people are pushed into it by economic necessity (Glenn 2010, p. 7).

These two different paths towards care work echo the intrinsic dichotomy between the relatives and the migrant care-givers. This is a dichotomy between high-level moral qualities, which are expressed in terms of 'love', and the inferior dirty duties traditionally assigned to people at the lower echelons of the social scale, who take up care because of 'money'.

Concluding Remarks

As mentioned in the introduction, this chapter is an attempt to go back to the classic question in the debate on paid domestic work: 'is this job a job like any other?' When examining this question from the position of the employers, the perspectives presented in this chapter corroborate the argument that no, indeed, it is not a job like any other.

First of all, there is an ambiguity in the division of roles between employers and workers. This division comes to the fore when relatives of sick, elderly persons take the role of the 'managers' of care and supposedly assign to paid care-givers the face-to-face, everyday and interactive assistance. However, despite being 'managers', the interviewees still claim to maintain an intimate connection with the care-recipient and see themselves as the best interpreters of their relatives' desires. Ultimately, employers portray themselves as the only ones that can actually assess the wellbeing of the care-recipients. This is especially so when the elderly are people with dementia and thus the interpretation of their needs are more heavily put on the shoulders of their relatives, who have to assess the service received 'on their behalf'.

Secondly, employers tend to portray migrant workers as not 'honestly' interested in the conditions of the care-receivers, or not capable of improving them – when not damaging them. Employers create a division in the qualities and motivations that one needs to foster in order to properly take care of sick elders: the high-level qualities, the prerogative of the 'loving family' and the low-level ones based on instrumental and money-led priorities. Thus, employers give emphasis to the relational character of this work for which, however, they do not consider migrant workers to be always suitable. At the same time, they are very concerned by the unreliability of their employees for the physical care of their relatives.

Another important issue has to do with the specific form of intimacy that employers would wish to have with their workers: they would like to find in them allies that help them in recuperating the resilient capacities of their sick relatives, at the mental and physical level. Employers expect the workers to give shape to the gestures, small activities and caring attitudes that, in their wishes, are possibly improving the health of their relatives. This expectation, in my view, reinforces the qualities-based dichotomy between employers and workers by defining the first one as those who know better what is best for their relatives and being those who 'really' love them, while the others are in an ancillary position simply as wage earners.

References

Ambrosini, M., 2013. *Irregular Migration and Invisible Welfare*. New York: Palgrave Macmillan.

Anderson, B., 2001. Just another job? Paying for domestic work. *Gender & Development*, 9(1), pp. 25–33.

Anderson, B., 2000. *Doing the Dirty Work? The Global Politics of Domestic Labour*. London: Zed Books.

Atchley, R.C., 2000. *Continuity and Adaptation in Aging: Creating Positive Experiences*. Baltimore: Johns Hopkins University Press.

Boris, E., and Parreñas, R.S. (eds), 2010. *Intimate Labors: Cultures, Technologies, and the Politics of Care*. Stanford, CA: Stanford University Press.

Botti, C., 2000. *Bioetica ed etica delle donne. Relazioni, affetti e potere.* Milano: Zadig.

Chang, K.A., and Ling, L., 2000. Filipina domestic workers in Hong Kong. In: M.H. Marchand and A.S. Runyan (eds), 2000. *Gender and Global Restructuring: Sightings, sites and resistances.* London: Routledge, pp. 27–43.

Cranford, C.J. and Miller, D., 2013. Emotion Management from the Client's Perspective: the Case of Personal Home Care. *Work, Employment & Society*, 27(5), pp. 785–801.

Da Roit, B., 2010. *Strategies of Care: Changing Elderly Care in Italy and the Netherlands.* Amsterdam: Amsterdam University Press.

Da Roit, B. 2012. The Netherlands: the struggle between universalism and cost containment. *Health and Social Care in the Community*, 20(3), pp. 228–37.

Daichman, L.S., 2005. Elder abuse in developing nations. In: M.L. Johnson et al. (eds), 2005. *The Cambridge Handbook of Age and Ageing.* Cambridge: Cambridge University Press, pp. 323–31.

De Regt, M., 2009. Preferences and Prejudices: Employers' Views on Domestic Workers in the Republic of Yemen. *Signs*, 34(3), pp. 559–81.

Degiuli, F., 2010. The burden of long-term care: How Italian family care-givers become employers. *Ageing and Society*, 30(5), pp. 755–77.

Douthit, K., 2006. Dementia in the Iron Cage: the Biopsychiatric Construction of Alzheimer's Dementia'. In: J. Baars et al., (eds), 2006. *Aging, Globalization and Inequality: The New Critical Gerontology.* Amityvill: Baywood Publishing Company, pp. 159–82.

Esping-Andersen, G. 1999. *Social Foundations of Post-industrial Economies.* New York: Oxford University Press.

Folbre, N., 2012. *For Love and Money.* New York: Sage.

Fraser, N., 1989. Talking about needs: Interpretive contests as political conflicts in welfare-state societies. *Ethics*, 99(2), pp. 291–313.

George, D. and Whitehouse, P., 2010. Dementia and Mild Cognitive Impairment in Social and Cultural Context. In: D. Dannefer and C. Phillipson (eds), 2010. *The Sage Handbook of Social Gerontology.* London: Palgrave, pp. 343–56.

Glenn, E.N., 2010. *Forced to Care: Coercion and Caregiving in America.* Harvard, MA: Harvard University Press.

Hochschild, A., 2012. *The Outsourced Self: Intimate Life in Market Times.* New York: Henry Holt.

Hochschild, A., 2002. Love and Gold. In: B. Ehrenreich and A. Hochschild (eds), 2002. *Global Woman: Nannies, Maids, and Sex Workers in the New Economy.* New York: Henry Holt, pp. 15–30.

Kitwood, T., 1997. *Dementia Reconsidered: The Person Comes First.* Philadelphia, PA: Open University Press.

Kofman, E., 2012. Gendered labour migrations in Europe and emblematic migratory figures. *Journal of Ethnic and Migration Studies*, 39(4), pp. 579–600.

Ligabue, L., 2010. *Diade: Attività svolte ed elementi emersi dal progetto.* Carpi: Anziani e non solo.

Lutz, H., 2008. *Migration and Domestic Work: A European perspective on a global theme.* Aldershot: Ashgate.

Mahon, R., and Robinson, F., 2011 *Feminist Ethics and Social Policy: Towards a New Global Political Economy of Care.* Vancouver: UBC Press.

Marchetti, S., 2014. *Black Girls. Migrant Domestic Workers and Colonial Legacies.* Boston: Brill.

Marchetti, S., 2013. Domestiche, assistenti o dame di compagnia? Identità performative e pratiche lavorative di cura nelle narrative di donne migranti. In: E. Bellè, B. Poggio and G. Selmi (eds), 2013. *Attraverso i confini del genere. Atti del convegno.* Trento: Università di Trento, pp. 415–28.

Marchetti, S., and Scrinzi, F., 2011. The gendered construction of a 'caring Otherness'. In:

Caponio, T., et al., (eds), 2011. *World Wide Women: Globalizzazione, Generi, Linguaggi. Volume III.* Torino: CIRSDe, pp. 29–38.

Olshansky, S.J. et al., 1991. Trading off longer life for worsening health. The expansion of morbidity hypothesis. *Journal of Aging and Health,* 3(2), pp. 194–216.

Parreñas, R.S., 2001. *Servants of Globalization: Women, Migration and Domestic Work.* Stanford, CA: Stanford University Press.

Pasquinelli, S., and Rusmini, G., (eds), 2013. *Badare non basta. Il lavoro di cura: attori, progetti, politiche.* Roma: Ediesse.

Passuth, P. and Bengston, V.L., 1996. Sociological theories of aging. Current perspectives and future directions. In: J. Quadagno and D. Street (eds), 1996. *Aging for the Twenty First Century.* New York: St Martin's Press, pp. 333–55.

Phillipson, C., 2013. *Ageing.* Cambridge: Wiley.

Posner, R.A., 1995. *Aging and Old Age.* Chicago, IL: University of Chicago Press.

Rusmini, G., 2013. I progetti di sostegno del lavoro privato di cura: un bilancio. In: S. Pasquinelli and G. Rusmini (eds), 2013. *Badare non basta. Il lavoro di cura: attori, progetti, politiche.* Rome: Ediesse, pp. 155–82.

Skeggs, B., 1997. *Formations of Class and Gender. Becoming Respectable.* London: Sage.

Stuckey J. Neundorfer, M. and Smyth, K., 1996. Burden and Well-being. The Same Coin or Related Currency? *The Gerontologist,* 36(5), pp. 686–93.

Timonen, V. and Ebrary, I., 2008. *Ageing Societies: A comparative introduction.* New York: Open University Press.

Triandafyllidou, A. (ed.), 2013. *Irregular Migrant Domestic Workers in Europe: Who Cares?* Aldershot: Ashgate.

Tronto, J., 1993. *Moral Boundaries: A political argument for an ethic of care.* New York: Routledge.

Vega Solís, C., 2009. *Culturas del cuidado en transición: Espacios, sujetos e imaginarios en una sociedad de migración.* Madrid: Editorial UOC.

Williams, F., 2011. Towards a transnational analysis of the political economy of care. In: R. Mahon and F. Robinson, 2011. *Feminist Ethics and Social Policy: Towards a New Global Political Economy of Care*. Vancouver: UBC Press, pp. 21–38.

Wolkowitz, C., 2006. *Bodies at Work*. New York: Sage.

Yeates, N., 2009. *Globalizing Care Economies and Migrant Workers: Explorations in Global Care Chains*. New York: Palgrave Macmillan.

Yeatman, A., 2009. *Individualization and the Delivery of Welfare Services: Contestation and Complexity*. New York: Palgrave Macmillan.

Zelizer, V., 2010. Caring Everywhere. In: E. Boris and R.S. Parreñas (eds), 2010. *Intimate Labors: Cultures, Technologies, and the Politics of Care*. Stanford, CA: Stanford University Press, pp. 267–79.

Zelizer, V.A., 2009. *The Purchase of Intimacy*. Princeton, NJ: Princeton University Press.

PART II
Employers and the Changing Policies on Domestic and Care Work

Chapter 7
Employment Without Employers?
The Public Discourse on Care During the Regularisation Reform in Austria

Bernhard Weicht

Introduction

The employment of migrant workers caring for elderly people in Austrian private households has received substantial attention in the literature over the last years (Österle and Bauer 2012; Bachinger 2010; Weicht 2010). While this phenomenon had existed for a long time, the illegality of the arrangement meant that the public and political engagement with the topic was only very limited. This suddenly changed in the summer of 2006, when during a pre-election campaign the phenomenon of the undocumented and illegal employment of migrant workers in people's homes became an issue of highly emotional public discourse (Weicht 2010). Since then the live-in arrangements with migrant carers have been a widely discussed topic in the political realm, as well as in newspapers and other public media. In Austria there are approximately 40,000 people employed as carers in private settings (Bilger et al. 2006). The large majority of these people are women from Eastern European neighbouring countries (in particular Slovakia; see Bahna, forthcoming). The live-in arrangements are usually organised by specialised agencies (both from Austria and abroad) and the carers work on a fortnightly cycle. In this example of circular or rotational migration (Triandafyllidou and Marchetti 2013; Bettio, Simonazzi and Villa 2006) migrant workers fill the gap of both public arrangements and informal availability of care. The suddenly arising public interest in the matter and the formal illegality of the arrangements subsequently required policymakers to create new employment and working regulations for this sector, starting with a legal amnesty and followed by the creation of a new law to regularise this form of employment (Bachinger 2010). Contrary to many other national contexts live-in migrant care workers in Austria are today mainly working legally, where, theoretically, two options are available: being employed by the care-receiver (or his/her family), or working as a self-employed care worker and 'selling' your services to the person in need of care. In practice the vast majority of care workers 'opt for' the latter option and work as self-employed care workers, often being registered with an organisation in their country of origin. Bettina Haidinger (forthcoming) reports data from the Austrian chamber of commerce that shows that at the end of 2012, 50,000 care workers were registered as self-employed (of which more than 38,000 were listed as active) while only 500 care workers were registered as employees. Almut Bachinger (2010) thus sees the political interventions such as regularisation and the introduction of subsidies as the factual establishment of the model of the self-employed carer which, in turn, allows a continuation of the Austrian elder care regime (Österle and Bauer 2012).

However, even though policymakers reacted to the challenges by creating legal possibilities for migrant care arrangements, their employment was never fully recognised as such. In public discourses migrant care workers were depicted as 'angels' or 'heroes' that help families care and thus function as 'fictive kin' (Barker 2002; Weicht 2010). This discursive construction allowed a continuation of Austria's care ideal in which care is provided within private family settings and in which the migrant carer completes the family solutions rather than challenging them. Consequentially, the employer of care workers is largely absent from the equation. This means that while the introduced legal regulations recognised a form of employment, this employment paradoxically seems to take place 'without employers'.

This chapter therefore investigates the roots and reasons for the particular political answers during the process of regularisation. Policymakers were confronted with two aspects that required interventions: a care system that obviously could not rely exclusively on families and irregular, illegal employment relations in private households. Both challenges urged political measures in a realm that is defined as the private sphere of families and households. It will thus be argued that the definition of this realm, the relations between people in the context of care and care work and the state's role in intervening in people's caring relations are crucial for an understanding of the Austrian process of regularisation (and subsidisation) of migrant care work. These aspects, which Jane Jenson and Mariette Sineau (2003) called 'citizenship regimes', frame and shape the possibilities for policymakers both practically and politically. In order to investigate the boundaries and demarcations of the citizenship regime in relation to care Critical Discourse Analysis (Reisigl and Wodak 2001) will be used. Drawing on newspaper articles and parliamentary speeches the reasons for the deficient position of migrant care workers' employers in public and political discourses will be analysed. Hence, three main questions will be tackled in this chapter: firstly, who is identified as embodying the functions, tasks and identities of an employer? Secondly, what does the relative absence of the employer mean in a working context which takes place in private, intimate settings within a care regime that is highly characterised by informal family relationships? And thirdly, which role do political arrangements play in shaping the construction of these 'employer-less' employment relationships?

Who's the Employer?

The particularities of migrants providing labour in people's households have received much attention over the last decades (Anderson 2000; Lutz 2004; Parreñas 2001; Baxter, Hewitt and Western 2009). It has been demonstrated to what extent economic and social power relations shape the specific situation of domestic work. The employment of migrant workers in general can typically be linked to the demand side of those actively providing this employment. People and/or organisations acting as employers seek migrant workers to fulfil certain needs which can be related to labour shortages or a lack of available people with the required skills and qualifications (Ruhs and Anderson 2010). However, in the field of care the role of the employer is much more diffuse. Not only are different actors and agencies, such as the care-receiver, the family, the state or a care organisation involved in the employment process, the question of who is acting as an employer, which includes tasks such as controlling time and work practices, can often not be answered directly (Moriarty 2010). Nevertheless, the relationship between employer and employee is crucial for understanding the practices in this particular field. Obvious power differences (Anderson 2000) can be intensified by phenomena such as racism and prejudices (Doyle and Timonen 2009), problems of illegality (Lutz 2004), problematic dependency relations between the care worker and the cared for elderly person (Degiuli 2007) and the unevenness of language abilities (Brush and Vasupuram 2006). Fine and Mitchell (2007) point out in the Australian context that the vulnerability of migrant care workers is linked to class, gender and ethnic power relations and differences between the employer and the employee. Importantly, since the work is usually taking place in the private home, domestic work is often not recognised as labour, equally to other forms of employment. Additionally, familialistic care ideology means that domestic workers are often included into family settings and this recognition as part of the family often implies that migrant workers are not necessarily paid to deliver specific tasks; rather their personhood and time is bought (Weicht 2010; Anderson 2000). Barbara Da Roit (2007) shows in this context how intergenerational relations within the family also affect the (employment) relationship between care workers and the families. Additionally, the construction of care work itself, characterised 'as a hybrid of love and instrumentality' (Ungerson 2000, p. 627) in which love itself becomes part of the commodification (Hochschild 2012), leads to a clouding of the employment arrangement by situating the practices within people's homes and families. Care workers are then often not described as employees but rather as 'new heroes' (Bonifacio 2008), 'the ideal housewife' (Akalin 2007), 'angels' (Weicht 2010) or 'fictive kin' (Barker 2002).

While these characteristics of care work within people's households are universal, there are still national differences with regards to the employment of migrants in informal, domestic settings. Recent work has emphasised how national care and migration regimes are the route for different migrant care work patterns (Da Roit and Weicht 2013). The specific situation in Austrian households has received considerable academic attention over the last years. Bettina Haidinger (2008) and Margareta Kreimer (2006) provide some institutional context of the particularities of the Austrian long-term care system and its policy responses to demographic developments. An important aspect of the Austrian care system is the availability of a relatively generous cash-for-care scheme. Jandl et al. (2007), Da Roit et al. (2007) and Österle and Hammer (2006) provide some information on the specifics of the Austrian cash-for-care scheme and its relation to the employment of migrant carers. Internationally cash-for-care schemes have gained prominence, not least because of their goal to strengthen the autonomous citizenship rights and to provide choice for citizens in arranging necessary care (Rummery 2009). Isabel Shutes argues that the possibilities of choice and control over care, having power or being dependent, are not only tied to the binary opposition of carer and care-receiver but constitute shifting social relations between care users, care workers, their families, employers and the state – social relations that need to be interrogated with regard to questions of choice and control over care provision. The construction of care users and care workers as individual consumers within welfare/labour markets obscures those relations (Shutes 2013, p. 56).

Shutes' description is indicative of more general changes in the relationship between individuals and the (welfare) state through which the former are more and more defined as (individual) citizens who execute their rights of choices within the welfare mix. The organisation of how individuals relate to each other and how that state relates to the individuals and their private relations is constitutive of the arrangement of citizenship and the role of the state in people's private lives (Lister 1997; Kivisto and Faist 2007). Arrangements of care need to be understood as a crucial part of citizenship itself (Knijn and Kremer 1997). How a country defines the respective relations can be described by the concept of citizenship regimes which includes institutional arrangements, national rules but also problem definitions, concepts and assumptions about the conception of identities of the (model) citizen, the second class citizen and the non-citizen (Jenson and Sineau 2003). As Ruth Lister (1997, p. 43) points out, since the possibility to perform agency is crucial for functioning as a full citizen, different groups 'enjoy different degrees of substantive citizenship'. Acting independently in the market, being in charge of one's life and being able to act as an employer are closely tied to the identity of being a full citizen. The context of care, however, presents a very specific setting. Firstly, different actors embody different notions and levels of citizenship. Dependent, elderly people are not regarded as being able to fully perform their rights and duties. Similarly migrants do not enjoy full citizenship rights. Secondly, care as work performed in people's houses and its close link to family relations clouds the applicability of general conceptions of citizenship, like being able to engage in employment relations equally. Jenson and Sineau's conception of a citizenship regime thus provides an ideal conceptual framework for the analysis of the construction of the employment situation for migrant care workers in Austrian households:

A citizenship regime encodes within it a set of identities, of the 'national' as well as the 'model citizen', the 'second class citizen', and the non-citizen. It contributes to the definition of politics that organizes the boundaries of political debate and problem recognition in each jurisdiction. It encodes representations of the proper and legitimate social relations among and within categories and the borders of public and 'private' (Jenson and Sineau 2003, p. 9).

Political interventions and regulations in the field of care touch upon the definition of which realms are regarded as 'public' or 'private'. The employment of migrant carers challenges Austria's conception of the field of care as a private field. Since paid employment obviously is a field of public concern an evaluation of the particular constructed roles and identities of the actors involved in these practices is significant. In the analysis of the construction of the employment relations and the construction of the employer of migrant care workers it will be investigated in how far different sets of identities are applied to the various actors. Additionally it will be asked how far political discourses engage with the private realm of care and to what extent general citizenship rules apply to this context.

Methodological Remarks

Identities, common understanding and political decision-making processes are produced and shaped in and by public discourses. Critical Discourse Analysis (Reisigl and Wodak 2001) is used to identify and analyse the portrayal of employers in the very discourses and to understand the effects of the intersection of social and migration policies in shaping an employment situation which is characterised by the absence of the employer. Discourses must not be understood as abstract structures and processes; they rather happen within concrete circumstances and a particular discursive context (Wodak 2001). The social context of the employment of migrant care workers in Austrian households is constituted by a care system which is strongly based on informally provided care, usually within family settings. Approximately 80 per cent of people are cared for at home by close relatives, of whom 80 per cent are women (Österle and Hammer 2004). Only between four and five per cent of people 65 or older live in institutional settings (retirement homes and nursing homes) and five per cent of those 65 and older receive some form of formal home help (Ibid. 2004). This exemplifies the general tendency in Austria of 'de-institutionalised' care arrangements (Ibid. 2004). In Austria long-term care is formally organised by a cash-for-care scheme, the payment of 'Pflegegeld', a financial benefit based on the needs of the care-receiver and one explicit goal of the implementation of this law was to financially secure and support the possibility of care within the family (Badelt and Österle 2001). The fact that care is still largely seen as a family issue, which is also reflected in public and political discourses, is challenged by demographic developments related to an ageing society and changing family structures. Care work, and in particular the organisation of round-the-clock care, place a large burden on family members, emotionally, financially and physically.

This chapter draws on two sources of data to analyse the discursive construction of the employment relationship and the person of the employer in the field of migrant care work in Austria: firstly, the political discussion will be analysed on the basis of the transcripts of the parliamentary discussions in the time of the introduction of the current political and legal regulations (June 2006–December 2008). Secondly, the public discourse on the topic will be mapped through the analysis of four major Austrian daily newspapers and their coverage of the topic (June 2006–December 2008). I used a newspaper sample, based on Martin Reisigl and Ruth Wodak's (2001) study. The sample consisted of four national Austrian daily regular newspapers, covering the whole spectrum in terms of political orientation and socio-economic characteristics of the readership. The goal of using newspapers is their capacity to capture 'what is both acceptable and socially thinkable' (Aldridge 1994, p. 35) and what could be called reflecting the social mainstream.

The analysis follows in particular two strategies, as established by Reisigl and Wodak (2001): firstly, the analysis of so-called nomination and predication strategies. How are the employers of migrant care workers named, referred to and described in the discourses and which characteristics are ascribed to them? Several actors, such as the elderly care-receiver, his/her family, the state, the care worker him/herself, agencies/organisations, both from Austria and abroad, are constructed as those being at least partly in charge of the employment situation (including hiring, supervising, arranging the financial remuneration and so on). Secondly, the analysis of argumentation strategies will try to identify the reasons for the absence or clouding of the role of employers. Argumentation strategies link certain roles and situations to so-called conclusion rules, that is, arguments for what should be done as consequences of the discursive construction. The aim of this step is to identify various available discursive *topoi*, such as the discursive mechanisms in place to establish the particular conclusions and arguments (Reisigl and Wodak 2001). It will be analysed why social policy has strongly emphasised the model of self-employment and the consequences of these argumentations are evaluated.

In Search of the Employer: Nomination and Predication Strategies

Analysis of the public discourses demonstrates that the role of the employer of migrant care workers is not defined explicitly. Rather the role is clouded and the responsibilities attached to being an employer are hidden and denied by the various actors involved. The first step of the analysis is therefore to identify the nomination and predication strategies in relation to the position of the employer. While nomination strategies show who is named and referred to as (potentially) being an employer predication strategies provide a characterisation of these actors. It will be analysed who is seen as being an employer of migrant care workers, and how these people are described and characterised. In the following extract from a parliamentary speech given during an early discussion of the legalisation and potential subsidising of migrant care work, Sabine Mandak discusses the problems arising in relation to financing care work offered by migrants in people's homes:

> With your proposal you take all those protection provisions for employees and employers away from those who are caring. I want to draw your attention to the fact that this also concerns aspects such as the right for an own room. And even worse: it also concerns the right for an own bed. Not even that is secured according to the proposal you're offering here. What – and this is here the question! – happens, if somebody registers the person caring? They would have to accept 30 per cent higher costs. Who is going to bear these costs? The families themselves? You know that these are often on the edge of their financial possibilities and that they can hardly afford the costs for the carers. Should the costs be shouldered by the cared-for themselves? My colleague ... has calculated for you how that is not possible at all – or should the carers themselves bear the costs? (Sabine Mandak, Green Party, 29 November 2006).

Three (groups) of people are nominated as potential employers: those being in need of care, their families and migrant carers themselves. Additionally, an actor absent in this quote but implicitly referred to is the state as a possible party acting as employer. The particular constructions of the relevant actors will be discussed in more detail below.

The Cared-for

Those directly affected and having a specific, direct interest in the employment regulations are the people in need of care. However, in the discursive construction this group is largely excluded from the possibility of acting as an employer. This can largely be explained by the fact that those in need of care are construed as dependent, vulnerable non-actors and positioned in contrast to those executing their rights and duties as ideal citizens (Weicht 2013). In relation to the employment situation the people to be cared for are thus mainly depicted as victims of political, economic and social arrangements. The following extract from the newspaper *Kurier* shows how the cared-for are nominated as potential employers and how, at the same time, they are excluded from this group by the use of predication strategies: 'Most of the foreign home helps do not have a work permit. The clients, who are old-age, bedridden pensioners, face charges and substantial fines' (*Kurier*, 5 August 2006).

By describing the *clients* as *old-age, bedridden pensioners* they are constructed in opposition to those being able to bear responsibility for employment regulations. Important discursive processes (Reisigl and Wodak 2001) such as exclusion and passivation can be identified. The care-receivers do not figure as acting subjects but rather as passive receivers of benevolence and support. As a consequence the cared-for are presented as a clearly defined group, whose wishes, needs and desires are established as an objective matter of course. The care-receiver thus functions as a second-class citizen who cannot, or is not supposed to, demonstrate agency, responsibility and duty. In the following extract from a parliamentary speech the process of passivation and exclusion is supplemented by a process of othering. The care receiver is the *other* for whom *we* have to find solutions:

> Dear colleagues, please imagine yourself to be in the position of those affected! They don't know which administrative steps are necessary for the legalisation of their support worker. Which steps do they have to take, which ones the workers? (Barbara Riener, ÖVP [Österreichische Volkspartei – Christian Democratic Party], 6 June 2007).

Administrative work is one part of carrying out citizenship rights and duties and a prerequisite for being able to embody the tasks of the employer. Through the discursive construction of the other, however, the care-receiver himself/herself is excluded from those being regarded as 'normal' citizens who are imagined to be, and practically expected to be, employers in their own right. People involved in care are constructed in opposition to a conception of citizenship in which normality is identified by self-sufficiency and in which full citizens do not require care (Sevenhuijsen 1998).

The Families

In addition to the care receivers themselves, their families are described as being directly affected by the care arrangements. Since elderly care in Austria is strongly based within family settings, relatives are crucial actors in the arrangement of care services. In the discourses families are nominated as a potential employer of migrant care workers. In the following newspaper extract from *Die Presse* which refers to a discussion on the fact that public figures (mainly politicians) have frequently relied on the then illegal employment of migrant carers, it becomes clear that families are seen as those being responsible for the hiring of migrant care workers:

> On Wednesday ÖVP [Österreichische Volkspartei – Christian Democratic Party] State Secretary Kukacka and the former SPÖ [Sozialdemokratische Partei Österreichs – Social Democratic Party] Minister Caspar Einem confirmed that they made use of Slovakian support workers for the care of their parents ... "My brother and I have done this. I admit that", Kukacka said. His parents wanted it like that ... Also Einem confirmed that there was a Slovakian help with the care for his father ... Last Saturday it became public that before her death, Chancellor Schüssel's mother-in-law was cared for illegally by a Slovakian carer. On Wednesday the story came up in 'Kurier' that also the father of the president received such help at home. (*Die Presse*, 24 August 2006)

Analysing the nomination strategies it becomes obvious that families are seen as the responsible actors. The migrant care workers are regarded as support for the family on the one hand and fulfil particular moral roles and associations related to the family on the other. In a study in the US, Judith Barker (2002) shows that within households care workers often act similarly to family. Consequentially they are constructed as 'fictive kin', a process which can also be observed in Austria (Weicht 2010). This process of inclusion in the family is based on emotional proximity and social intimacy which in turn allows closeness and a moral feeling of responsibility. The analysis of the predication theories furthermore shows the reproduction of the image of migrant care work as support for families. On the one hand the families are described as facing a crisis situation, as being desperate to deal with an enormous challenge, as exemplified by the following newspaper extract: 'The relatives draw on these services out of desperation. That's a very sensitive area' (*Kronen Zeitung*, 16 August 2006).

On the other hand families are characterised as trying to do the best for the person in need of care. Since they face a crisis situation, every possible action is seen as courageous action. Facing charges or fines would then mean that relatives' personal, emotional involvement is attacked, as can be seen in the following newspaper extract:

> What are we going to do with old Dad? After the stroke? Family P has found the following solution: home care for Dad by a foreign nurse. You almost feel like a criminal but it's the only possibility we can just as well afford without shifting off our father completely (*Kronen Zeitung*, 8 August 2006).

In this quote family relations and values such as love and responsibility are emphasised. Families care for their elderly members with the help of a migrant care worker. They fulfil their responsibilities as main carers by enabling the father to stay at home. The way families are characterised and constructed disregards their function as employers. Acting as an employer, being responsible for administrative work, calculations and control does not neatly fit into the image created of the very actor. While in Austria the responsibility of arranging the care for elderly people is situated with the care receiver's family, the responsibility for the employment situation is thus less obvious and clear. The emphasis on the familial relations and the kin-like associations often cloud the actual employment relations and also exclude families from the conception of the employer's role within the citizenship regime.

The State

As has been mentioned, the state is also seen as an actor being responsible for the employment regulations of migrant care workers. However, while the state is clearly confronted with certain demands in relation to care, the discourses also show important critical remarks. The following newspaper extract demonstrates how the state as an actor of policy-making is constructed in opposition to civil society:

> Between law and humanity. Those affected have long ago found a solution for the care misery – what's missing is a legal version … There is no care crisis (as those affected have long ago solved the crisis caused by the old laws), rather there is a legal emergency. The laws need to be changed, not the practice. Civil society is more innovative than that state and the unions together (*Die Presse*, 14 September 2006).

So while the state and state representatives are nominated as potential employers of migrant care workers, the analysis of the predication strategies shows that by discursively creating a dichotomy the state is excluded from the realm of care. The request to adapt laws according to existing practices is related to a critical understanding of the state and bureaucracy. The dichotomy of human agency and inhumane involvement of public agencies reproduces Austria's traditional situation of placing care within the private family context. The following newspaper commentary also shows the creation of this dichotomy. Care on the one hand includes the care-receiver, his/her family *and* the migrant care worker, and the state on the other hand is characterised by laws, fees and bureaucracy:

> The only problem with the Slovakian carers seems to be that according to Austrian laws the thing is illegal. All those directly involved – the carers as well as the cared-for and their relatives – are very happy with it. Is this exploitation of foreign workers? I have talked to many carers. Not one sees it like that, on the contrary. The only ones who are not ok with it are the state, some agencies and various interest groups. This private, illegal care support is a beautiful example for how something can work well without the state … The problem about the legalisation of this area is that politicians will make sure that in the future everything is covered with an immense number of bylaws, prescriptions and fees and that at the end the result will be a bureaucratic super welfare state monster (*Der Standard*, 26 August 2006).

The concept of citizenship regimes focuses on the state's role in interfering with private relations and the demarcation of the public and the private. The quote above illustrates how the state (and with it laws, regulations, administration and financial costs) becomes a challenge to the realm of care and families. The individuals involved in the care process (the cared-for person, the carer and the relatives) are positioned in opposition to any agency executed by the state. Both the care-receiver and his/her family are thus constructed as *other* in relation to the expected conceptualisation as an ideal citizen who engages in publicly recognised employment relations in this situation. The analysis of the nomination and predication strategies demonstrates that the state's involvement is seen as fundamentally different, both socially and morally, to the understanding of care in Austria. The debates of political representatives therefore take place in a very specific discursive context. Since the state's interventions and politicians' involvement are seen critically from the outset, the discursive space for manoeuvre is restricted. Due to the particularities of the citizenship regime in relation to care, clearly defined employment structures that would also require a dedicated employer cannot easily be implemented from 'the outside', that is – politics. Both care-receivers and their families are thus liberated from their potential roles as employers. This is then furthermore reflected in the regularisation process itself. In a first step, political parties agreed on a decriminalisation of families that had hired irregular migrants as care workers and decided to aim for regulations that did not compromise the familial conceptualisation of care in Austria. The state in these arrangements is clearly seen as a support for families in their endeavours to arrange care for elderly relatives. According to the discursive construction, rules and regulations are indeed required but should not intervene with actual practices and relations; they rather should aim to provide security for families. The state is not perceived as being responsible for the employment situations but is asked to find solutions that allow the continuation of the current system even without a clearly defined role of the employer.

The Care Workers

Consequentially care workers themselves come into the spotlight as being responsible for the employment relationship. Self-employment becomes the logical focus for the arrangement of migrant care work. Both discursively and politically, self-employed care workers do not interfere with the construction of care itself. The analysis of nomination strategies gives some indication of this process. In the following extract from a parliamentary speech of the minister for economy and labour, it can be seen how self-employment is seen as the logical arrangement which captures best the current practices:

> The reality is that care at home is de facto, in many cases, in the majority of cases performed by foreign carers. After everything we know on the basis of the free rendering of services which is in place in Europe and on the basis of the position of our ministry of finance it is absolutely arguable to speak of a self-employed practice in the context of the free rendering of services and that we can assume that social insurance as well as taxes will be paid in the country of origin (Martin Bartenstein, ÖVP [Österreichische Volkspartei – Christian Democratic Party], 6 June 2007).

While I have argued elsewhere (Weicht 2010) that migrant care workers are not constructed as employees in the Austrian discourses but rather as 'angels' or 'fictive kin', the introduction of regulations for the employment relations required an actor responsible for the employment relation itself. While in the public discourses migrant care workers are described as being part of the family, as embodying particular family values and virtues, the legal arrangements built on the discursive context of the particular citizenship regime necessitates a dedicated employer. Since the care workers, due to their migrant status, do not function as full citizens, the inherent discursive challenges and contradictions can be tackled and resolved more easily. This means that not only do migrant care workers function as non-citizens with restricted rights, but that they are also unable to acquire proper citizenship identity from their employment. Additionally, not referring to migrant care workers as professional employees leads to a reproduction of care outside the normal citizenship realm. Self-employment might then also be seen as a logical consequence – it is not constructed as establishing rights and duties related to a conception of (social) citizenship.

The analysis of nomination and predication strategies has shown that neither the care-receiver, their families, the state nor the carer are situated within the usual construction of the full citizen engaging in employment relations. Being able to act as an employer is therefore questioned and challenged. Both newspaper discourses and political speeches show that the practices are not disputed but rather recognised as families' answers to particular care-related challenges. The state's role is recognised as enabling current family practices. In the following section the argumentation strategies will be analysed which depict political demands as logical consequences of the discursive construction described above.

Enabling Employment without Employers: Argumentation Strategies

The political debates show that representatives of all parties aim to continue the current practiced situation in people's households. At the same time it is recognised that the illegality of the situation (related to citizenship rights) requires actions and answers by the political arena. The argumentation strategies establish 'conclusions rules' by linking the various discursive constructions of agents with particular inevitable and logical conclusions and actions; by that rules and laws are justified and explained (Reisigl and Wodak 2001). The particular construction of the employment relation (or rather the clouding of this relation) requires interventions by policymakers. Here also the inter-relationship between public and political discourses becomes clear. In that sense it is argued that due to people's wishes and desires, it is the state's responsibility to provide the necessary possibilities for migrant care in people's households. Any other interventions are described as interference with civil society's ability to solve problems themselves and within the families, as the following newspaper extract shows: 'It's crazy: A highly civilized country threatens those who solved social problems within the civil society with criminalisation and fines, instead of awarding them honorary medals of the republic for innovation' (*Die Presse*, 14 September 2006).

The argumentation strategy is that the state should adapt the legal regulations according to those who had been identified as the 'victims' of the care crisis, that is the people in need of care and, even more importantly, their families. Politicians are asked to provide the necessary laws, regulations and financial means that allow for the continuation of existing employment patterns. The following quote is taken from a parliamentary speech of Theresia Haidlmayr in which she argues for the state to allow for a humane solution by letting people stay in their own houses with the help of migrant care workers:

> So are we not better off if we leave people at home, let them live where they want to live and pay for the difference so that they can also afford the assistance? I think everyone's benefitting from that. Everyone who's active in disability politics knows that it is not only more humane but also a right of all people to live and be at home where they want to (Theresia Haidlmayr, Green Party, 29 November 2006).

This quote demonstrates three important arguments shaping the discourses: first, it is argued that *we*, referring to politicians in particular and society in general, know what everyone wants and what the best treatment is for every person requiring care and support. Secondly, the arrangements that allowed people to stay home (in many cases the employment of migrant workers) in fact benefit everyone involved. Thirdly, staying at home is not only seen as a preferred possibility but as a right of every person. Here the link to the construction of citizenship becomes obvious again. Politics defines the rights for those who are (at least partly) excluded from properly acting out citizenship rights – people in need of care, their families and migrant workers. In this context the sphere in which care takes place is equally significant. As has been argued earlier in the chapter, the construction of citizenship includes a differentiation between the private and the public sphere. An intervention in the private sphere is seen critically and since care is closely tied to the domestic setting, politics is meant to not interfere with particular (employment) relations. Lister (1997) shows how the separation between the public and the private spheres is closely linked to a separation between the full citizen and the *other*, the second-class citizen or the non-citizen. The discourses on the employment of migrant care workers equally demonstrate this split. The home is discursively separated from the sphere of financial exchange and political regulations and hence, paid domestic labour challenges the socially accepted meaning of home and its association with the private and familial (McDowell 1999).

The construction of Austria's elderly care system can be seen as being based on two main assumptions: family relations as the most important source for care and the private home as the intimate realm of care. Viviana Zelizer's (2005) concept of 'two hostile worlds' draws attention to the discursive and ideological separation of the private sphere of love, closeness and intimacy and the public sphere of financial exchange, markets and paid labour. The ideological separation also shapes the meaning of political involvement and the political processes more directly. In the following extract Ridi Steibl, from the ÖVP [*Österreichische Volkspartei* – Christian Democratic Party], criticises the political debate and political disagreements about this particular topic. Since migrant care work has been constructed as a form of support for families providing care in the private sphere, politics should only secure the possibilities and, importantly, not intervene with the practices: 'This topic is way too delicate to talk about it polemically. This topic is a family policy and social policy concern which we all should more than take into our concerns and about which we should debate seriously' (Ridi Steibl, ÖVP, 29 November 2006).

This argumentation shows the interconnection between politics and the construction of citizenship regimes. Peter Kivisto and Thomas Faist (2007, p. 13) argue that 'citizenship establishes the boundaries of the political community. It defines that which is public and that which is private'. Since all those involved in the provision of care (the care-receiver, the families and migrant care workers) are denied full citizenship in relation to their involvement in care the setting in which this care takes place is regarded private itself. This means that the political community does not directly intervene or change the setting itself.

Concluding Remarks

The discourses in the context of the regularisation process of migrant care work in Austria have shown that four parties could possibly be identified as employers: the care-receiver, his/her relatives, the state or the migrant care worker him/herself. However, the analysis of nomination and predication strategies has demonstrated that all are denied the role of acting as a full citizen in an employment relation and are therefore not seen as embodying or being able to embody the employer. Due to the demarcation of the public and the private in the context of care, care-receivers and their relatives cannot be identified as employers. The state's role, on the other hand, is also restricted and politics can only marginally interfere in people's private relations. This means that in the realm of care, the family is regarded as the main unit and actor and the state's task is seen to enable the family to continue their own care efforts (which, however, in many cases includes the use of migrant labour). The discourses construct the regulations about the provision of care in people's households as tackling a problem that arises for families and thus as a solution for the families. The families are thus the (model) citizens who are seen to have the right to be supported with their own caring arrangements. Again taking up Zelizer's discussion of the model of 'two hostile worlds' (2005), it needs to be emphasised that in practice the employment relation and the sphere of care, family and love are inherently intertwined. Any ideological separation limits the possibilities to imagine and construct an employer-employee relationship in people's homes. Live-in care workers are thus constructed as support to help families care.

Politically it has then been affirmed that self-employment of care workers is the desired (and cheapest) option and political interventions in people's homes should be reduced to providing the necessary regulations and supporting families through financial subsidies. In this chapter, it was argued that the absence (or at least the clouding) of the employer both in the discourses and in the policies introduced can be seen as both a consequence of and reason for the prolongation for the current ideological construction of elderly care in Austria. Using the concept of citizenship regimes, the relationship between the political constructions and the discursive associations with care could be highlighted. Several actors involved in care are found at the margins from citizenship (older people; those caring informally) or even excluded (migrant care workers). Melanie Eichler and Birgit Pfau-Effinger (2009) confirm that in the context of care decisions, they are hardly ever taken by autonomous actors but are rather situated within complex family relations. Finally, work, which crucially defines the full citizen, is not recognised fully when it is performed in private, domestic settings.

The focus on the absence of the employer sheds light on the fact that there is no real employment situation to be found – the work is not fully defined and constructed as employment itself. While the current legal and practical regulations might be (economically) attractive for both care-receivers and migrant care workers, they cover or obscure the employment relationships and therefore the power relations. Since both the discursive and political construction of the employment situation completely lack a conception of someone being the employer, migrant care workers are still mainly seen as 'supporting' families in caring for their elderly relatives. While migrant care workers' status as non-citizens already situates them outside the focus of the Austrian citizenship regime, their function as workers within the private realm only reinforces this role. Constructing and arranging the care work practices as self-employment does thus not challenge the boundaries of public and private spheres and the state's intervention in private relations.

References

Akalin, A., 2007. Hired as a caregiver, demanded as a housewife – Becoming a migrant domestic worker in Turkey. *European Journal of Women's Studies*, 14(3), pp. 209–25.

Aldridge, M., 1994. *Making Social Work News*. London: Routledge.

Anderson, B., 2000. *Doing the Dirty Work? The Global Politics of Domestic Labour*. London: Zed Books.

Bachinger, A., 2010. 24-Stunden-Betreuung – Gelungenes Legalisierungsprojekt oder prekäre Arbeitsmarktintegration? *SWS-Rundschau*, 50(4), pp. 399–412.

Badelt, C. and Österle, A., 2001. *Grundzüge der Sozialpolitik: Spezieller Teil, Sozialpolitik in Österreich*. Vienna: Manzsche Verlags- und Universitätsbuchhandlung.

Bahna, M., forthcoming. Slovak care workers in Austria: Just another migration flow from Slovakia? In: B. Weicht and A. Österle (eds), *Im Ausland zu Hause pflegen: Die Beschäftigung von MigrantInnen in der 24 Stunden Betreuung*.

Barker, J.C., 2002. Neighbors, Friends, and Other Nonkin Caregivers of Community-Living Dependent Elders. *Journal of Gerontology*, 57B(3), pp. 158–67.

Baxter, J., Hewitt, B. and Western, M., 2009. Who Uses Paid Domestic Labor in Australia? Choice and Constraint in Hiring Household Help. *Feminist Economics*, 15(1), pp. 1–26.

Bettio, F., Simonazzi, A. and Villa, P., 2006. Change in care regimes and female migration: The 'care drain' in the Mediterranean. *Journal of European Social Policy*, 16(3), pp. 271–85.

Bilger, V. et al., 2006. *Migration und irreguläre Beschäftigung in Österreich: Ergebnisse einer Delphie-Studie*. Vienna: International Centre for Migration Policy Development (ICMPD).

Bonifacio, G., 2008. I Care for You, Who Cares for Me? Transnational Services of Filipino Live-in Caregivers in Canada. *Asian Women*, 24(1), pp. 25–50.

Brush, B.L. and Vasupuram, R., 2006. Nurses, nannies and caring work: Importation, visibility and marketability. *Nursing Inquiry*, 13(3), pp. 181–5.

Da Roit, B., 2007. Changing Intergenerational Solidarities within Families in a Mediterranean Welfare State: Elderly Care in Italy. *Current Sociology*, 55(2), pp. 251–69.

Da Roit, B., Bihan, B. and Österle, A., 2007. Long-term care policies in Italy, Austria and France: Variations in cash-for-care schemes. *Social Policy & Administration*, 41(6), pp. 653–71.

Da Roit, B. and Weicht, B., 2013. Migrant care work and care, migration and employment regimes: A fuzzy-set analysis. *Journal of European Social Policy*, 23(5), pp. 469–86.

Degiuli, F., 2007. A Job with No Boundaries. *European Journal of Women's Studies*, 14(3), pp. 193–207.

Doyle, M. and Timonen, V., 2009. The different faces of care work: Understanding the experiences of the multi-cultural care workforce. *Ageing & Society*, 29, pp. 337–50.

Eichler, M. and Pfau-Effinger, B., 2009. The 'Consumer Principle' in the Care of Elderly People: Free Choice and Actual Choice in the German Welfare State. *Social Policy & Administration*, 43(6), pp. 617–33.

Fine, M.D. and Mitchell A., 2007. Review article. Immigration and the aged care workforce in Australia: Meeting the deficit. *Australasian Journal of Ageing*, 26(4), pp. 157–61.

Haidinger, B. 2008. Contingencies Among Households: Gendered Division of Labour and Transnational Household Organization – The Case of Ukrainians in Austria. In: H. Lutz, ed., 2008. *Migration and Domestic Work: A European perspective on a global theme*. Aldershot: Ashgate Publishing, pp. 127–44.

Haidinger, B., forthcoming. Flexibilität, Absicherung und Interessenvertretung in der 24-Stunden-Betreuung … grenzenlos? In: B. Weicht and A. Österle (eds), *Im Ausland zu Hause pflegen: Die Beschäftigung von MigrantInnen in der 24 Stunden Betreuung*.

Hochschild, A., 2012. *The Outsourced Self: Intimate Life in Market Times*. New York: Metropolitan Books.

Jandl, M., Hollomey, C. and Stepien, A., 2007. *Migration and Irregular Work in Austria: Results of a Delphi-Study.* Geneva: International Labour Organisation.

Jenson, J. and Sineau, M. 2003. The Care Dimension in Welfare State Redesign. In: J. Jenson and M. Sineau (eds), 2003. *Who Cares? Women's Work, Childcare, and Welfare State Redesign.* Toronto: University of Toronto Press, pp. 3–18.

Kivisto, P. and Faist, T., 2007. *Citizenship: Discourse, Theory, and Transnational Prospects.* Oxford: Blackwell.

Knijn, T. and Kremer, M., 1997. Gender and the Caring Dimension of Welfare States: Toward Inclusive Citizenship. *Social Politics*, 4, pp. 328–61.

Kreimer, M. 2006. Developments in Austrian care arrangements: Women between free choice and informal care. In: C. Glendinning and P.A. Kemp (eds), 2006. *Cash and Care: Policy challenges in the welfare state.* Bristol: Policy Press, pp. 141–54.

Lister, R., 1997. *Citizenship: Feminist Perspectives.* Basingstoke: MacMillan.

Lutz, H., 2004. Life in the Twilight Zone: Migration, Transnationality and Gender in the Private Household. *Journal of Contemporary European Studies*, 12(1), pp. 47–55.

McDowell, L., 1999. *Gender, Identity and Place: Understanding Feminist Geographies.* Cambridge: Polity Press.

Moriarty, J., 2010. Competing with Myths: Migrant Labour in Social Care. In: M. Ruhs and B. Anderson (eds), 2010. *Who Needs Migrant Workers? Labour Shortages, Immigration, and Public Policy.* Oxford: Oxford University Press, pp. 125–53.

Österle, A. and Bauer, G., 2012. Home care in Austria: The interplay of family orientation, cash-for-care and migrant care. *Health and Social Care in the Community*, 20(3), pp. 265–73.

Österle, A. and Hammer, E., 2004. *Zur zukünftigen Betreuung und Pflege älterer Menschen: Rahmenbedingungen – Politikansätze – Entwicklungsperspektiven.* Vienna: Kardinal König Akademie.

Parreñas, R.S., 2001. *Servants of Globalization: Women, migration and domestic work.* Stanford, CA: Stanford University Press.

Reisigl, M. and Wodak, R., 2001. *Discourse and Discrimination: Rhetorics of Racism and Anti-Semitism.* London: Routledge.

Ruhs, M. and Anderson, B. (eds), 2010. *Who Needs Migrant Workers? Labour Shortages, Immigration, and Public Policy.* Oxford: Oxford University Press.

Rummery, K., 2009. A Comparative Discussion of the Gendered Implications of Cash-for-Care Schemes: Markets, Independence and Social Citizenship in Crisis? *Social Policy & Administration*, 43(6), pp. 634–48.

Sevenhuijsen, S. 1998. *Citizenship and the Ethics of Care: Feminist Considerations on Justice, Morality and Politics.* London: Routledge.

Shutes, I., 2013. The Employment of Migrant Workers in Long-Term Care: Dynamics of Choice and Control. *Journal of Social Policy*, 41(1), pp. 43–59.

Triandafyllidou, A. and Marchetti, S., 2013. Migrant Domestic and Care Workers in Europe: New Patterns of Circulation? *Journal of Immigrant & Refugee Studies*, 11(4), pp. 339–46.

Ungerson, C. 2000. Thinking about the Production and Consumption of Long-term Care in Britain: Does Gender Still Matter? *Journal of Social Policy*, 29(4), pp. 623–43.

Weicht, B., 2013. The making of 'the elderly': Constructing the subject of care. *Journal of Aging Studies*, 27(2), pp. 188–97.

Weicht, B., 2010. Embodying the ideal carer: The Austrian discourse on migrant carers. *International Journal of Ageing and Later Life*, 5(2), pp. 17–52.

Wodak, R., 2001. The discourse-historical approach. In: R. Wodak and M. Meyer (eds), 2001. *Methods of Critical Discourse Analysis*. London: Sage Publications, pp. 63–94.

Zelizer, V.A., 2005. *The Purchase of Intimacy*. Princeton and Oxford: Princeton University Press.

Chapter 8

Outsourcing Housework: Clients, Agencies and the Voucher System in Brussels[1]

Beatriz Camargo

This chapter investigates the nature of clients' work relationship in the formal domestic work sector in the city of Brussels (Belgium). The issue is explored within the context of the housework voucher policy (*titres-services*), which allows households to officially purchase weekly housework services from an authorised agency, through vouchers.

The Belgian policy introduced in 2004 is a triangular scheme (worker-authorised company-client), that replaced the former employer-employee direct relationship. This intermediation seems to bring better work conditions for workers, as they are less dependent on the households they work for (Devetter and Rousseau 2011). Attracted by interesting subsidies, many former employers in the informal domestic work market became clients in the new housework voucher service, while authorised agencies are the ones employing the workers.[2]

In our contribution, we will show that even though the housework voucher system creates a new formal sector, dynamics in the work relations are largely borrowed from the existing historical informal market. Furthermore, the triangulation of domestic work relations does not challenge the intrinsic characteristics of domestic work, especially proximity and interdependence between worker and employer. This chapter is therefore centred on two key questions, the first of which is twofold: who are the clients of domestic work in Brussels and what is the nature of their housework outsourcing? And how do work relationships function under the formal triangular system with the arrival of an intermediary agent?

We intend to shed light on an often neglected topic within the domestic work literature. If many scholars have discussed the possibilities of formalised or professionalised domestic work (Mendez 1998; Anderson 2000; Devetter

1   Special thanks to Andrea Rea, Cecília Magalhães, Sueli Fidalgo, the co-authors Maurizio Ambrosini, Majda Hrženjak, Živa Humer, Pilar Gonalons-Pons and the editors for their precious comments and revision of this chapter.

2   To avoid vocabulary mixing in particular with the word 'employer', we will use 'clients' for households purchasing housework services in the voucher system, 'employers' for direct employers, in formal or informal arrangements (they can become clients in switching to the voucher system), while 'purchasers' will indicate any person or household outsourcing domestic work; authorised 'agency' or 'company' will refer to service voucher intermediaries.

and Rousseau 2011), the analysis of State intervention and the discussion of a triangular work relationship remain largely unexplored. Moreover, purchasers (whether clients or direct employers) of domestic work and the choice to outsource domestic chores are frequently absent from domestic work literature.

In this chapter, we will first briefly explain our methodology. We will, then, introduce the functioning of the housework voucher policy. Thereafter, we will look at the specificity of the policy in the Brussels Region and introduce the actors of the triangular work relationship, mixing our findings with some available data. We will then describe clients' profiles when outsourcing domestic chores and, later, explain the interaction between clients and authorised housework voucher agencies. Finally, we will discuss the role of these authorised companies in the formal domestic work market in Brussels.

This contribution is part of a broader ongoing PhD research on the Brussels domestic work sector. This qualitative research is based on 73 in-depth or semi-structured interviews with domestic workers, domestic work purchasers and authorised companies, besides other interviews with stakeholders and social actors. The interviews were held between August 2011 and June 2013 in Brussels. Clients and workers were contacted through agencies, ads and personal contacts, and the sample was complemented by the snowball method. Interviews were held in French, English, Spanish and Portuguese and are translated by the author when quoted. Statistical data from the more recent housework voucher system annual assessment (Idea 2011–13) gives an overview of the sector and complements the findings.

The Belgian Housework Voucher System

Under the voucher policy, households can purchase weekly cleaning for €9/hour (2014[3]). They also benefit from a tax deduction of 30 per cent or a tax credit on the voucher value, up to the limit of €1,380 per person per year (which lowers the voucher price to €6.30/hour in the end). Differently from other versions of personal and household services that include care-related chores, in the Belgian housework voucher system, tasks are limited to the core of housework: cleaning, laundry, ironing, meal preparation, occasional sewing. It is also possible to have some outdoor services, such as small errands, having your ironing performed in an ironing centre (if the company has one) and also transport for disabled people (being the most 'caring like' activity which is offered by very few authorised companies). One person can purchase 500 vouchers per year, to a maximum of 1,000 per household (the equivalent of about 22h/week).

---

3   This voucher value refers to January 2014 (price will increase to €10 above 400 vouchers purchased). In 2013, the hourly price was €8.50. The most recent assessment published, however, is from 2012, when the hourly voucher cost €7.50 (Idea 2013). The government has progressively increased the voucher value to control its budget expansion, as the policy is heavily subsidised.

The policy is thus conceived for domestic workers paid on an hourly basis. For full-time employees, there is a domestic servant status under Belgian law, which is rarely chosen by employers because it is considered expensive (in terms of tax and social charges) and the employer is legally responsible for the worker. On the contrary, under the voucher system, clients have no legal obligation to remain attached to a worker or agency. Therefore, besides not being the workers' legal employers, the clients pay less for the same service. Additionally, the domestic servant status provides less protection and advantages or benefits to workers (Michielsen et al. 2013). Besides formal arrangements, informal labour might persist as well, in all types of domestic work in Brussels, whether *live-in*, or *live-out*. It is hard to show a reliable figure on how broad the shadow market is (Gutierrez and Craenen 2010; Michielsen et al. 2013).

Explicitly care-related aspects of domestic work (elderly or child care, for instance) were left out of the voucher policy, probably because an important part of the care services are still quite institutionalised, with public and private crèches, and homes for the elderly. In practice, however, public homes or day nurseries in the Brussels Region have become increasingly insufficient in the number of places available, or economically inaccessible. In parallel, other personal services emerging from social policies undertake care services at home, such as home-help (*aide-familiale*) or home nurses, with agencies being non-profit or public. They remain limited compared to demand, as their increase is restricted by a fixed State budget. On the opposite side, the housework voucher system answers to a client demand, which is not controlled by the State.

The triangular service relationship is actually a five-actor-scheme consisting of the following (see Figure 8.1): domestic workers get the vouchers from their clients and give them to the authorised agencies, which refer them to an issuing company (whose function is to manage the system). Companies then receive €22.04 per voucher from the issuing company and pay the workers their wages. The Belgian State plays a large role in costing workers' salaries (€13.04 of the amount of €22.04 per voucher) and the administrative expenses of the system. In 2012, the gross cost for the government was €1,858.9 million, of that, €1,594.9 was the direct intervention on the vouchers' price; 14.9 million the cost of the policy framing; and 248.9 million for the tax deductions (Idea 2013, p. 100). The government justified its investment by three enounced objectives: to create jobs for the 'low-skilled' unemployed, mainly women; to fight the informal market in the domestic work sector; and to support double wage-earner households to meet a work/life balance.[4] Interestingly, migrants were never mentioned in the official policy, as the government intends to target (nationals') long-term unemployment. As I will show later, however, the great majority of workers in Brussels are regular migrants.

---

4   In the 2012 Idea Consult report, this objective was exposed as follows, detaching the policy of the notion of family/work conciliation: 'Answer to a demand of persons willing to find a help for several domestic chores and at a concurrent price for them, comparing to prices practiced in the shadow market' (2012, p. 7).

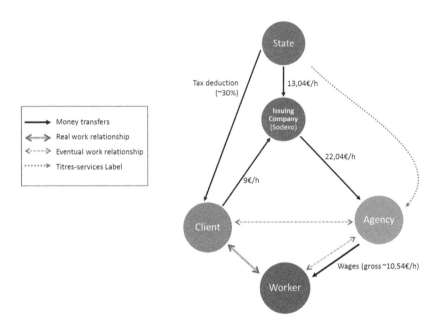

Figure 8.1   The housework voucher scheme

Although the system cannot be considered as a part of the process of monetisation of the welfare services, since there are no direct care-related tasks involved, the Belgian housework voucher policy shows, as it has been observed in other European countries, the evolution from a social policy to a labour market policy (Camargo and Rea 2013). In the name of creating (new) formal jobs and supporting work/life balance, the State delegates these services to the 'more efficient' private market, but subsidises them through significant tax reductions that clearly benefit middle and upper classes (Devetter and Rousseau 2011; Kofman 2013).

As for other similar initiatives in EU countries, the inspiration for the Belgian housework voucher system has its origin in the 1993 EU-White Paper 'Growth, competitiveness, employment: The challenges and ways forward into the 21st century'. The paper stressed the sources of jobs which could satisfy new demands such as housework, home-help for the elderly, children and dependent people and so on. It encouraged the development of a new sector to fight against unemployment while responding to new needs. This system would have the financial support of the State but would be implemented by private companies or by local public institutions. This policy was seen as a positive development also in boosting European competitiveness and avoiding the 'brain waste' of highly educated women as it would facilitate the employment of domestic workers and free native women from cleaning and caring tasks.

Almost ten years after its launch, the Belgian housework voucher system has grown significantly and it is seen as a success in policy terms by the government. In 2012, it employed 151,137 workers, had 2,753 authorised agencies, and was used by 899,558 persons, or 10.5 per cent of the Belgian population above 20 years of age (Idea 2013, p. 13). State subsidies have indeed attracted many domestic work employers and workers into the formal market, and even attracted people that had never outsourced their domestic chores before, those that we will call the *newcomers*. This achievement is mainly based on the voucher price, which is inferior to the average price of cleaning services off the books, about €10/hour in Brussels.

The voucher system also succeeded in providing better labour conditions to workers who had previously been employed in the informal domestic work market, as they can now access social benefits (work insurance, paid holidays, maternal leave and so on). The system also opens the possibility of being unionised, and the collective agreements bring some positive improvements to this expanding sector. Even though workers do lose financially in switching to the formal system, in a long-term rationale, most of them prefer their current situation in the formal market. It is worth noting that only nationals or migrants with a stay permit can join the housework voucher system. Besides, there is no possibility to immigrate to Belgium to work under the voucher system.[5]

The Specificity of Brussels as a Global City

In Brussels, growth rates of this sector are greater than in the regions of Wallonia and Flanders, with a client rate increase of 15.1 per cent from 2010 to 2011 and 10.9 per cent from 2011 to 2012, versus a national average of, respectively, 9.8 per cent and 6.4 per cent (Idea 2013, p. 16). Moreover, the profile of workers, clients and authorised agencies in the Brussels region is *suis generis*. This particularity might be understood under the light of the global cities literature, first addressed by Saskia Sassen (2007).[6] Accordingly, globalised financial centres need highly qualified and specialised professionals, but a great number of manual and low-paid jobs as well. In parallel, there is also a demand for (all kinds of) domestic services to guarantee the lifestyle of these highly qualified (and well paid) professionals, as Parreñas has also observed (2001, p. 26).

Available data on clients of the voucher system show that they are younger, wealthier and more educated in Brussels than the clients' national average, which also confirms the presence of highly qualified workers attracted to the global city (see Table 8.1 below).

---

5   For more on the irregular migrant domestic workers' situation, see Godin 2013; Michielsen and al. 2013; and Gutierrez and Craenen 2010.

6   Adrien Favell (2009) later placed Brussels amidst other global cities or as a global-city-region and was then followed by other authors (Kuzma 2012; Godin 2013).

Table 8.1   Clients of the housework voucher system (2010)

	Brussels (n=604)	Belgium (n=7,106)
Age*		
20–34	19.2%	14.4%
35–44	25.3%	24%
45–54	18.9%	21.1%
55–64	14.0%	14.0%
65–79	13.7%	16.1%
Higher than 80	8.8%	10.4%
Cohabiting (*versus living alone*)	67.2%	75.7%
Special needs' dependents	1.9%	5.2%
Professional situation		
Employee/State employee	56.6%	53.8%
Self-employed	14.6%	12.4%
Retired or pre-retired	23.6%	27.9%
Housewife	3.1%	2.3%
Work regime		
Part time	2.1%	1.8%
Between part time and full time	17.2%	21.4%
Full time	75.3%	71.4%
Educational level		
Completed High School	16.8%	22.6%
Completed Superior Education	75.8%	65.3%
Earnings		
Less than 1,000€/month	2.6%	3.2%
1,000€–2,000€/month	22.5%	25.4%
2,000€–3,000€/month	21.1%	23%
3,000€–4,000€/month	22.1%	21.8%
4,000€–5,000€/month	11.2%	10.4%
More than 5,000€/month	6.7%	4.9%
Don't know	13.8%	11.1%

* Age data is the only data from the registered clients database of 2011and represent real numbers (total n=834,959) (Idea 2012, p. 20).
Source: Idea Consult (own survey with clients of the housework voucher system) 2010 (Idea 2011, p. 18).

The elderly are an important group, as 22.5 per cent of clients in Brussels are above 65 years of age, despite the fact that this amount is inferior to the national average. Concerning purchased hours, clients from Brussels and people aged between 35 and 64 years of age are the most significant consumers within the system.[7]

---

7   Clients from Brussels purchase in average 150h/year, while people aged 35–64 years of age purchase 139h/year (national average) (Idea 2012, p. 22).

Our fieldwork with clients of the voucher system and some employers from the informal market is accordant with the available official data. Among 28 participating clients, most of them in the middle or upper classes, 16 are Belgian of Belgian origin, the others are from Brazil, France, Morocco, Portugal, Hungary, Italy and the United States. They are mainly women and often, they or their partners, are working within EU institutions or multinational companies. They come from a variety of professional backgrounds, such as: civil service, veterinary, housewifery, legal, secretarial, insurance service industry and academia.

People with more than 70 years of age are also an important group among the interviewed clients (five participants, all Belgian). There is a generational cut concerning clients' professional life: younger women are (fully or partially) employed in the labour market, while older women were mostly housewives. We will further explore this data in observing the kinds of demands emerging from these clients, in the next section of this chapter.

Similarly, concerning workers of the housework voucher scheme, if at a national level 71.7 per cent of them are Belgian, in Brussels the figure is the complete opposite: only 22.3 per cent of the 21,179 workers are Belgian nationals. Europeans from the EU-27 (all members minus Belgium) represent 56.4 per cent of the workforce and non-Europeans account for 21.3 per cent all together (Idea 2013, p. 35). These data do not take into account foreign naturalised Belgians, which could further increase the sector 'ethnicisation'. Workers of our sample come from 13 countries,[8] and only two out of 29 have Belgian nationality. Concerning gender, statistics show that the majority of workers in the voucher system are women, which confirms the reality found elsewhere. Brussels has more men than the national average: 4.9 per cent, for 2.6 per cent in all Belgium (Idea 2013, p. 35). Three migrant men were interviewed in the sample: two working through vouchers and one working informally.

High Competitiveness Between Authorised Companies

The range of intermediaries in the sector includes: individuals, non-profit organisations, temporary work agencies, commercial companies and local public organisations. According to Henry et al. (2009), this heterogenetic setting creates a quasi-market with disparities *a priori* in the policy application, since the authorised companies do not necessarily have a converging interest.

In Brussels, there is a majority of profit-making structures among authorised companies, whether commercial or temporary work agencies, and the competition between them is high (Idea 2012; Henry et al. 2009). In 2010, commercial enterprises held, for instance, 65.3 per cent of the housework voucher system authorisations in the Brussels Region, employing 64.1 per cent of the housework voucher workers (Idea 2011, p. 39).

---

8 Argentina, Bolivia, Brazil, Colombia, Benin, Ecuador, The Philippines, Macedonia, Morocco, Pakistan, Poland, Portugal and Romania.

Our fieldwork shows that housework voucher agencies in Brussels reflect the stratification of the sector into ethnic niches, or the concentration of nationals, ethnic, linguistic or religious groups in certain sectors or activities, as defined by Waldinger (1994). Indeed, many agency owners are non-Belgians or nationals with foreign origins.[9] Agency staff (human resources role) also reflects the significant presence of ethnic niches in Brussels compared to national averages: in 2011, they were composed of 45.4 per cent Belgians, 36.8 per cent EU-27 nationals and 17.8 per cent of non-EU nationals; while in the national level they were, respectively, 86 per cent, 10.4 per cent and 3.6 per cent (Idea 2011, p. 84). Similarly, recruitment practices are mostly informal (word of mouth) and based on ethnic networks (Camargo and Rea 2013). Some labelled agencies use small ads as well, in local or ethnic newspapers.[10]

Client Demand for Outsourcing Domestic Work in Brussels

Belgium, as other European countries, has seen demand for different kinds of domestic work increase, resulting from a complex combination of factors such as population ageing and articulations of the care, gender and migration regimes (Lutz 2008, p. 4). In many cases, outsourcing of care and household tasks became a condition for women in order to pursue a full career under a male work culture (Hochschild 2000, p. 140). Moreover, socio-economic inequality is an important aspect, since it allows households to afford the employment of domestic workers, according to the equation established by Devetter and Rousseau (2011, p. 80). The authors show that to choose outsourcing, a purchaser's hourly wages might be at a minimum of about four times higher than the worker's wages (or, in this case, to the voucher price). This relation will lessen in countries that subsidise domestic work, such as Belgium, which makes the 'income threshold mark' decrease.

Among all participants in a heterosexual relationship, the woman is the person responsible for the domestic tasks or their management. Among the interviewees, the commodification of domestic work did not change the fact that it is gendered as 'women's work' (Lutz 2011; Ehrenreich and Hochschild 2004) and hence did not bring changes whereby couples share the tasks. Partners were working for longer hours, had very demanding jobs and/or were often travelling for professional reasons. For some couples, tasks were more equally shared, while for others, male members of the household were responsible for some (minor) tasks, such

---

9   Sixteen managers or owners of authorized agencies were interviewed, seven of whom were non-Belgians or nationals with a foreign origin (Polish, Portuguese, Spanish, Brazilian, Moroccan, Romanian and Turkish).

10   By ethnic newspapers we mean ethnic or migrant minorities' publications, written in their mother tongue. In the Polish *Gazetka*, for instance, we found 21 ads for authorised companies in a 2012 edition.

as putting dishes in the dishwasher, throwing out the garbage and/or housework gendered as 'men's work': gardening, car maintenance and so on.

Clients' demands are, thus, shaped by their respective class (or the economic capital) and cultural capital (Bourdieu 1994), but also by gender conceptions that underlie daily actions and representations, or what Lutz has called 'doing gender' (2011, p. 28). For instance, some interviewees had their first experience in outsourcing domestic work when arriving in Belgium:

> Having somebody coming to clean the house is not part of Japanese culture. Neither for me as an American was it part of American culture, unless you were really rich. So I always cleaned my house myself … until I came to Belgium (Cintia, American, 59 years old, works in the European Commission: Partner, English, retired from the European Commission).

From our fieldwork, three main profiles have emerged, mainly divided by the salient category of social class:[11] households with high economic capital, the *upper-class* group; middle-class clients, with medium or high cultural capital and with different levels of economic capital, or the *intellectual middle-class* group; and finally the *dependents*, a cross-class group, which cannot do their domestic chores by themselves.

The *dependents* group is mainly composed of elderly people (over 70 years of age). Some of whom always purchased domestic work and have employed the same domestic worker for over 20 years (earlier in the informal market and later in the housework voucher system). In this case, bonds of loyalty and interdependence are very strong, creating a very singular relationship. A few others started to employ someone for the housework only recently, due to the increased effort it took or inability to perform these tasks any more.

The difference for this group is essentially its dependence on the outsourcing of domestic work. Based on the distinction between *necessary care* (caring for vulnerable persons) and services following comfort or lifestyle preferences, that the authors call 'cleaning' services (Devetter and Rousseau, 2011, p. 18), this group comes closer to the former aspect of domestic work. Unlike the other two groups, the notion of being in need for the service puts this group's demands in a different moral and emotional dimension: they have no free choice in the decision of employing a person to do (some or all) of their domestic tasks.

Often at home, *dependents* expect not only housecleaning but to talk with workers. At the interviews, many clients mentioned they usually have coffee with the worker. Depending on the person's level of requirement, the social aspect of the work is as important as the cleaning part. For this reason, this group can be more demanding on the emotional and care work expected. Moreover, language is for this group an important issue in order to better communicate.

---

11   The typology refers to housework voucher clients, but can contribute to the understanding of the more broad scope of domestic work purchasers in Brussels.

Within the other two groups (*upper class* and *intellectual middle class*), boundaries are considerably more blurred. The main factor defining the *upper-class* group is its high economic capital: householders are much above the Brussels income average. Societal conceptions of domestic work and lifestyle are also an important divider.

With some exceptions, the choice of outsourcing domestic chores amidst the *upper class* appears as 'natural' for many participants of this group: there is often very little self-reflection of being a purchaser of domestic work, or what it means to outsource domestic chores and engage in a work or service relationship with a domestic worker. Francine describes the outsourcing as a personal lifestyle choice:

> Interviewer: How do you feel not having to do the housework?

> Client: Pleasure. I value it each day. We value it a lot. We say very often that it's really a pleasure that we don't spend our weekends cleaning the house and that ... It's a life choice, as well. We work a lot but we like when these things are done.

> Interviewer: It's more a matter of wasting your time or of doing tasks that are really unpleasant?

> Client: It's a bit of both, that's it. You wouldn't think, but we're already doing lots of things [in the house] (Francine, Belgian, mid-forties, lawyer, partnered, five children).

Francine has always had domestic help, even if she currently does the shopping, manages the dish washer, cooks almost every evening and eventually does the laundry. She and her partner work about ten hours a day, and they live with their dog and five children (three of hers and two from her partner, in shared custody situations with the respective ex-partners) in a large house in Brussels. She used to have *live-in* workers but since some years ago there is a worker under the housework voucher system coming for 30 hours per week. This decision came about mostly because Francine could not find workers willing to fulfil the position, and since the children are older, they do not need so much assistance. The new arrangement is by the way more costly: she used to pay about €800 cash to a *live-in* worker, while she now pays about €1,000 a month for six hours per day. Francine also informally employs a 'nanny', who picks the children up from school and takes them to extra-curricular activities.

The *upper-class group* reflects a more traditional demand for housework. In Brussels, it is also the demand of the highly skilled employed in top positions of the global city for servants to support their lifestyle (Parreñas 2001). Clients here are mainly employees from the EU or important national or multinational companies or, like Francine, they are self-employed professionals (for example lawyers, doctors, engineers). Children are studying mostly in the European school or in traditional Catholic schools (considered as better than public schools).

Participants in this group (all working women except one housewife) have invested in outsourcing to fulfil their life with work and 'quality time' with family and friends. Outsourcing domestic work is coupled with other kinds of outsourcing as was often mentioned in the interviews, such as internet shopping, gardening, ready meals and so on (Kofman 2013).

Many of the interviewees in this group counted on the domestic workers to 'do everything': the '3 Cs' for cooking, caring and cleaning (Anderson 2000), but mostly, managing and 'taking the initiative' for what needs to be done. They must meet expectations of an 'ideal worker', as collected among domestic work employers in Los Angeles by Hondagneu-Sotelo (2007). The description some interviewees of the *upper-class* group give of the outsourced tasks shows the contradiction between the conception of an unskilled job and the capacities needed to perform it efficiently, as it has been argued by Anderson (2000).

It is worth noting that the demand described in the *upper-class* group is not part of the target demand of the (heavily subsidised) housework voucher policy. To have 30 hours per week, about eight more than the allowed ceiling, Francine and her partner buy vouchers from friends and family members. Many householders from this group might supplement their vouchers with informal arrangements or be employers in the informal market, considering their high demands of work and the partial inadequacy of existing formal options. Diplomats employing domestic workers have a similar kind of demand, and their employee's status is similar to those of domestic servants, with the difference of having immunity before Belgian justice (Gutierrez and Craenen 2010).

The *intellectual middle-class group* includes 'old' employers of domestic work for some hours a week in the informal market and *newcomers* from the housework voucher system. The last are people who had never outsourced their domestic chores before. Purchasing about four hours per week, group members vary from upper to lower middle class. They are 'closer' to the practice of domestic tasks than the previous group: many have done it themselves for years, shifting to an outsourced model with changes in life stages and/or changes in the load of work due to child birth, moving to a bigger house, financial and employment situation. The client's profile shows, accordingly (see Table 8.1), that most of Brussels' clients are between 20 and 44 years old, an age bracket where working couples might have (small) children and are therefore great users of domestic help.

Equally, clients of this group can move back to unpaid housework if the household situation changes: with the crisis, for instance, many clients diminished their hours or stopped employing a cleaner. As argued by Lutz (2011, p. 8), this switch between paid and unpaid poles of domestic work according to the household economic situation is one of the factors that challenge professionalisation of this sector.

Clients of the *intellectual middle-class* group experience some self-reflection and justify resorting to an outsourced model. In some (female) discourses, one can even identify a hint of guilt in outsourcing housework, as other authors have verified (Lutz 2011, p. 95). This group's demand is linked to the cleaning itself, the *dirty work* chore, as other domestic tasks commonly continue to be performed by the (female) householders, such as cooking, laundry and ironing. In the participants' view, their practice, of employing a housecleaner for some hours a week, is seen as a 'help', something very distant from having a 'domestic employee', which denotes for them archaism. Many interviewees' stories illustrate the entrance of women in the masculine professional world, meaning that they must 'find someone else' to take over, at least partially, the job in the domestic sphere (previously carried out by housewives) (Hochschild 2000, p. 140). During the interviews, nevertheless, none of the interviewees evoked gender equality as an issue, and explanations were turned to personal reasons.

They usually justify their choice by the lack of time to accomplish domestic tasks or by a 'small comfort' they dare to confer themselves, as Céline explains:

> It's a question of life choice. If it's to ruin my life, as long as I'm able to afford it ... I don't buy lots of things, we don't go to the restaurant a lot, and we don't have expensive tastes, but ... The house has to be clean, it's nice to think that there's someone that has spent three, four hours cleaning, because I don't find three, four hours all at once, I don't have the courage to clean for three, four hours all at once ... With the kids, during day time, inevitably when they're not here, I'm not either, and when they're here, either they sleep, either they ask for attention, or I want to give them some attention (Céline, Belgian, early thirties, part-time employee, lives with partner, two small children, pregnant).

Publicity distributed by many authorised agencies in mail boxes in Brussels is very in line with customers' desires, as they mostly market the purchasing of free time more than the efficacy of a professional cleaner. Mendez (1998, p. 121) observed that cleaning companies in the USA used the motto: 'Your time is precious. Ours is affordable'.

Clients of both the *intellectual middle* and *upper-class* groups agreed in the interviews that the housework voucher system, being part of the formal market, brings several advantages to workers and that it is worth paying more for. Shadow market prices, or slightly above, appear nevertheless as the accepted limit.

Households' motivations to outsource the domestic work converge amid the *upper* and *intellectual middle-class* groups, with the difference being the workload and hours purchased and the absence of questioning the outsourcing decision by the *upper class*. The *dependents* differ in the sense that they cannot do without this help and are for this reason 'hostages' of the outsourcing price (be it formal or informal).

Establishing Trustful Relations: The Triangular System Scales

The most particular characteristic of domestic work is the social sphere where the work is performed: the client's private house, as many authors have defined previously. The work relationship is thus built on the bricks of confidence, loyalty and intimacy (constrained or not), being 'highly emotional, personalised and characterised by mutual dependency' (Lutz 2008, p. 1). At the same time, the social inequality between employee and employer makes this relationship fundamentally asymmetrical.

The housework voucher triangulation, shown in the scheme, should be able to guarantee, on the one side, better job conditions for workers and, on the other side, quality of the cleaning service for clients. Notwithstanding, essential aspects of the domestic work relation, such as proximity and interdependence, cannot be challenged by this triangular arrangement.

Firstly, the work within a formal labour market continues to be performed in a private sphere. Agencies can hardly control if the job is indeed carried out and in how much time, nor can they verify the quality of the service given as well as the work conditions. These intermediaries depend on the communication of each part of the triangle to do so.

The intimacy of domestic work is then maintained and housework tasks do not change essentially with the shift to a formal work relationship.[12] This situation is especially true for clients that were previously employers in the informal market with the same workers. Moreover, many workers started to work in a household by a reference from the employer's friends, thus establishing a trustful relationship *a priori* with their new employers or clients (and perhaps not with the agency, their real employer).

Secondly, clients are very often physically closer to workers than to the agency, particularly if they are at home when the worker comes. Very often, interviewed clients have never been to the agency and some of them do not know its name. A great majority of clients interviewed hardly had any contact with the authorised company, as Sarah explains:

> Zero relation … actually I've got it through Janaina [worker], she was already in the voucher system, and I told her I would like to switch to it as well. So she was the one that put us in contact. I sent them an email, I pay them regularly and that's it. I don't have any relation with them (Sarah, French, 43 years old, employee for a multinational company, two children with partner).

Many of the clients interviewed give a bonus in cash or in extra vouchers to the workers, to add up to the total amount they used to disburse informally. In some arrangements, the bonus value is maintained even with the increase of the voucher price. In others, the difference diminishes, which in practice signifies a decrease in the net income of the workers. Another loyal practice from clients to workers is to 'follow' the worker that wishes to change the authorised company employing her, thus moving with the worker to different agencies.

---

12   For more on the change from informal to formal work relations in the Brussels domestic work market, see Camargo, Freitas and Godin (forthcoming in 2014).

The *newcomers* subgroup, nevertheless, can eventually have a trustful relationship established with the authorised agency and not with the worker as recounted below:

> I don't like the idea of giving the key, even though … I have no fears because it's a voucher company. If it would be someone on her own, I would fear it a bit, as they can suddenly disappear … Here, it's different. But as I'm very often at home, not giving the key fits me better (Céline, Belgian, early thirties, part-time employee, partnered, two small children).

This situation was found in the case where *newcomers* enter the housework voucher system through agencies: by word of mouth, because they live nearby, or received a flyer.

Frequently, interviewed agencies paid special attention to these *newcomers* in trying to establish their loyalty. They described their effort in 'finding a good match' between workers and the equivalent client in terms of exigency or expectation level. Some of them call to survey if clients are satisfied. Mostly two groups of clients appreciate this practice: the *newcomers* subgroup whose entrance door is the company, and elderly people, who are mostly in the *dependents* group. Whenever the match of worker-client 'fits', clients seem to be less in contact with the agency. With time, even for *newcomers*, confidence and loyalty is reinforced and interdependence sets in the private sphere.

For the *newcomers* that do not have any contact with the worker coming to clean their houses, however, agencies can remain as the privileged contact. Many clients hardly see the worker and, even, prefer to not have any relationship with the cleaner (Mendez 1998). Several workers interviewed confirmed the frequent absence of the householders.[13]

The fact of being a client (paying for a service) without ever having had the experience of being a domestic work employer (having a direct employment relationship) tends to put *newcomers* in a 'distanced hierarchy', which is a manner to set a boundary between employers and workers (Lutz 2011, p. 93). Paying for the cleaning hours can thus exempt purchasers from giving 'something else', such as simply being kind or respectful (treating the worker properly, tidying up before the worker arrives, offering a coffee and so on), or showing recognition for the worker's labour. Outsourcing the housework in this case also signifies outsourcing all concerns linked to household tasks, including the worker's wellbeing. The client has no responsibility as he/she is 'doing his/her part of the agreement': paying the fixed-price vouchers in exchange for a clean house. If this behaviour is more explicit among *newcomers* entering the system through agencies, one could ask if it is not favoured by the formalisation of domestic work.

---

13 Many workers didn't want to ask their clients to give us an interview because they hardly knew them, or argued that clients were 'too busy'.

Coming back to the client's typology, *upper-class* purchasers have a closer relationship with the worker than with the authorised company, mainly due to the implication of the worker in so many essential tasks to the household functioning. Similarly, within the *dependents* group, the proximity and the emotional work needed contributes to establish strong trust bonds. The work relationship can, then, be more passionate and conflicting as result of intimacy (Hondagneu-Sotelo 2007; Lutz 2011). Amidst the purchasers sample, however, people from all groups have demonstrated acknowledgement and/or a close relationship with workers.[14]

Therefore, clients do not equally trust the agency and the worker, but rather privilege one of the actors in this relationship, as shown by the cash bonus example. The place of a trustful relationship for each actor cannot be at the same time equally balanced between both ends of the scale.

Quality of Work and of the Service: The Role of Authorised Agencies

Even if the triangulation of the work/service relationship is often theoretical, authorised agencies do have, nevertheless, an important role in the formalised domestic work sector in Brussels. Firstly, they allow workers to be less dependent on their clients; workers feel they are supported by a structure and no longer alone in direct one-to-one negotiations. Secondly, the setting of rules for the sector regarding domestic chores, security measures and pay (fixed price) somehow seem to help in framing clients' expectations and preventing abuses.

Many authorised companies in Brussels act as a 'cashier', simply paying workers and receiving State subsides. However, some agencies, for competitive reasons (keeping the workers happy so they won't go to rival company), attempt to upgrade the quality of the work for their employees, trying to adapt both sides to the new framework. Many company managers or staff members interviewed described situations in which they were confronted with abusive requests by clients, such as cleaning windows outside in winter time, or polishing shoes continuously for hours.

Interviews also revealed many examples of lack of respect for the workers, as Valérie records:

> Even when the worker's mother died suddenly in Morocco and she had to catch a plane, I had this furious client on the phone! ... But they forget that if the girl is not coming, they save their money and they will take their vacuum, and this will not be the end of the world! Whereas the girl that couldn't come, she loses a part of her salary (Valérie, Agency staff, Belgian; Commercial authorised agency).

---

14   In methodological questioning, one could ask if purchasers of domestic work willing to give interviews weren't precisely those with more empathy and good relations with workers. In our sample, only one elderly participant avowed having a tense relationship with the worker at the time of the interview.

Interestingly, according to authorised companies and workers, abusive demands or excessive exigencies tend to come mostly from *newcomers*. On the one hand, this could signify that trust bonds previously established in the informal market would block each side of the work relationship from appealing to authorised agency mediators. As described above, many workers carry out their 'old' tasks without change when they enter the formal system. Conflicts and tension may arise, but they remain (solved or unsolved) within the private sphere, just as in the shadow market.

On the other hand, as the housework voucher system is the first experience of the *newcomers* in outsourcing their housework, they cannot estimate how much time or effort it means for someone else to clean their house 'in a professional way' and might seem too demanding, as argues this manager:

> I'm telling you, in three hours each two weeks, they would like the cupboards to be emptied each time, that all the dishes are done ... Demands like that are the limit of slavery! Because they don't know how long it takes to do things (Halima, Belgian from Moroccan origin, Manager/Owner, small commercial authorised agency).

Differences between authorised companies also do have an impact on building better work conditions and, by consequence, providing a better quality service. Amidst commercial authorised companies, for instance, large companies can give workers better access to training (both job skills and personal development workshops), whereas smaller agencies tend to be closer to workers, creating a more 'familiar' environment. In this kind of small firm, newly employed workers are often trained by the senior workers of the agency.[15]

For non-profit authorised agencies, following workers closely is part of the mission and of the additional label of 'social organisation of labour market inclusion' or 'help to families' that authorises supplementary funds. According to their legal mission, a significant proportion of the hiring of 'labour market inclusion' companies must be from former long-term unemployed or beneficiaries of a social allowance from the municipality. In this profile, there is an over-representation of single mothers trying to escape the so-called 'employment trap'.[16]

Agencies' roles are also to bring about changes in the domestic work picture. Nowadays even if workers are generally satisfied with a formal employment arrangement and enjoy social rights, there is still a lack of professional honour: being proud of their job of cleaner is yet to be achieved! But there are some that will say: 'I'm proud of my job because I help a family in which the parents work

---

15   In the authorised companies where the manager was an ex-domestic worker, this coaching was often given by the manager herself.

16   Employment trap (*piège à l'emploi*) defines situations where wages are so low that they hardly exceed unemployment allowances, so financially it is worth more not to work, especially for single parents.

a lot and the children are a little bit messy, so when they come back they will be happy to be at home, and I know I've helped them', some few people will think like that (Caroline, Manager, Belgian, small non-profit authorised agency with a 'labour inclusion' label).

In spite of the great potential of the authorised companies in moulding better work conditions and service quality in the sector, actions seem to be intrinsically linked to the personal commitment of the manager or of the agency staff members. As many aspects in the domestic work sector, relations are personalised, and a great part of Brussels agency managers and staff members, just as domestic work employers previously, do not necessarily have professional experience in human resources or management.

Concluding Remarks

The housework voucher policy, launched in 2004 in the Brussels region, achieved unquestionable success in formalising domestic work relations. This client-oriented policy (subsidising the demand) attracted many 'old' and new (*newcomers*) domestic work clients to the formal system, even if the informal sector may continue to persist. Authorised agencies, the new actor in the triangular scheme, have the possibility to become important 'power regulators' and mediators in case of conflict, while increasing the recognition of the domestic work profession. The figure of the intermediate in the housework voucher system distinguishes the Belgian experience from other initiatives of personal services (such as 'cash for care' policies, for instance), and should receive more attention from scholars and policymakers.

The housework voucher system does not, however, automatically transform work relations in domestic work, but rather reproduces in the formal agreement the personalised and emotional relations typical of the informal sector. This is observed in all the client's groups (*upper class, intellectual middle class* and *dependents*), mostly in the case of former informal work relationships. Besides, the formal domestic work sector remains profoundly ethnicised and marked by women's presence, as was/is the shadow market.

With the maintenance of work in the private sphere, the balanced triangular scheme appears as merely theoretical. Agencies are thus unable to exercise a true mediation, due to the properties of the domestic work itself: the characteristic of the workplace as private reinforces the complex and intimate client-worker relationship. Moreover, time spent together and clients' entrance to the voucher system can also influence for whom the scale will tip, worker or agency. A partial exception to this personalisation is the behaviour of some clients, principally *newcomers*, which can cultivate a distanced hierarchy regarding the worker rather than a closer relationship. Whether this behaviour is intrinsic or not to a formal triangular relationship needs yet to be analysed.

The increasing demand for vouchers in Brussels is primarily due to the *upper-class* group, namely highly skilled national and foreign professionals, and shows the specificity of a global city regarding the application of a national policy. The *newcomers* subgroup of the *intellectual middle class* are critical as well to success of the voucher policy in Brussels, even though they are more unstable in outsourcing their domestic chores and can eventually go back to doing the domestic chores themselves.

We have discussed some aspects of the outsourcing of domestic work within the voucher system in Brussels, describing who domestic work clients are and what the nature of their housework outsourcing is like. We also explored the functioning of the triangular relationship of the voucher policy and its theoretical balance, as well as the role of authorised agencies. However, the phenomenon deserves further investigation. Questions of where the line between *dependents* and *non-dependents* in public policy should be drawn, and how to deal with the different and complex needs of clients in an ageing city are for instance of the highest pertinence to be pursued in this debate. Policy-making cannot evade the question of *who* is doing the housework, and should also look at the interaction of care, gender and migration regimes. Otherwise, gender equality in the labour market will continue to be met only by (domestic work) outsourcing.

References

Anderson B., 2000. *Doing the Dirty Work? The Global Politics of Domestic Labour*. London and New York: Zed Books.

Bourdieu, P., 1994. *Raisons pratiques: sur la théorie de l'action*. Paris: Seuil.

Camargo, B. and Rea, A., 2013. Belgian policy supporting domestic work: Who gets benefits? Migrant domestic workers, outsourcing companies, Belgian and international households in Brussels. In: *Council for European Studies, The 20th International Conference of Europeanists-CES*. University of Amsterdam, 25–27 June 2013.

Camargo, B., Freitas A. and Godin, M., forthcoming in 2014. Networking et entreprenariat: transformations des pratiques professionnelles des femmes migrantes dans le marché formel du travail domestique bruxellois. In: P. Devleeshouwer, M. Sacco and C. Torrekens (eds), *Bruxelles, ville mosaïque: Entre espaces, diversités et politiques*. Bruxelles: Éditions PUB (Université libre de Bruxelles – ULB).

Devetter, F., and Rousseau, S., 2011. *Du Balai: Essai sur le ménage à domicile et le retour de la domesticité*. Dijon-Quetigny: Raison d'Agir.

Ehrenreich, B., and Hochschild, A., 2004. *Global Woman: Nannies, Maids, and Sex Workers in the New Economy*. New York: Henry Holt and Co.

Favell, A., 2009. *Eurostars and Eurocities. Free movement and Mobility in an integrating Europe*. UK: Blackwell Publishing.

Godin, M., 2013. Domestic work in Belgium: Crossing boundaries between informality and formality. In: A. Triandafyllidou (ed.), 2013. *Irregular Migrant Domestic Workers in Europe. Who Cares?* Aldershot: Ashgate.

Gutierrez, E. and Craenen, S., 2010. *Le travail domestique: un autre regard. Rapport. OR.C.A vzw, avec le soutien du Groupe de Recherches Interdisciplinaires sur l'Amérique latine (GRIAL), Université catholique de Louvain (UCL)*. Brussels: OR.C.A vzw.

Henry, A. et al., 2009. *Economie Plurielle et régulation publique: le quasi–marché des titres-services en Belgique*. Gent: Academia Press.

Hochschild, A., 2000. Global Care Chains and Emotional Surplus Value. In: A. Giddens and W. Hutton (eds), 2000. *On the Edge: Living with Global Capitalism*. London: Jonathan Cape, pp. 130–146.

Hondagneu-Sotelo, P., 2007. *Domestica: Immigrant Workers Cleaning and Caring in the Shadows of Affluence*. Berkeley, CA: University of California Press.

IDEA CONSULT, Gerard, M., Neyens, I. and Valsamis, D., 2013. *Évaluation du régime des titres-services pour les services et emplois de proximité. Rapport Annuel 2012*. Bruxelles: Service public fédéral Emploi, Travail et Concertation Sociale, Direction générale Emploi et Marche du Travail.

IDEA CONSULT, Gerard, M., Neyens, I. and Valsamis, D., 2012. *Évaluation du régime des titres-services pour les services et emplois de proximité. Rapport Annuel 2011*. Bruxelles: Service public fédéral Emploi, Travail et Concertation Sociale, Direction générale Emploi et Marche du Travail.

IDEA CONSULT, Gerard, M., Valsamis, D. and Van der Beken, W., 2011. *Évaluation du régime des titres-services pour les services et emplois de proximité. Rapport Annuel 2010*. Bruxelles: Service public fédéral Emploi, Travail et Concertation Sociale, Direction générale Emploi et Marche du Travail.

Kofman, E., 2013. *Privileging the Household: Policy and Academic Analysis in the EU*. In Council for European Studies, The 20th International Conference of Europeanists-CES. University of Amsterdam, 25–27 June 2013.

Kuzma, E., 2012. *Émergence d'une communauté transnationale dans l'espace migratoire européen. Analyse de la migration polonaise à Bruxelles (2002–2009)*. Ph.D. Thesis. Université libre de Bruxelles.

Lutz, H., 2011. *The New Maids: Transnational Women and the Care Economy*. London: Zed Books Ltd.

Lutz, H. (ed.), 2008. *Migration and Domestic Work: A European Perspective on a Global Theme. Introduction*. Aldershot: Ashgate.

Mendez, J., 1998. Of Mops and Maids: Contradictions and Continuities in Bureaucratized Domestic Work. *Social Problems*, 45(1), pp. 114–35.

Michielsen, J. et al., 2013. Promoting integration for migrant domestic workers in Belgium. International migration paper, no. 116. International Labour Office (ILO), Centre for Migration and Intercultural Studies (CeMIS). Geneva: ILO. Available on-line at: http://www.ilo.org/wcmsp5/groups/public/---ed_protect/-

--protrav/---migrant/documents/publication/wcms_222293.pdf   [accessed: 7 April 2014].

Parreñas, R., 2001. *Servants of Globalization: Women, Migration and Domestic Work*. Stanford, CA: Stanford University Press.

Sassen, S., 2007. *Sociology of Globalization*. New York: W.W. Norton.

Waldinger, R., 1994. The Making of an Immigrant Niche. *International Migration Review*, 28(1), pp. 3–33.

Chapter 9

An Employer *Sui Generis*: How Placement Agencies Are Changing the Nature of Paid Childcare in the Czech Republic

Adéla Souralová

Introduction

This chapter deals with a newly emerging actor among paid childcare suppliers in the Czech Republic: care placement agencies (further referred to as: agencies). Delegated care work is a relatively old phenomenon worldwide (Momsen 1999; Hoerder 2013; Sarti 2008), and it reached a new boom in the 1970s (Ehrenreich and Hochschild 2003). A similar sphere of services emerged in the Czech Republic after 1989, as the 1990s were marked by a decline in the number of State nursery schools (for children up to three years), and slow proliferation of private (migrant) domestic and care workers and care placement agencies. While State nursery schools are diminishing, private care and care placement agencies are formalising, professionalising and becoming experts in the Czech Republic. These agencies, which are the subject of our focus here, removed care work from the illegal framework and placed it in the regular labour market, where the agencies became the dominant (if not the only) force providing legal, formal individual care work. In addition, they generate expert knowledge on care work which is presented as specialised, qualified and professional. In doing so, a new kind of commodification of caregiving occurs in the market, which impacts on the nature of paid childcare as well as the character of the relationships between concerned actors. The following excerpt from the web presentation of an agency is telling of their approach to care work:

> Every mum needs to solve personal and family matters quietly, go shopping, or just rest for a while from her beloved child; and she also needs to take care of herself or her partner. We are here to help you by providing professional babysitting whenever needed. Our babysitters have healthcare and social care backgrounds. All have passed psychology tests and special healthcare courses, have pedagogy education, and are ready to substitute for you in the role of a mother of the best quality (Web presentation of a care placement agency).

In one of her latest books, *The Outsourced Self,* Arlie Hochschild elaborates on many examples of the proliferation of intimate services, which turn acts that were once ordinary into services that require the help of paid *experts* (Hochschild 2012). She states that while on one hand the new market services are very welcome, on the other hand they raise 'the spectre of a profound shift in American culture: the commodification of intimate life, which may be the great unnoticed trend of our time' (Ibid., p. 12). Inspired by Hochschild's insight, we perceive agencies as subjects, the paid expert that moves the process of commodification further, beyond the simple commodification of caregiving, to promoting new kinds of commodified relationships. The point is that agencies do not simply commodify the performance of the childcare itself, but above all allow care-recipients to outsource the whole procedure of caregiving, which includes the selection of nannies, the definition of their tasks, as well as logistics during caregiving.

Drawing upon an analysis of interviews with owners of agencies and of their website profiles, this chapter shows what happens to delegated childcare when it is offered by business-run care placement agencies. The chapter will illuminate how caregiving shifts from an ordinary activity to a complex procedure which includes expert knowledge on caregiving and care work. Analysing these processes, this chapter focuses on the double commodification of childcare which entails: (1) making care work a job that strictly follows the employment logic of the professional relationship, and (2) selling the services of a particular *type* of care worker to customers. By type we mean a care worker who follows a specific profile – she is young, educated, Czech, with skills and able to provide professional services. We argue that in so doing, agencies offer a working relationship which is different from the more widespread direct relationship between employer and employee. The agencies do not operate as intermediaries between a family and a nanny. Over the course of the whole service provision the nanny is an employee of the agency, paid by the agency with money received from clients. The agencies are the employers of the care-givers, and from them the customers buy caregiving services. The agency becomes an employer *sui generis* providing work positions, which are based on a written work contract, for nannies who are protected by labour law and who perform this type of work with sufficient skills and the proper work ethic. This logic of employment should guarantee to customers that they are buying a 'professional' service (as apparent in the introductory quotation). Consequently, parents no longer look directly for a nanny; instead they look for an agency from which they can buy the services of the desired nanny. Studying the care placement agencies, hence, brings important contributions to the care work scholarship as it reveals how care work can be organised, defined and performed when it is transformed into the professional service to be bought or sold. Above all, it illuminates the process through which the care work may be decoded as a 'natural(ly) female activity' and turned into a work suitable only for particular women being endowed with the skills and qualifications needed.

The following section will examine the contextualisation of care placement agencies within Czech social policy and will provide basic information on the way they are run. After a brief outline of the researched institutions, the focus will be on two complementary processes, the transformation of care work: first into 'work' and second into 'service'. Focusing on the perspective of agency owners (as verbalised in interviews and as visualised on their websites), this chapter illuminates what happens when the traditionally two-sided employer-employee relationship is replaced by a three-sided cooperation between customers, expert employers and employees.

Care Placement Agencies and their Place in Czech Society

The aim of this section is to place the service provided by care placement agencies within the context of childcare arrangements in the Czech Republic. The chapter will depart from the fact that individual private childcare is a relatively new phenomenon in the Czech Republic, where only 1 to 2 per cent of families with pre-school children employ an individual care worker (Hašková 2008). Given this low statistic, this chapter will explain the position of care placement agencies and their service with reference to family policy, as well as other solutions for childcare that are present in the Czech Republic. Then we will describe who the care placement agencies are, how they function and to whom they offer their services.

In their introduction to the analysis of family policy in the Czech Republic, Tomáš Sirovátka and Steven Saxonberg write:

> When the communist walls came tumbling down, Central European women found themselves in a historically unique situation. On the one hand, they experienced the highest employment levels in the entire world, with only the Scandinavian social democratic countries coming close. On the other hand, in contrast to the Scandinavian countries, little discussion arose about the need for men to share in the household and child-rearing chores (Sirovátka and Saxonberg 2006, p. 185).

Family policies in former Czechoslovakia after 1989 could have gone in two directions: either to promote gender equality at work and at home, or to induce women to return to the home. Sirovátka and Saxonberg argue that the latter was actually chosen (Ibid.).[1] The authors examine three key areas of family policy: childcare leave schemes, access to day care, and labour market policies that influence the work-family balance for women and men. Their observations in post-1989 Czechoslovakia and the Czech Republic lead them to conclude that there has been an explicit re-familisation of social policy.

The new direction of family policies in practice has led to the prolongation of paid parental leave, and a radical reduction in State nursery schools. This common institution, which prior to 1989 provided collective day care for children up to

---

1   See also Szelewa, Polakowski (2008) and Lister et al. (2007).

three years old, was labelled as inappropriate and harmful (Dudová and Hašková 2010),[2] and the number of facilities decreased from 1,043, with almost 40,000 places for children in 1990 to 45 facilities placing 1,425 children in 2011.[3] Only 3 per cent of children attending day care at the end of 1980s can attend nursery schools today, which means that only 0.5 per cent of children up to three years old are placed in State nursery schools (Hašková 2008). The re-familisation of policies incorporated 'the conservative, separate gender role model, based on a combination of low level lump-sum benefits for parental leave and inadequate support for daycare' (Sirovátka and Saxonberg 2006, p. 190). One of the main messages was that childcare is best performed by mothers at home, very much resembling what has been described in the Western world since 1970s as 'the myth of motherhood' (Oakley 1974) or 'the ideology of intensive mothering' (Hays 1996). As Dudová and Hašková (2010) pointed out, four-fifths of all mothers of children up to three years old are at-home primary care-givers for their children. The widespread ideal is that it should be the mothers in particular who stay home with young children. However, for many parents this ideal is harder and harder to accomplish, due to rising pressure on the labour market, prolongation of retirement age and internal migration, the latter two of which make it impossible to rely on grandparents, and have created a space for the emergence of a new sector – care placement agencies.

The agencies are private companies run according to a business plan; this was very often stressed in the interviews with owners, who accentuated that they are entrepreneurs, not a charity or non-governmental organisation providing social services. All agencies must be registered at the Trade Licensing Office. A prerequisite is that their representatives must have qualifications either in the medical sphere, they must be nurses, midwives or paramedics or in social work. Like the discursive framing of nursery schools, childcare here is legally defined in the medical context. Their owners are usually women whose incentives to establish such businesses usually centre on their own experience of mothering. They compensate for the lack of State institutions, the barriers in the work-family balance, and thus take advantage of these market gaps professionally. According to an extensive study on childcare arrangements in the Czech Republic, care placement agencies are a rather marginal actor in the field of childcare (Kuchařová et al. 2008). In 2008 there were 93 agencies operating, 50 of which were in Prague. Nowadays the number of agencies is increasing, and so is the range of services they provide. Still they remain rather a supplemental actor, functioning alongside the irregular market, kinship support and above all the traditional model of at-home mothering.

Care placement agencies offer their customers individual caregiving (one nanny to one child/siblings) in the household of the customers. The agency selects a number of nannies (the process of selection will be analysed later in this chapter)

---

2   See also Saxonberg, Hašková, Mudrák (2012).
3   Institute of Health Information and Statistics of the Czech Republic.

who are available when the agency is contacted by clients. Then a contract for the work is signed between the agency and the nanny, while at the same time a contract for the service is signed between agency and client. The nanny is therefore not only mediated to the family, she is an employee of the agency, and the service of caregiving is bought by customers from the agency, not from an individual nanny (see Chapter 8 in this volume). The most common model in the region where research was conducted (see below) is that childcare is scheduled three times a week for four hours. Usually the nanny is hired for the time when mothers want to return to work after maternity leave, when they study and must attend university lectures or foreign language lessons, when they want to have leisure time for themselves, or occasionally when they need to go to the doctor or government offices. The price for care is three times higher than the average price on the irregular market (one hour of babysitting costs around six euros; the minimum hourly wage in the CR is 3.4 euros). By contrast, the hourly cost of a place in private nursery school in the region is around 1.3 euros. It is therefore clear that the service provided by agencies is relatively expensive, and is hence offered to middle-class or upper-middle-class families – as reflected in the interviews. For instance, Ms Rose explained with reference to the commodification of care work: 'of course this service is not for everybody. ... It is the same as when you cannot buy a jacket so you don't buy it. And it's the same in the case of nannies, if I may say so directly' (Ms Rose, Elephant agency, February 2010, place of interview).

Research Design and Methodology

In the research, we aimed at covering a particular geographical area and the care placement agencies that run their businesses in that area. For these purposes a city which is the administrative and cultural centre of the region and has more than 100,000 inhabitants was chosen. Since the intention was to capture the developing market in order to see how these agencies negotiate their position in the childcare market, it was decided not to choose Prague where the situation is different than in the rest of the Czech Republic. When the research began there were around 10 care placement agencies directed to children under the age of three. The first agencies were established here between 2005 and 2006, and the year 2009 was described by the interviewees as the 'heyday of this service'. The peak of service in this region can also be seen as the result of the decline in the number of public nurseries: at the time of the research, there were only three State nursery schools. Nowadays, there is a boom in private 'mini-kindergartens' for children one to three years old. In fact, some of these kindergartens were established by the owners of agencies.

Between 2010 and 2011 nine agency owners were interviewed, and an analysis of their website profiles was also conducted. All owners were women in their 30s and their own experience with mothering and the lack of public childcare facilities led them to start their business in this area. All of the interviews were recorded with the consent of the interviewees, and transcribed. All the names used in this text are changed to preserve anonymity. Analysis of transcribed data and website profiles focused on the conceptualisation of care work, how agency owners define the particular aspects of their service, in what context their services are shaped and where they draw their inspiration as to how to do (or not do) their business. Since interviews with clients or with nannies were not conducted, the aim was not to capture the phenomenon from all three perspectives. Instead, the construction and presentation of care work as shaped by the agencies was researched in depth. The findings presented in this chapter must hence be seen as an interpretation of one perspective, which is part of a more complex relationship.

Making Care Work *Work*: From Girl to Care Worker

This section will analyse the necessary steps that agencies take to make care work strictly a matter of employment by creating the care worker who personifies the profile of the agency. Care placement agencies started their business in a field which was internationally and historically reserved for other actors: mothers and/or other relatives, and later State nurseries (before 1989 in the former Czechoslovakia), and (usually) for immigrant women working in the shadow economies of Western Europe. These different kinds of actors appear in the interviews as imagined past, current and future competitors vis-à-vis whom the agencies define the particularity of their services, and build up an image and principles of the care work they provide. They pervade all of the interviews as examples of how the agencies do *not* work. This binary framework will be used to illuminate how agencies present their caregiving as individual, qualified and professional; and how, by doing so, they promote the definition of care as *work*.

First, agencies are not nurseries, and they provide *individual* care. The stress on individual care springs from the negative discourse on collective care for children under three years old, as discussed above. The discrediting of nurseries supports the neoliberal rhetoric of free choice, as Dudová and Hašková (2010) pointed out. Additionally, many care placement agencies, being the embodiment of this neoliberal discourse, nourish the discourse of the unsuitability of collective care provided in State nurseries. They do so by repeating in the interviews the argument about its harmful effects on children's emotions and health, or by citing interviews with authorities (psychologists or doctors) who oppose collective care. Providing individual care, the agencies offer the service of nanny-to-family caregiving, not caregiving for other children (such as a couple of children from the neighbourhood, and so on). The emphasis on individual contact also means that they specialise only on care work, not domestic work. The interviewees argued that this was so, because the nanny must focus on the child only (and not on ironing or dusting), and because care work requires a different set of qualifications than domestic work does.

Second, agencies are not informal and unskilled domestic workers or au pairs; instead they provide *qualified* care. The word 'qualified' became a mantra repeated in the interviews, just as it is placed in the foreground on the website profiles. The notion of qualification appears very often in the scholarship on domestic and care work, and is considered to be an essential step toward the professionalisation and recognition of the job itself (Anderson 2000; Lutz 2011; Scrinzi 2011). The reason why this step has not been taken so far is, according to many scholars, is that defining the set of skills is an extremely difficult task. The feminist critique points out that domestic work is in public discourse considered as being performed on the basis of 'everyday skills' (Lutz 2011, p. 8), and hence the persisting assumption is that care work is a 'skill that requires little formal training, relying instead on a special combination of "natural" characteristics' (Bakan and Stasiulis 1995, p. 310). It is 'something that women naturally do; it is an extension of their culturally-sanctioned caregiving roles as mothers' (Murray 1998, p. 15). Such suppositions are rejected by the agencies, and very complex definitions of the skills and competencies necessary for paid caregiving are formulated.

In the context of researched agencies, the qualification for care work is portrayed as a response to increasing demands on the part of parents and a reaction to changing strategies of mothering as well as changing definitions of childhood. These demands are the outcome of the increasing stress on actively spent time with the child, which is also apparent in the quotation introducing this section: the Czech families are said to be 'very demanding', 'not lowering their sights' and wanting 'cultivation of the child'. The interviewees argued that this creates major expectations as to the quality of qualified care they provide. 'The nannies must be able to do something; they go to work there, meaning that they enter the household equipped with some content, with an aim to be fulfilled so that the child is cultivated', explained Ms Violet, owner of the agency Teddy. Her statement mirrors two discourses on qualification concerning the agencies' activities: the qualifications of nannies ('the nannies must be able to do something', referring to the personal traits of nannies) and the qualification of care work provided by the nannies ('content', 'aim' and 'cultivation', referring to the performance of care work).

The agencies hence define the set of qualifications indispensable for work as a nanny, and remove the activity of caregiving from the general framework where it is considered an 'intuitive' or 'natural' activity which can be performed by every/any woman. A woman must meet many requirements to become a nanny, as evident in the following account:

> The basic thing is that Czech families are very demanding, they do not lower their sights when they decide for paid care giving, they really want their child to be worked with, that something is happening, not just to put their child to one side but to cultivate him/her. ... There are demands for education; very often the care givers are university students, they are trained as care givers. There are demands they have a driver's license, a foreign language, it is like the requirements for a managerial position. ... So it is about the professional relationship between parent and care giver; when you don't like something about the care giver, you

will reproach her. … Another thing is that the care givers do not share with you their own problems, they just report to the workplace, and you will never hear any complaints. The care worker can give an advice to a mother, but she must do it tactfully. She does not interfere in her household, while when you have grandma, you cannot choose whether she tells you what she thinks about your household or not (Ms Rose, owner of the Elephant Agency, February 2010).

The competencies that any nanny employed by the agency must have can be classified into three groups. First is the requirement that nannies achieve a particular kind of formal education: all nannies must be educated either in pedagogy or in medical care. Usually they are either university students in a particular discipline (pedagogy, psychology) or they graduate from specialised vocational school (for nurses or kindergarten teachers). The second set of requirements concerns competencies and experience with caregiving. Each nanny 'must have something to offer to clients', be it playing a musical instrument, drawing, dancing and so on. Also, she must have experience with childcare: former au pairs or older sisters of younger siblings are welcomed. And third, there are personal traits and characteristics which are in demand. The nanny must prove that she possesses qualities such as empathy or flexibility in her work (which are usually connected with youth in our society). All these are the basis for the definition of a 'good nanny' and the professional screening described in next section.

Defining the qualifications for care work starts with specifying what it means to be a qualified nanny: only such nannies can perform what agencies regard as qualified care. Qualified care, as it is described in the interviews, is care that cultivates the children, pushes them further along in their development and transmits to them skills and cultural capital. Qualified caregiving is not only looking after the child, it is implicitly an educational process performed by qualified experts (the nannies). In addition, these experts, in order to be able to cultivate the child, are further cultivated and educated themselves when they pass a curriculum created by the agency owners. In all agencies such a curriculum includes a Red Cross first aid course that the nanny must pass. Some agencies teach their nannies the basics of developmental psychology, the idea behind this being that the nanny should scientifically understand the various aspects of childhood so that she can accommodate her approach to the child. As for developing the competencies that the nanny is supposed to use to cultivate the child, these entail various types of training in leisure-time activities and handwork. The photo galleries in the agencies' websites (one of the most important and fullest sections) are filled with snapshots taken during workshops on different kinds of handicraft work, which is meant to illustratively and explicitly show customers that the nannies are equipped with the competencies which make their caregiving educational.

And third, it is important to note that agencies are not relatives: they provide *professional* care. This feature becomes prominent in the excerpt above; it is the first information that a potential customer can find on all the website pages. The professionalism of the care work consists not only in the qualification of nannies and care, but also in the nanny's attitude towards caregiving, to clients and to the child. The nanny's concept of caregiving can be summarised by referring to the account cited above that 'nannies report to the workplace'. Trained as caregivers, nannies are considered to be professionals in terms of the performance of caregiving, which has certain (qualified) aims and which is based on a strict division between private and public, between personal and work/professional. The nanny's relationship to the clients is characterised by distance and professionalism. It means that the nanny not only knows what to do with the child and how to perform 'fulfilling' caregiving; in addition, such a nanny can also give advice to the mother, because it is she (and not the mother) who is trained in caregiving and hence is expert in the field. As an expert she must be able to follow the rules of detached attachment (see Nelson 1990; Macdonald 1998, 2010), meaning that she must like the child she cares for, but must simultaneously keep in mind that that it is her skills not her emotions which are being sold here.

In this section we have seen evidence that agencies shape a particular type of definition for 'appropriate' and 'good' care work as offered in the legal (labour) market. Their practice creates a new segment of childcare, one which is sanctified, *inter alia*, through the business license, and by the fact they are actually the only legalised subjects providing individual care work. Placing their work within a binary framework, the interviewees argue that legal care is better than illegal, individual is better than collective, qualified is better than unskilled and professional is better than ad hoc. In doing so, the agencies define their care work at the top of the hierarchical ladder of delegated childcare arrangements.

What do these characteristics of care work as presented by the owners of agencies tell us about care work and the care worker concept? Agency owners strongly reject the idea that all women are good care-givers: being a mother is not a sufficient prerequisite to become a nanny in their agency. Instead, their view of the issue could be described by paraphrasing Simone de Beauvoir (1949): one is not born, but rather becomes, a nanny. Becoming a nanny is a long-term process which entails the acquisition of skills, competencies and experiences. Only after having achieved the basic prerequisites can a nanny become an employee of an agency (with a signed work contract and labour law protection included) which follows the ethics of work, and carries out a pre-set description of the work.

Making Care Work a Service: A Trustworthy Match in Four Steps

During the interviews the owners of agencies were asked to describe how they are able to attract customers. One example of their answers is presented below by this agency owner:

> Adéla: Why do some parents prefer the agencies?
>
> Ms Yellow: The certainty!

Adéla: Certainty of what?

Ms Yellow: The certainty that if anything happens, the agency is insured. The certainty that the care giver is not a girl from the street and that agencies are insured; and when the child breaks his or her head, it will not be 'so what, your child broke his/her head', but there will be a solution. And it's also the certainty that somebody has put together a team, the girls and women are being guided, that somebody takes care of them, teaches the caregivers and pushes them further. And that they really are not randomly-picked-up girls (Ms Yellow, owner of Turtle Agency, November 2011).

Key phrases such as 'the care giver is not a girl from the street', 'professional screening', 'guidance/training of care givers' or 'the agency is insured' are echoed through the interviews, reflecting the public relations strategies of agencies that are also reflected in their web pages. 'The agency does the things you cannot manage on your own. It professionally screens the nanny, it trains her, it is in permanent contact with her, and guarantees you a substitute when the nanny gets ill' (Ms Rose, owner of Elephant Agency). The interviewees like that with Ms Rose articulate the essential role of the agency in establishing a trustworthy match between customers and nannies, which will be discussed below. If the previous section illuminated how the agencies construct care work as work, here light will be shed on how the care work is turned into a trustworthy service offered to customers.[4] The notion of trust is crucial in the delegation of childcare, and it figures as a critical point in the very decision to hire a paid care-giver (Ruijter, van der Lippe and Raub 2003). Analysis of the interviews indicates that the issue of trust is central to the definition of professional caregiving and makes the service provided by agencies unique compared to other possible alternatives.

To address the process of shaping good care work service, it is necessary to elaborate on the expert process of matching nanny and customers. Four elements are analysed in this section: the definition of a 'good nanny', professional screening, creating a proper match between nanny and customer and the establishment of trust in daily caregiving.

First Step: Definition and Cultivation of a 'Good Nanny'

How the agencies define a 'good nanny' was examined in the previous section when the issue of qualifications and skills was studied. However, besides these competencies, the definition of a good nanny includes other characteristics, notably age (younger women are preferred) and ethnicity (all the women are Czech). That nannies be of Czech origin is an important factor, unlike Western countries where most of the care workers are foreign-born migrant women.

---

4   Relying on the accounts of the agencies, this chapter analyses the presentation of services which agencies provide, not how the customers respond to the services offered.

Interviewees derive their preference for Czech women from three sources that are mostly related to prejudices and stereotypes. First, they assume that Czech clients are too xenophobic to hire a migrant woman to take care of their child. Second, they build upon the current European division of reproductive labour, which creates the image of women from Central-Eastern Europe as the best care-givers and domestic workers. 'Abroad, Western families are satisfied with Czechs, Slovaks, or Polish women', concluded one of the interviewees, articulating her explanation in the logic of 'why to carry coals to Newcastle'.[5] A third argument is formulated in terms of linguistic socialisation, one of the most important processes inherent in caregiving for children up to three years old, as the interviewees argue. Fluency in Czech is required: this excludes not only Slovak women but also Czech women with a speech impediment.

Second Step: Professional Screening and Reaffirmation of the 'Good Nanny' Image

Susan Cheever identified one of 'the nanny dilemmas' as the pressure put on the working mother who must 'find reliable childcare in an unreliable market' (Cheever 2003, p. 32). In a similar spirit the interviewees point out that you give the most precious thing you have, your child, into someone else's hands and these hands must be selected carefully. Professional screening is the central topic in the interviews as well as the website pages, and this becomes the main added value of agencies (Bakan and Stasiulis 1995). If a woman wants to become a nanny, she must pass through professional screening during which her qualifications and competencies are tested. The admission procedures focus on the woman's characteristics as described above (education, skills, experiences and so on) as well as on practical tasks. The candidate is usually taken to the small day care (in supermarkets or gyms) and observed by the employer who focuses on the woman's approach to children, how she speaks to them and whether her attitude is appropriate to the children's needs. Besides these observations and checking competences, agencies also use expert methods to analyse not only the woman's prerequisites to be a nanny, but her entire psychological profile. In some agencies the woman must pass a psychological test; some employ the services of a graphologist to professionally screen the personalities of potential nannies.

By emphasising the need for professional screening, the agencies send three important messages to potential customers. The first is that the paid care work cannot be done by just anybody and only careful selection can ensure good caregiving. The need for professional screening, as Bakan and Stasiulis (1995) stress, is *created* by the agencies. They conclude that 'part of the role of the agency, therefore, is to manufacture greater demand by impressing upon potential clients the need for professional screening' (Ibid., p. 309). Second, when highlighting the necessity for professional screening, agencies portrayed themselves as erudite experts that

---

5   For a similar image of Polish women in Norway see Isaksen (2010).

– unlike parents – possess particular knowledge essential to making qualified and quality choices. Such knowledge is then presented as coherent (the agencies screen for the significant and relevant features) and dominant (their selection of features is confirmed by practice as noted above). Nor do customers question, explore or monitor the process of professional screening: they are not interested in how and what is screened, they trust in the expertise of agencies' competencies to select what is important and relevant for a professional nanny. Third, there is a dialectic process between the definition of a 'good nanny' and professional screening: when the characteristics of the good nanny are defined, they serve as the basis for professional screening and professional screening reaffirms this definition. The definition of a good nanny is therefore self-fulfilling because it is both the basis on which the screening is performed and the outcome of this screening, and of course then the selected nannies are marketed as the suitable women for the job.

Third Step: Matching Nanny to Family

Customers trust agencies not only to select a good nanny, but to select a nanny that meets the particular requirements of the family. Bakan and Stasiulis (1995, p. 309) quote many examples of metaphors which are used in the matching process, for instance 'making a placement in a client's home is almost like a marriage. It has to fit', or 'getting a nanny is like getting a custom-made dress. You don't just take it off the rack'. Far from being 'love at first sight', the match between clients and nannies resembles an arranged marriage mediated by the agency, where the initiative of both clients and nanny is minimised. As Ms. Blue from Ladybird agency described the procedure:

> The clients contact us and they say 'I need a nanny for this and this age, for these and these days and for such time' – and we simply say 'this nanny will come to you'. We do not give them any choice in the matter, and they even do not want it from us. They rely on us and trust us that the nanny we send will be the right one (Ms Blue, Ladybird Agency, April 2010).

Here again, matchmaking is organised by the agency alone which collects the requirements from the side of customers, and profiles of the nannies from the other, which are matched together after rational consideration by the agency who needs neither help nor initiative from either the clients or the nannies. The task of pairing nannies and clients shows how much burden of activity lies on the agencies' shoulders. Altogether, this leads to the depersonalisation of the activity of caregiving, as the main outcome of its expertise.

Fourth Step: Depersonalisation of Caregiving and Trust in (External) Authority

The last step in making a trustworthy match is to present a set of 'certainties' that are guaranteed when the match between nanny and customer is made. These certainties are defined by agencies in terms of reliability and safety. These are ensured by two simultaneous processes: depersonalisation of caregiving, and depersonalisation of trust. When the service of caregiving is offered by an agency, the caregiving not only changes into a qualification-necessary activity, but an activity that can be performed by any woman who passes professional screening and training. The customers, in other words, do not look for a nanny, but for a service provided by a certain *type* of nanny who embodies the qualifications prescribed by the agency. Consequently, the nannies are replaceable, reducible to each other – and in practice it happens that one nanny can be substituted by another when one is ill. In such cases, the customers do not change agencies; they 'only' change the person performing the caregiving. The trust is established not between customer and nanny, but between customer and the agency, which is able to find a qualified, screened, trained, suitable and reliable nanny when her service is needed.

Such a depersonalisation of caregiving inevitably leads to the depersonalisation of trust in the nanny-client relationship. This occurs according to the following logic: if the nanny is interchangeable, so is the trust when customers shift from trusting an individual nanny to trusting in the procedures and expertise behind the service. Likewise during the screening process, here too expertise reaches beyond the walls of the agencies, and external authority is employed to support the already-expert activities of the agencies. All the interviewees stressed the role of insurance in the quality of their services (see the quotation introducing this section). Each agency must be insured in case the child is hurt or there is damage to the household, and being shielded by a big insurance company gives them (as interviewees believe) the biggest credibility, and serves as an important cornerstone on which trust is constructed. In this context, the understanding of trust broadens from being a 'simple' belief that neither party in the relationship will hurt the other (Lutz 2011), to trust in covering the consequences (in financial terms) of possible harm 'if something, God forbid, should happen'. As such, it shifts from being embodied in the relationship itself, to being guaranteed by an external authority.

In summary, the fourfold process of making a trustworthy match builds upon the expert knowledge that agencies create to ensure their position vis-à-vis the irregular market, as they offer the services which are more expensive than those found in the illegal market segment. Agencies not only professionally select nannies, they also reproduce the normative image of the good nanny whom all parents, when they decide to delegate the job of childcare, want in order to ensure the safety of their children and the comprehensive reliability of the service. When the traditionally two-sided employer-employee relationship is replaced by a three-sided cooperation between customers, expert employers, and employees, a transformation of the trust in the relationship occurs. It is not the individual nanny who is trusted by customers, but the institution of the agency and its expert knowledge (as well as the knowledge of other cooperating subjects such as psychologists or insurance houses) which makes the service trustworthy, reliable and attractive (despite the cost) for particular customers. In doing so, the agencies operate as Giddensian disembedding mechanisms (Giddens 1991), lifting social relations out from local contexts of face-to-face interaction between nannies and clients, and making them part of expert systems and putting them in the hands of professionals instead.

Concluding Remarks: Formalisation, Expertisation, and Depersonalisation of Caregiving

In her essay on 'The Nanny Dilemma', Susan Cheever writes: 'We teach our kids that money can't buy love, and then we go right ahead and buy it for them – hiring strangers to love them, because we have more important things to do' (Cheever 2003, p. 31). When conducting research, this quotation was shown to interviewees; they were asked to comment on it or simply share the associations that came to their minds when reading these words. One of the interviewees, who did not try to hide her disagreement even as she was reading it, replied: 'I do not agree with this. You are not buying love, you are buying a service'. This reaction, effectively, concludes the main findings presented in this chapter.

The chapter dealt with the process through which care placement agencies transform paid childcare into *work* on the side of the nannies and a buyable, qualified *service* on the side of customers. It illuminated how paid childcare is transformed from an intimate activity into a relatively rigid sequence of tasks that are defined by expert knowledge (which the owners of the agencies declare themselves the possessors of) and carried out by professionals (nannies selected, trained and supervised by those experts). The way the agencies operate challenges the traditional image of care work as being a natural activity for any/ all women. Even if all the nannies in agencies are women, not all women are good nannies for the agencies – only those who pass the screening process are accepted. Agency owners provide paid childcare services as an expert activity, the fulfilment which depends on expert knowledge and the women who possess it. In this regard, agencies take paid childcare out of employment illegality and invisibility, elevating it to an activity that requires qualifications and (to a certain extent) symbolic recognition. This logic inherent in the process of making care work *work* can have a 'destabilising effect on a core area of feminine identity work', as Lutz (2011, p. 187) and Anderson (2000) have stated.

The final question remains: departing from the perspective of agencies and their definition of services, what kind of service *exactly* are customers motivated to buy from agencies? Or, in other words and with reference to Arlie Hochschild (2012), what kinds of activities are they outsourcing to paid experts? And what kind of childcare activities do the parents still perform? Considering the image of the service as presented by agencies, the simple (and simplistic) answer may be that when the decision to contact an agency is made, the only task the clients need to do is to choose a particular agency; from this moment on, all activities and responsibilities are transmitted to the shoulders of the selected agency. Hence it would be misleading to confine the services that agencies provide only to caregiving itself. What is outsourced here is not only the childcare, but rather the entire set of steps that childcare seekers are supposed to do both before and after they find the desired nanny. Including the trust that is removed from the immediate interaction, and which becomes a commodity buyable together with the skills of nannies.

In conclusion, when care work becomes *work* on the one hand, and a *service* on the other, the caregiving itself is thus based on principles which transcend the inter-personal relationship. These principles, being the depersonalisation of trust, the interchangeabilty of the nanny, and her reduction to a set of characteristics and competencies, indicate a possible shift in the conceptualisation of care work. This occurs at a particular time (the beginning of the twenty-first century), a specific socio-cultural context (the Czech Republic as a former socialist country that is now witnessing the re-familisation of social policies), and in the peculiar organisations (business-run agencies) which are found in a particular segment of the market (the regular market of the service society, and the labour market creating job positions).

References

Andall, J., 2003. Hierarchy and Interdependence: The Emergence of a Service Caste in Europe. In: J. Andall (ed.), 2003. *Gender and Ethnicity in Contemporary Europe*. Oxford: Berg, pp. 39–60.

Anderson, B., 2000. *Doing the Dirty Work? The Global Politics of Domestic Labour*. London and New York: Zed Books.

Bakan, A.B. and Stasiulis, D.K., 1995. Making the match: Domestic placement agencies and the racialization of women's household work. *Signs*, 20(2), pp. 303–35.

Beauvoir, S. de, 1949. *Le deuxième sexe*. Paris: Gallimard.

Bourdieu, P., 2001. Forms of Capital. In: M. Granovetter and R. Swedberg (eds), 2001. *The Sociology of Economic Life*. Boulder, CO: Westview Press, pp. 96–111.

Cheever, S., 2003. The Nanny Dilemma. In: B. Ehrenreich and A. Hochschild (eds), 2003. *Global Woman: Nannies, Maids, and Sex Workers in the New Economy*. New York: Metropolitan Books, pp. 31–8.

Cox, R. and Watt, P., 2002. Globalization, polarization and the informal sector; the case of paid domestic Workers in London. *Area*, 34(1), pp. 39–47.

Dudová, R. and Hašková, H., 2010. Diskurzy, instituce a praxe péče o děti do tří let ve francouzsko-české komparativní perspektivě. *Gender, rovné příležitosti, výzkum*, 12(2), pp. 36–47.

Ehrenreich, B. and Hochschild, A., 2003. Introduction. In: B. Ehrenreich and A. Hochschild (eds), 2003. *Global Woman: Nannies, Maids, and Sex Workers in the New Economy*. New York: Metropolitan Books, pp. 1–13.

Giddens, A., 1991. *Modernity and Self-Identity. Self and Society in the Late Modern Age*. Cambridge: Polity Press.

Hašková, H., 2008. Kam směřuje česká společnost v oblasti denní péče o předškolní děti? In: A. Křížková et al. (eds), 2008. *Práce a péče: Proměny rodičovské v České republice a kontext rodinné politiky Evropské Unie.* Prague: SLON, pp. 51–70.

Hays, S., 1996. *Cultural Contradictions of Motherhood.* New Haven: Yale University Press.

Hoerder, D., 2013. Historical Perspectives on Domestic and Caregiving Work: A Global Approach. In: International Conference of Labour and Social History. *Towards a Global History of Domestic Workers and Caregivers, 49th International Conference of Labour and Social History*, Linz, Austria, 12–15 September 2013.

Hochschild, A., 2012. *The Outsourced Self.* New York: Picador.

Isaksen, L.W., 2010. Transitional care: The social dimensions of international nurse recruitment. In: L.W. Isaksen (ed.), 2010. *Global Care Work. Gender and Migration in Nordic Societies.* Lund: Nordic Academic Press, pp. 139–58.

Kuchařová, V. et al., 2009. *Péče o děti předškolního a raného školního věku.* Prague: VÚPSV.

Lister, R. et al., 2007. *Gendering Citizenship in Western Europe: New Challenges for Citizenship Research in a Cross-National Context.* Bristol: Policy Press.

Lutz, H., 2011. *The New Maids. Transnational Women and the Care Economy.* London, New York: Zed Books.

Macdonald, C.L., 1998. Manufacturing motherhood: The shadow work of nannies and au pairs. *Qualitative Sociology*, 21(1), pp. 25–53.

Momsen J.H. (ed.), 1999. *Gender, Migration and Domestic Service.* London: Routledge.

Nelson, M.K., 1990. *Negotiated Care: The Experience of Family Day Care Providers.* Philadelphia, PA: Temple University Press.

Oakley, A., 1974. *Woman's Work: The Housewife, Past and Present.* New York: Random House.

Parreñas, R., 2001. *Servants of Globalization: Women, Migration, and Domestic Work.* Stanford, CA: Stanford University Press.

Romero, M., 1992. *Maid in the USA.* New York: Routledge.

Ruijter, E., Van Der Lippe, T. and Raub, W., 2003. Trust Problems in Household Outsourcing: New Hypotheses. *Rationality and Society*, 15(4), pp. 473–507.

Sarti, R., 2008. The Globalisation of Domestic Service: An Historical Perspective. In: H. Lutz (ed.), 2008. *Migration and Domestic Work: A European Perspective on a Global Theme.* Aldershot: Ashgate, pp. 77–98.

Sirovátka, T. and Saxonberg, S. 2006. Failing family policy in post-communist Central Europe. *Journal of Comparative Policy Analysis*, 8, pp. 185–202.

Saxonberg, S., Hašková, H. and Mudrák, J., 2012. *Péče o nejmenší. Boření mýtů.* Prague: SLON.

Scrinzi, F., 2011. Gender, migration and the ambiguous enterprise of professionalizing domestic service: the case of vocational training for the unemployed in France. *Feminist Review*, 98, pp. 153–72.

Szelewa, D. and Polakowski, M.P., 2008. Who cares? Changing patterns of childcare in Central and Eastern Europe. *Journal of European Social Policy*, 18(2), pp. 115–31.

Stiell, B. and England, K., 1997. Domestic distinctions: constructing difference among paid domestic workers in Toronto. *Gender, Place and Culture*, 4(3), pp. 339–59.

Chapter 10

When the State Steps In: An Experiment of Subsidised Hiring of Domestic Workers in Slovenia

Živa Humer and Majda Hrženjak

Introduction

The chapter brings insights on regulated, paid domestic work under live-out arrangements in Slovenia. The empirical material analysed here was gathered during the *System of Household Assistance* (SIPA) project, whose aim was to contribute to alleviating the precarious situation in the field of care service on the supply and demand side by introducing the public subsidised system of paid domestic work, thus reinforcing the welfare state in this respect. The purpose of the chapter is to analyse the 'employer's' perspective, both women's and men's views on their needs for paid domestic work, their reflection on the work when performed by the 'other' and their views on what the paid domestic work brought to their homes. Special attention will be devoted to how families and workers negotiated power relations, intimacy, scope of work and class issues as well as how domestic work was redefined during the process.

Contextualisation of Paid Domestic Work in Slovenia

Slovenia represents a particular context for exploring paid domestic and care work in private homes since the Slovenian family model was never tied to the notion of a bread-winner model because men and women were equally financially responsible for providing for the family. In contrast to the dominant Western discourse about women's economic inactivity and attachment to the home, even before WWII, when Slovenia was mostly rural, women always were economically active. After WWII, the 'adult worker model' (Lister et al. 2007), which was a norm in Slovenia where economic gender equality was constructed, as a trade-mark of socialist gender equality was only put into practice in Northern Europe from 1970s onwards. As disclosed by Burcar (2009, p. 7), in accordance with the socialist policy encouraging overall employment for all and giving a special emphasis to women's emancipation, women for the first time gained the right to full-time and long-term employment. This also brought with it important individual rights to social, health and pension insurance. Along with that, women also gained the right to maternity leave before and after giving birth, which was paid as a regular salary with all the regular supplements.

Prohibition of dismissal of pregnant women and nursing women entered into force. The legislation ensured social security and economic independence for mothers with a special clause which enabled women to return to the same full-time work position after maternity leave. Thus women as full-time employees and mothers became entitled to diverse individually based social transfers, assistance and allowances, instead of being dependent on the employment of the men.

Women entering the labour market would not have been possible without the concurrent establishment of an extensive network of publicly available social services, such as kindergartens, nurseries, extended childcare, children's colonies and homes, initially also milk and later on school kitchens, organised care for the elderly and the ill. Workers' kitchens and canteens were also established to relieve women of household chores and full-time care for children, elderly, the ill and other family members in need of help (Ibid., p. 8). Although this socialisation of care work that was institutionalised by the socialist state did not bring women full equality in politics, economy and in family, it did however considerably improve their position in society.

The 1991 transition from the socialist socio-economic regime to the capitalist system brought a reorganisation of the social system which resulted in a constant reduction of rights deriving from work and motherhood, for instance the lowering of parental allowance[1] and making access to public kindergartens increasingly harder and more expensive. Reduction of the public care system together with the abolition or downsizing of a series of social rights that were universal within the socialist regime and enabled women to reconcile their full-time employment with their family obligations has had negative consequences for all women. More so for certain groups of women, that is those mostly from economically weaker circumstances and the working class, single mothers and mothers with small children who cannot afford private childcare. At the same time, research shows that after 1991, labour market conditions have been changing drastically, for example youth full-time, long-term employment is becoming rather exceptional whereas intensity, precarity and flexibility of work is on the rise. In Slovenia and in Eastern Europe, working hours are relatively long in comparison to Northwestern Europe. In Slovenia, the volume of overtime work, weekend work and shift-work is increasing rapidly. In 2002, the relation between empirically executed hours and contractually mandatory hours of work was 45.8 to 40.5. The Cranfield Network on International Human Resource Management (CRANET)[2] international research showed that overtime work is being carried out in 96 per cent of businesses, whereas shift-work only used in 14.8 per cent of businesses and weekend work occurs in only 17.4 per cent of businesses in Slovenia (Ignjatović 2002, pp. 183–4).

Despite the fact that the research on values shows that the traditional roles of women as housewives and mothers are an important identity for Slovenian

---

1   The parental allowance has been reduced from 100 per cent of the salary to 90 per cent in 2012, which affects mainly women as they take the leave in majority (95 per cent).

2   Information on CRANET is available on-line at: http://www.cranet.org [accessed: 18 April 2014].

women, the emancipation deriving from full-time employment and economic independence remains a highly valued priority and equally an important source of identity for women in Slovenia (Šadl 2006). Therefore part-time employment is not as common an option as it is in many other EU countries. In 2011, 13.3 per cent of Slovenian women worked part time, while the EU average was 32.3 per cent (Eurostat 2011). On average, women and men in Slovenia devote more time to paid work compared to other EU member states. Women in Slovenia work in paid labour on average 39.5 hours weekly, compared to 42.4 hours weekly for men, while in the EU, women work 34.3 and men 41.7 hours (Eurofound 2009). In Slovenia, women (84.9 per cent) and men (94.9 per cent) with children below 12 years of age are also represented in a greater share in the labour market compared to women (83.0 per cent) and men (81.9 per cent) without children (Eurostat 2011). The data for unpaid work in households confirms gender inequality as employed women in Slovenia spend 42 hours for household tasks and childcare compared to men who spend 28 hours for these tasks, this adds up to a 'second shift' for Slovenian women (Eurofound 2009). Along with the data confirming gender disparities in the field of paid and unpaid work, the OECD (2011, p. 25) estimates that informal, unpaid work in households represents around 33 per cent of GDP of EU member states, while in Slovenia it adds up almost 40 per cent of GDP.

Such contradictory gender norms lead to a work and family conflict as women have to combine career with motherhood, household work and partnership, which in general creates a chaotic life, constant lack of time and, above all, overburdening, fatigue and exhaustion. Household chores, such as cooking, cleaning, tidying and ironing, are time-consuming, intensive and hard work, and as women are lacking energy (because of exhaustion from paid work), transfer of the above mentioned tasks is becoming increasingly more frequent as one of the adaptation strategies (of women with higher education) to contradictory requirements of family, paid work and gender norms.

Also deep structural changes during the (post)-transition period, such as wealth polarisation, unstable and more demanding working conditions, relocation of public care into the family realm while the population is rapidly aging, all influence the growing supply of and demand for informal paid care work in Slovenian middle-class households. It happens despite the fact that social egalitarianism, also because of the socialist tradition, is high up on the value scale in Slovenia.

Figures of Paid Domestic and Care Work in Slovenia

In Slovenia, paid domestic and care work remain unregulated and part of grey economy. The empirical research[3] shows that in 2009, approximately 4.5 per cent

---

3   In March 2009, public opinion research was carried out via telephone poll by the Public Opinion and Mass Communication Research Centre (CJMMK) at the Faculty of Social Sciences (University of Ljubljana). A statistically representative sample included

of Slovenian households had in-home help: 81 per cent for cleaning, 10 per cent for childcare and 23 per cent for care of the elderly (Hrženjak 2010).[4]

Because the majority of this work is done in the sphere of the grey economy and the workers and users may end up being sanctioned, it can be assumed that these figures may be higher but remain invisible by criminalisation. Eight per cent of households use the services of commercial care companies, 21 per cent of the services are provided by the public home-care system, and as much as 71 per cent of services are provided by the informal care market. The share of paid care work provided by the informal care market in Slovenian households considerably surpasses the share of the public and commercial services.

In 98.3 per cent of the households using the informal economy for in-home help, this work is performed by a woman, of which 81.4 per cent are of Slovenian ethnic origin. In 16.3 per cent of the households, help is provided by a person from the former Yugoslavia and, while none of the households answered that they employ a person from another country, 2.3 per cent do not know the ethnic origin of their cleaner, nanny or care-giver. These data show that in Slovenia, 'local care chains' (Hrženjak and Humer 2011) prevail over 'global care chains' as the level of feminisation of immigration to Slovenia is relatively low compared to other European countries. Nevertheless, 'other' ethnicity in intersection with female gender remains an important category also in 'local care chains' because local care chains include many members of the 'non-recognised' ethnic minorities.[5] These minorities include internal migrants from former Yugoslavia, who are now Slovenian citizens. From the 1960s onwards, Slovenia was the economically most prosperous republic within Yugoslavia, it was already dependent on internal economic migration and the recruitment of female workers in unskilled manual and poorly paid jobs in cleaning, care and the service sector from the 'less developed' rural regions of Yugoslavia. Today this is reflected in ethnically segregated elderly care in the public sector as well as in the informal care market. Since these jobs are also poorly respected and undervalued, they contribute to the growing number of the working poor (Hrženjak 2012).

In 44.2 per cent of the households, the help at home is provided by a pensioner, in as many as 24.4 per cent of the households informal paid care work is provided by a fully employed person as additional work and in 17.4 per cent of the households

---

7,536 households, 2,677 interviews were carried out, and the level of sample realisation was 36 per cent. In addition to demographic questions, people were asked about their opinion of paid home help, whether they were using it, and if so, why, in what form, for which services and on what scale it took place. They were also asked what was the ethnic, gender and employment structure of the workers.

4 Some services concur, for instance, cleaning and elderly care.

5 *Constitution* defines special rights for the recognised Italian and Hungarian minorities in Slovenia, however, the *Constitution* and any other anti-discrimination regulations do not refer to the 'non-recognised' minorities, which are mostly made up of people from the former Yugoslavia who constitute approximately 10 per cent of the Slovenian population.

the pay for care work represents the basic income of an unemployed woman. This shows that informal paid domestic work is provided by the social groups that are structurally highly exposed to poverty: female pensioners, female workers in labour-intensive jobs requiring low qualifications and paying low salaries and unemployed women. These data, in parallel with the data on how the frequency of use of home-care services increases along with household income and education level, show that informal paid care work is a phenomenon of class inequalities.

The main motive for hiring an in-home care worker is an ill family member in 50 per cent of the households, family and work conflict in 37.8 per cent, while 11.8 per cent of the households cite status and life-style-related reasons. The main reasons for the revival of informal paid care work therefore appear as the lack of available alternative forms of care for the elderly and those requiring care; the lack of mechanisms for balancing work and family life in families with small children, and economic inequalities, that encourage the wealthy to seek services and force the poor to provide them. Within this situation two categories stand out: households with small children, which, being overburdened, already buy care services on the informal market, and long-term unemployed women for whom paid care work already represents a main survival strategy. With the SIPA project we focused on the precarious situations of these two social groups.

Research Design and Methodology

The SIPA[6] project aimed at putting to the test the idea that the introduction of a public system of household assistance would reduce work-family conflict in households with pre-school children and enable new, quality workplaces for long-term unemployed women.

The main conclusion drawn from the empirical survey[7] was that there is a high demand for paid domestic work on the side of households (80 per cent) with pre-school children and a high level of interest (70 per cent) on the side of long-term officially unemployed women to regularise their 'illicit' work as domestic workers. Based on the analysis of the questionnaires, a pilot experiment on paid domestic work was organised in 2006, whereby five long-term unemployed women were employed for a period of six months in 30 households in Ljubljana.

---

6   The project was carried out in 2004–07 within the EQUAL Initiative of the European Social Fund.

7   The empirical part of the study was implemented in 2005 and consisted of two questionnaires aimed at two target groups: households with pre-school children and long-term unemployed women in Ljubljana. The survey wanted to investigate whether there is a need for paid care work in households with pre-school children and if there is an interest for employment in the field of paid care work among long-term unemployed women. The survey included 400 mothers with pre-school children, and 100 long-term unemployed women.

After six months of the pilot experiment, a quantitative and qualitative evaluation was implemented in both target groups to detect the advantages and disadvantages of such a system of paid domestic work. The empirical material includes four focus groups with women and men with small children and two focus groups of long-term officially unemployed women, who got paid job as domestic workers in the pilot project. Four focus groups were conducted with 23 household members, involving 19 women and four men (employers) and five domestic workers (employees). The focus groups aimed to evaluate the regulation of paid domestic work, its advantages and disadvantages. The focus groups with the domestic workers were divided between the beginning of the pilot project and the end of it. This material represents the basis for the analysis presented in this chapter.

It was an action-oriented project, which in terms of increasing individualisation and privatisation of care work, aimed to politicise and reinstate care work as a public affair. On one hand, it encouraged women to increase public awareness of care work and social inequalities related to it, while on the other hand, it acted preventively against discrimination and exploitation in the field. The fundamental problems frequently identified in the field of paid care work centre around irregular live-in forms (Anderson 2000), the global care-chain (Hochschild 2000) and the privatisation of care (Williams and Gavanas 2008). The pilot project presented here introduces regulated, paid domestic work under a live-out arrangement. It disrupts the global care-chain by engaging long-term unemployed local women, and proposes the socialisation of care work through the development of a public network of agencies, rather than its privatisation. Despite the regularised situation, the pilot and the project's evaluation showed many unequal and diverse faces of paid domestic work from the 'employer's' and 'employees' perspective, which will be discussed in the sections below.

Paid Domestic Work: The Employer's Perspective

Needs for Paid Domestic Work and Gendered Reflection of It

The literature on paid domestic work confirms that the needs of households for paid services increase with the arrival of children as the amount of household work increases, and this increase falls on the shoulders of women (Bianchi et al. 2000; Tijdens et al. 2003). As stated by Tijdens et al. (2003), and families with small children between four and 12 years of age are the ones that require the most paid help, mainly with cleaning. As revealed in the questionnaire survey conducted in the SIPA project, women devote 28.8 hours for household work and 46.6 hours for care of children weekly, while their partners spend 17.6 hours for household tasks and 33.5 hours for care of children.[8] More than half (55.5 per cent) of the

---

8   The data show a greater amount of hours spent for household work in comparison with other surveys. The difference is due to the fact that in the sample of the SIPA project

women confirm they share domestic work with their partners, while 60.1 per cent of women estimated their share is prevailing in their households.

The existing gendered gap in individual everyday situations is evident in the number of hours spent by women and men for domestic and care work and in their attitudes and values towards these types of work. The 'family myth' about the division of domestic work between partners is common, as stressed by Hochschild (1997, p. 101), particularly among middle-class families and successful business women who are for the majority responsible for the 'second shift'.

In the focus groups, both women and men stressed the difference before and after having a child in relation to household work. When children come along, firstly, the amount of household work increases and, secondly, the time to perform the household work needs to be reorganised. As one male participant explained, 'we used to do it on Saturdays, we turn on the music and we started to clean. Now you have to tidy up, first, you need to pick up the toys lying around ...' (Marjan, Ljubljana, 10 October 2006).

A common pattern can be observed in the households of the SIPA sample: the amount of household work increases, while gender equality between the partners decreases as women take over more responsibilities and the household workload. Household work is integrated in a certain ideology of motherhood. Women usually do several tasks in parallel, such as cooking, cleaning and playing with the child(ren). Doing many activities at the same time can be stressful in terms of the amount of work, however they are involved only partially in these activities. For example, they are cooking and playing with a child, but in this case they are more focused on cooking and are only partially engaged with the child (Rener et al. 2008; Humer 2009). As a female participant explained:

> We used to, before having kids, to clean once a week in the evening. We used to say, 'ok, let's go' and we did it together and cleaned the flat in two hours and Saturdays were dedicated to the family. Now, my partner has a lot of work and I'm not waiting for him to clean together. We have rather classical division of work, I have the household and he has a firm. I don't blame him, because it is like it is, he has a firm and has to continue the work in the firm and I accepted the situation (Polona, Ljubljana, 5 October 2006).

She legitimised the change in the division of household work between the partners from more equal to a traditional one as a consequence of the changed working arrangement of her partner and of having children which brings more responsibilities for women. The gap between the perceptions, wishes, expectations and everyday situations is also seen in the negotiations regarding family and work responsibilities. The perception of the need to negotiate pressures of workload in family and paid work is evident and realised in a gendered way, where one of

---

only women with pre-school children participated, and that with young children the amount of hours for household tasks and childcare increases to a great extent.

the partners builds the career (usually men) and the other one (usually women), besides paid work, also takes care of the family (Humer 2009).

Slovenian parents of pre-school children who are forced to choose between household work and socialising with children, which is at the heart of the work and family conflict, give priority to children (Hrženjak 2008). Usually women choose to spend time with children and postpone household work until late evening hours, or usually men spend time with the children while women do the urgent household work. Those who can afford it increasingly choose to outsource household work. As one female participant said:

> We want to spend afternoons with children, because in the morning they are in the kindergarten anyway. Those few afternoon hours to hire nanny ... it is actually unnecessary and in my opinion even harmful ... It's really fine when you don't have to worry about the hygiene of the apartment; otherwise it is postponed until Saturday morning (Amanda, Ljubljana, 10 October 2006).

The participating domestic workers kept a diary recording the tasks accomplished; analysis of these records revealed the types of work that were most frequently required. The services required involved the activities needed to maintain basic household hygiene and tidying up, meaning the tasks that are never in a short supply in households with small children. The list is topped by vacuum cleaning, cleaning of the bathroom, ironing, dusting, kitchen cleaning, washing up, window cleaning, garbage disposal and washing of clothes. It is evident from the diaries that the majority of duties were repetitive cleaning tasks, meaning the labour-intensive activities that are the most physically strenuous and the most time-consuming category of domestic work. Since most of the workplaces remain rigid in terms of adjusting to the needs of families, the reconciliation of work and family is a one-way process meaning that the family has to adjust to the workplaces entirely. Our participants asserted that the issue here was the balancing of household tasks and time spent with children, and by no means the balancing of work and family life. A male participant stated:

> Cleaning is a problem when children are around. I don't know if anyone can do cleaning when kids are at home. In our home, one went out with the kids while the other did the cleaning. But that leads to partners increasingly drawing apart from each other. I no longer saw my wife. All you can do is say 'hi' at around 10 p.m. when you sit down to watch TV, exchange a few sentences and you are already asleep. You have 10 minutes a day to spend with your partner, and that is the main problem (Boštjan, Ljubljana, 10 October 2006).

Paid domestic work represents an amortisation for the conflicts between the overburdened partners about the share of unpaid domestic work and facilitates an easier balancing of paid work, household tasks and family time.

In this vein, paid domestic work was reflected as an appreciation, gratitude towards the domestic workers who disburdened the female participants, who consequently gained few additional hours of family time in the afternoons and free time in the evenings. Exclusively female participants stressed their recognition of household work as a tiring, time-consuming and a never-ending task. The male participants reflected on paid domestic work solely in terms of the additional time devoted for family and in terms of disburdening their female partners from household work. In particular, the women in the households with no previous experience with paid domestic work revealed recognition of what domestic work entails in practical terms of time-consuming work. As one of the female participants stated: 'I only now see how much time you need for such work. Only now, when we had someone who did it instead of us, I realise it' (Jana, Ljubljana, 5 October 2006).

Apart from the recognition of the nature of household work, the female participants also revealed that they changed their negative opinion about paid domestic help as a status symbol, as if it were a sign of women's laziness and lack of 'feminine competences' and confirmed that the quality of their lives improved. One of the female participants clearly rejected the idea of paid domestic work before, but when she had a possibility to be involved in the pilot project, she changed her understanding of the work, when done by an 'other woman'. As she explained:

> Before I didn't appreciate that someone comes to your home and tidy it up, what does it mean and how it disburdens me in the evening when I'm free of household work. ... But then you see, how one part of your life improved, the quality of life improved for a bit (Petra, Ljubljana, 10 October 2006).

Strikingly, neither women nor men who participated in the focus groups reflected on paid domestic work from the perspective of gender equality. On the contrary, legitimisation of gender inequality took place whereby it is 'normal' that when having a family, men devote more time to paid jobs, while women usually do a 'triple shift', meaning their paid job during the day, childcare in the afternoons and in the evening they accomplish household tasks. Therefore, paid domestic work was reflected as a practical solution, which enabled women's negotiation between household work and childcare, while men 'gained' less stressful partners and more family time.

Employer's Perspective: Gendered and Classed Expectations

As paid domestic work is part of informal care markets, employers most often find workers through personal contacts. Studies reveal that employers' expectations regarding the care worker refer mainly to the worker's personal characteristics, such as being warm, honest and friendly (Rollins 1985; Cox 2006). Differentiation occurs in the type of care work, where employers who employ nannies expect them to be good with children, while for household work the employers only expect the worker to be reliable and honest. Alongside the personal characteristics of the care worker, gender also plays an important role as the employers prefer a female over a male care worker.

Domestic work, either paid or unpaid, is a gendered work, as illustrated by one of the female participants in SIPA project who illustrated the following situation: 'For instance, an unknown man who would come to clean my home, well ok, but I don't have that picture in my mind, because I've never seen it' (Polona, Ljubljana, 10 October 2006).

Employers' expectations refer also to the appearance of the worker being clean and groomed, which in a way presupposes that people dealing with dirt are dirty and of a lower class. It points to the relationship between dirt, cleaning and status. The status of a care worker encompasses the status of work, which in Cox's view (2006, p. 7), 'is impossible to impose dramatically the standing of either without challenging deep-seated feelings about dirt'.

Personal characteristics alongside the gender and appearance of the domestic worker, as the main qualifications for performing paid care work, legitimise the status and the value of gendered work as a type of work that a woman knows by her nature. Domestic work is constructed as work which every woman can do by nature, given that no qualifications are required for performing it.

Households reflected they usually didn't take enough time to introduce the domestic worker with the employer's home, to discuss the tasks that needed to be done and the expected results. As it was revealed in the focus groups, clear communication was sometimes absent, in particular what tasks and how they needed to be done. A male participant, for instance, describes the first visit of domestic worker in their home, 'I have to admit that I don't know where we have cleaning products and my wife only wrote a note for the domestic worker and when she came I just showed her the note and said "bye" and went for work' (Boštjan, Ljubljana, 10 October 2006).

It became obvious in the focus groups that neither female nor male participants recognised themselves as an employer of the domestic worker. Cox (2006) stressed that the nature of care work, in particular the content of the work and the private location of the work, point to the fact that the relationship is hardly professional and is difficult to manage. A few minutes a week to explain what needs to be done is not enough to introduce someone in to the full scope of the work needed. Employers expected that domestic workers would know 'by heart' and 'see' what needs to be done and to a certain extent to initiate the work. Doing paid domestic work obviously requires several tasks from the domestic worker, like 'creating a system of order (ordering), re-establishing that order (tidying) and, finally, the cleaning of various objects' (Lutz 2011, p. 53). This means that the worker needs to be familiar with the household and needs to know what and how the tasks should be accomplished in order to fulfil the employer's expectations. What was missing on the part of employers was exactly their input on managing the work relationship. As one of the female participants highlighted: 'I expected that as a woman she would see things that needed to be done' (Simona, Ljubljana, 11 October 2006). Similarly, a male participant noted: 'you like to have your own place tidy under your system, but we were a bit disappointed, because she didn't see it. You have to tell her, "do this and that" and she didn't clean systematically' (Janez, Ljubljana, 10 October 2006).

The focus groups with male and female participants revealed their contradictory position where, on the one hand, the employer's expectations regarding the employee refer mainly to the personal characteristics and gender of the worker, and to 'see' what needs to be done. While, on the other hand, they ignored their own role as employers as they didn't recognise themselves as being in this position. Reasons for that are mainly due to the de-professionalisation of paid domestic work, in particular the work relations in the private sphere, which can hardly be named as professional, the nature and the status of the domestic work and domestic worker.

Work Relations: Warm, Friendly and Unequal

The literature on paid domestic and care work reports extensively on patronisation, exploitation, discrimination and humiliation, which occasionally turns into real abuse and a slave-like relationship (Ehrenreich and Hochschild 2002; Anderson 2000). The negative and risk factors of paid domestic work give way to many forms of abuse including non-payment, breach of agreements regarding the working conditions and the working hours (Tronto 2002). If demand and supply of paid domestic work are taking place in the grey economy, domestic workers are not entitled to the rights arising from formal employment agreements. The work takes place in the employer's private sphere in isolation from the public, which is also recognised as an aggravating circumstance in the relations between employer and employee (Lutz 2011). The prevailing notion in the literature on employer-employee relations in the field of paid care work is the existence of multilayered inequalities intersected by gender, class, race and ethnicity (Cock 1984; Rollins 1985). Nevertheless, Lutz (2011, p. 110) emphasises the multilayered and complex nature of the relationship between employer and care worker, which 'cannot be shoehorned into a straightforward exploiter – exploitee schema'. Despite the existence of the legal contract, which was also the case in the SIPA project, trust is still the crucial element of the relationship. Trust must exist on both sides: on the employer's side that the care worker will not steal, damage the property and/ or will treat children and elderly with care; while the employee must rely on the employer that he/she will pay and in case of the illegal status of the care worker, that the employer will not report the worker (Ibid.). Therefore trust replaces the contract when paid care work is performed on illegal basis (Ibid.). As Lutz (2011, p. 84) notes, 'this prerequisite of trust operates along a scale with fluid transition between friendship, loyalty and professionalism within the private sphere'.

In general, both parties found it easier to establish the needed trust, in fact, 66 per cent of the households thought that they had established a pleasant relationship with the domestic workers. Most often the relationship they established with the domestic worker was described as warm and friendly, based on the crucial element of trust. Domestic workers, however, were slightly more reserved in describing their relationships with the households as friendly or based on friendship. In particular, one worker put a strict limit between paid domestic work in households and friendship. She stressed, 'with my clients I don't develop genuine friendship, I came there to work' (Ana, Ljubljana, 25 September 2006). Likewise, Cox (2006) critically points to an employer's efforts for friendship as intrusive. Relationships based on friendship to a certain extent blur the social boundaries between the employer and the employee and de-professionalise the employer-employee relations and care work (as any other paid work). Also the employer's efforts for a friendly relationship with the employee can mask the employer's uncomfortable feelings, shame and/or guilt of letting another woman in to one's own privacy to do her own 'dirty job' and for class inequality. The domestic worker allegedly becomes very close with the employer, 'one of the family' (Bakan and Stasiulis 1997), due to performing care work related to the employer's intimacy, while at the same time the distance between them exists and is based on structural inequalities (Cox 2006).

Domestic work in the SIPA pilot involved the household chores and attendance of and escorting children. However, at the end of the pilot project it was revealed that the service of child-minding amounted to only 10 per cent of all the accomplished tasks in the pilot experiment. The reasons were twofold: firstly, because the needs for household tasks prevailed over the needs for child-minding, and, secondly, the lack of trust to leave the child to an unknown person.

As one of the rare households which also used paid domestic work for child-minding, the female participant explained that she trusted the worker from the beginning, which also resulted in her request for child-minding, as she describes below:

> ... now at the end I also asked her for child minding ... I was thinking that nothing bad could happen, but I also trusted her and she told me after that she liked it that I trusted her, and I was actually the first one who trusted her child (Eva, Ljubljana, 5 October 2006).

Nevertheless, uncomfortable feelings on the side of households existed, in particular at the beginning. As one of the female participants underlined, she asked for the employee's c.v., which was for her an indirect way to get familiar with the employee's working experience before meeting in person. Besides, a c.v. is usually the first item requested by the potential employer, and by requesting it from the domestic worker, she recognised domestic work as a regular paid job. She explained:

> Yes, I asked for her c.v., just as when you apply for a job. Her working experience, well basic information about her and I was very happy with her. Because at the beginning I was, 'hm, I don't know the person'. And then I was calmed when I read her c.v. She worked in hospitals and had experience with that, and you already had a feeling that you know her a little bit (Pupa, Ljubljana, 5 October 2006).

Despite the confirmed overall estimation of the households in the quantitative evaluation, where 70 per cent of them stated that they trusted the domestic workers from the beginning, and 60 per cent of the households gave door keys to domestic workers, the focus groups showed more diverse perspectives on work relations in the households. Even when the work was organised through the mediation of an agency, which was an additional element of security for both sides, uncomfortable feelings and fear existed both among households and domestic workers. They expressed partly similar and partly different views on paid domestic work in someone's private sphere. One of the workers explained she felt uncomfortable at the beginning when entering the private sphere and could also sense these feelings with her households, especially the suspicious looks and questions, where certain items were. As she describes below:

> I was afraid at the beginning and also my households; they also were afraid of me. At least I saw it like that. When I was wiping something and would remove something, after that I went ironing and the lady would come and ask me, 'oh, where is that thing'. I felt like I stole something, and I also didn't know where that thing was. Maybe I removed it from here to there, I wasn't sure, and then I saw it, but she didn't (Ana, Ljubljana, 25 September 2006).

In the course of time trust developed on both sides. One of the female participants explained: 'At the beginning I didn't feel comfortable to give her the keys ... I had a nanny, so she wasn't alone or also my parents came. After that I also trusted her with keys' (Sabina, Ljubljana, 11 October 2006).

Despite the regularised and controlled situation in the SIPA pilot, the households rarely but still tested the domestic worker by setting the 'servant trap', putting valuable items lying around in order to test their honesty. 'Honesty tests' were a popular tool in times of maidservants, while it might still be present today as Lutz explains (2011). However, no household mentioned this 'honesty test' at the focus groups, while the domestic workers stressed they experienced it. One of the interviewed workers said, 'there was some golden jewellery on the tables and in the bathroom. But I'm not interested ...' (Božica, Ljubljana, 25 September 2006). Another tool used by the households to cope with the lack of trust and uncomfortable feelings of invasion in the private sphere is co-working between mostly female participants and domestic workers, which plays a double role. First, co-working was used by the households as a motive for accomplishing a master clean, which is usually done once/twice per year. A female participant explained that on several occasions she worked together with the domestic worker due to the workload:

> Few times we worked together, especially these master cleanings, because it seems fair to me that she wouldn't be alone there, because she is not familiar, I took some time for cleaning and it was also easier if I have someone who comes and I know 'ok, now we'll do it' (Amanda, Ljubljana, 10 October 2006).

Second, co-working is also an expression of the lack of trust, to check if the work will be done as expected and as a way of exercising control over domestic worker.

A male participant explained that at the beginning he would work together with the domestic worker due to the control of the performed work. He said: 'At the beginning for sure you have to be with the person. We were with her four, five times. ... I start working on certain tasks and she did the basic cleaning in parallel' (Marjan, Ljubljana, 10 October 2006). Co-working also involved the household's engagement on how the work should be performed, but it nevertheless was aimed as a control over the worker, based on the lack of trust and as a household's 'excuse' to task occasionally the workers with a more intense workload.

Relationships in households are fundamentally different from other work relationships and they are not 'exclusively professional' (Lutz 2011, p. 82) as was observed in the SIPA project. Working relations between the employer and employee are characterised by multiple asymmetries addressing power relations, working conditions and work location, which need to be considered in the context of the regulation of paid domestic and care work.

Concluding Remarks

In this chapter, paid domestic work from an employer's perspective was explored in the Slovenian context, which is particularly interesting due to changes in gender, employment and care regimes experienced in last decades in two different socio-economic and political systems – socialism and Capitalism. During the Socialist period, from the 1950s onward, women's employment was promoted by the State, which led to well-developed public day care, favourable maternity leave and other social benefits. However, economic gender equality did not go hand in hand with gender equality in the private sphere where women have remained until today in the main role of homemakers, home-managers and caregivers, devoting a disproportionate amount of time to family life compared to men. In the post-socialist period, after 1991, Slovenia has not faced a process of re-traditionalisation in terms of withdrawal of women from the labour market in order to take care of the family, as happened in other Eastern European countries. However, the structural changes during the transition period extending to the neoliberal conditions tend towards intensification of work, deterioration of working conditions and shrinking the welfare state, that is, the relocation of public care into the family sphere. This resulted in the 'double' and 'triple shifts' performed by mothers with small children and boosted demand for paid care work in informal care markets which are sustained by a growing number of long-term unemployed native women.

In the SIPA project from where the material for this analysis was drawn, regulated and subsidised systems of household assistance were tested in order to tackle the conflict between work and family and older female long-term unemployment. The aim was to transform the currently existing informal market of paid domestic work into a publicly subsidised regular employment market for long-term unemployed women and to relieve the burden of domestic work shouldered by full-time employed women with pre-school children. The pilot experiment proved that despite the regulation of paid domestic work in private households, asymmetries and inequalities between employees and employers still persist. Nevertheless, when the State steps in to regulate this kind of work some advantages can be recognised. Access to care services is restructured by subsidies and becomes more inclusive and open to individuals and families (such as single-parent families, families with a child with special needs and so on) who could not otherwise afford such assistance, but are in a great need of it. The mediation of an agency gives both sides a better feeling of security and trust, and it simultaneously enables supervision and organisation. Hence, the regulation of work enables better protection of domestic workers from abuse while affording a level of security to the households that hire the workers. It is of paramount importance also from the perspective of poverty prevention in the future, in a regulated system care workers are ensured the social and pension rights together with defined payment and working conditions. A regulated system of paid care work made care work visible as a regular job, which also enables the professionalisation (to a certain extent) of work relations and working conditions. Further, it enables both sides, employers and employees, to be legally covered in terms of employer-employee relations and problematic/abusive situations on both sides.

The SIPA project's standpoint was that the marginalisation of care work, which is intrinsic to a capitalist system, leads to the invisibility of contemporary domestic and care workers. This is especially problematic considering that this invisible type of work is performed under informal conditions primarily by those groups of women who are already socially excluded in one way or another (that is older women, long-term unemployed women, first time workers, single mothers, migrants) (Hrženjak 2007). The SIPA project inspired public awareness and political action, which is particularly important in light of the aging population and the increasing needs for care. The overburden caused by (non)-paid reproductive work cannot be considered only as women's private problem, but must be regarded as a public issue. In order to avoid a situation in which the burden of reproductive work is borne by certain social groups only, the State must encourage gender equality within the private sphere and social responsibility among employers, so that they provide working conditions that enable the reconciliation of work and family. Last but not least, the State should stimulate the development of a regulated and accessible public service providing care work. The pilot experiment proved that when more recognition and assurance of basic social and labour rights and a concrete definition of the working conditions for domestic and care workers are present, the better it is for both parties.

References

Anderson, B., 2000. *Doing the Dirty Work? The Global Politics of Domestic Labour*. London: Zed Books.

Bakan, A.B. and Stasiulis, D.K. (eds), 1997. *Not One of the Family. Foreign Domestic Workers in Canada*. Toronto, Buffalo: University of Toronto Press.

Bianchi, S. et al., 2000. Is anyone doing the housework? Trends in the gender division of household labor. *Social Forces*, 79(1), pp. 191–228.

Burcar, L., 2009. Od socialistične k (neoliberalni) kapitalistični družbenoekonomski ureditvi: redefinicija državljanstva žensk. *Borec*, 61(657/661), pp. 296–331.

Cock, J., 1984. *Maids and Madams. A Study in the Politics of Exploitation*. Johannesburg: Ravan Press.

Cox, R., 2006. *The Servant Problem. Domestic Employment in a Global Economy*. London: I.B. Tauris & CO Ltd.

Ehrenreich, B. and Hochschild, A.R. (eds), 2002. *Global Women: Nannies, Maids and Sex Workers in the New Economy*. London: Granta Books.

European Foundation for the Improvement of Living and Working Conditions, 2009. Second European Quality of Life Survey. Overview. Available on-line at: www.eurofound.europa.eu/pubdocs/2009/02/en/2/EF0902EN.pdf [accessed: 5 April 2014].

Eurostat, 2011. Tables, Graphs and Maps Interface (TGM) table. Employment rate by gender, age group 15–64. Available on-line at: http://epp.eurostat. ec.europa.eu/tgm/table.do?tab=table&init=1&plugin=1&language=en&pcode =t2020_10 [accessed: 5 April 2014].

Hochschild, A., 2000. Global Care Chains and Emotional Surplus Value. In: W. Hutton and A. Giddens (eds), 2000. *On the Edge: Living with Global Capitalism*. London: Jonathan Cape. pp. 131–46.

Hochschild, A., 1997. *The Second Shift*. New York: Avon Books.

Hrženjak, M., 2012. Hierarchization and segmentation of informal care markets in Slovenia. *Social Politics: International Studies in Gender, State and Society*, 19(1), pp. 38–57.

Hrženjak, M., 2010. (Neformalno) skrbstveno delo in družbene neenakosti. *Teor. praksa*, 47(1), pp. 156–71.

Hrženjak, M., 2008. Expanding the public system of household assistance: A pilot experiment in Slovenia. Suvremene teme (Spletna izd.), pp. 34–49. Available on-line at: http://contemporary-issues.cpi.hr/journals/281fde39ed4b69183021 61795945d448.pdf [accessed: 5 April 2014].

Hrženjak, M., 2007. *Nevidno delo*. Ljubljana: Mirovni inštitut.

Hrženjak, M. and Humer, Ž., 2011. Informal care work market from the perspective of local care workers. In: M. Hrženjak (ed.), 2011. *Politics of Care*. Ljubljana: Peace Institute, pp. 99–119.

Humer, Ž., 2009. Etika skrbi, spol in družina: procesi relokacije skrbi med zasebno in javno sferom (Ethics of care, gender and family: the processes of the relocation of care between private and public spheres) Ph.D. Thesis. Ljubljana: Fakulteta za družbene vede.

Ignjatović, M., 2002. *Družbene posledice povečanja prožnosti trga delovne sile.* Ljubljana: Znanstvena knjižnica FDV.

Lister, R. et al., 2007. *Gendering Citizenship in Western Europe. New Challenges for Citizenship Research in a Cross-National Context.* Bristol: The Policy Press.

Lutz, H., 2011. *The New Maids. Transnational Women and the Care Economy.* London/New York: Zed Books.

OECD, 2011. Society at a Glance 2011: OECD Social Indicators. OECD Publishing. Available on-line at: http://dx.doi.org/10.1787/soc_glance-2011-en [accessed: 5 April 2014].

Rener, T. et al., 2008. *Novi trendi v starševstvu – analiza očetovstva ter predlogi za izboljšave družinske politike na tem področju. Raziskovalno poročilo.* Ljubljana: Fakulteta za družbene vede, Center za socialno psihologijo.

Rollins, J., 1985. *Between Women: Domestics and Their Employers.* Philadelphia, PA: Temple University Press.

Šadl, Z., 2006. Plačano gospodinjsko delo v Sloveniji. *Družboslovne razprave,* XXII (53), pp. 33–54.

Tijdens, K., van der Lippe, T. and Ruijter, E., 2003. Working Women's Choices for Domestic Help. The Effects of Financial and Time Resources. Working Paper 03/17. Amsterdam: Amsterdam Institute for Advanced Labour Studies. Universiteit van Amsterdam. Available on-line at: http://www.wageindicator. org/documents/publicationslist/w17/view [accessed: 5 April 2014].

Tronto, J., 2002. The 'Nanny' Question in Feminism. *Hypathia,* 17(2), pp. 34–51.

Vojnovič, M., 1996. *Situacijska analiza o položaju otrok in družin v Sloveniji.* Ljubljana: Slovenski odbor za UNICEF 1995.

Williams, F. and Gavanas, A., 2008. The Intersections of Childcare Regimes and Migration Regimes: A Three-Country Study. In: H. Lutz (ed.), 2008. *Migration and Domestic Work. A European Perspective on a Global Theme.* Burlington, Hampshire: Ashgate Publishing, pp. 13–19.

PART III
From Host Parents to Employers: Recent Developments in Au Pair Schemes

Chapter 11

Au Pairs and Changing Family Needs in the United Kingdom

Lenka Pelechova[1]

> Full-time childcare costs working parents across Britain £722 a month, it's not surprising many families decide it doesn't make sense financially for both parents to work. So what can you do to cut your childcare costs? A live-out nanny costs up to £500 a week and you must pay tax and National Insurance on their behalf, so even a nanny share can be pricey. By contrast, an au pair will work 25–30 hours a week for as little as £65, along with food and board. Use the British Au Pair Association's directory to find a local au pair agency.

This quote, taken from the newspaper *The Guardian* (29 January 2013), is reminiscent of the current atmosphere in the UK, reflecting not only the high cost but also the lack of availability of childcare provision. The hiring of au pairs as a form of childcare and domestic work is being promoted as one of the low-cost alternatives to employing a nanny or using nurseries. The exact number of au pairs currently working in the UK is unknown, however the estimate for the year 2000 was 60,000 (Addley 2002). More than a decade later, and with the EU having undergone two enlargements, these numbers are likely to be even higher.

This chapter will consider the dynamics of au pair families. Drawing on examples from our research project, it will initially identify some themes underlying the sector of au pair work. Following this, two examples from our current research will be provided. In particular, this chapter will focus on the perspectives of the host parents and their attempts at renegotiating 'family time' as well as the effect of au pair employment on family members' responsibilities, whilst bearing in mind that these are intertwined within highly gendered and classed notions. This chapter will conclude with a suggestion that the role of an 'employer' is approached not only from the viewpoint of domestic work, but also from a family studies perspective, hence the classification of host mothers and host fathers. By introducing the concept of family studies into the subject of domestic work, the focus shifts towards a greater understanding of family roles, family time and family boundaries, and how these are renegotiated in this case by the employment of an au pair.

1 Acknowledgements: I am particularly grateful to Dr Elisabetta Zontini and Dr Christian Karner who supervised my PhD, and Dr Diane Trusson and Dr Elisabetta Zontini for their helpful comments on this chapter.

The Growth of the Domestic Work Sector and the Debate on the Au Pair Scheme

Over the last two decades, there has been an increase in academic literature addressing contemporary changing patterns of migrant domestic workers (see Triandafyllidou and Marchetti this volume). According to Bridget Anderson (2001, p. 27) it is a combination of factors that encourage the recent growth of the paid domestic sector; such as an ageing population and the increase of women entering the paid labour market. These factors have thus lead to a 'reproductive labour gap', together with changes in family forms and reduction in social provisions. Similarly, Rosie Cox (2006) notes that in the case of the UK, the supply and demand of domestic work is sustained on the one hand by the rise in working hours and the high cost of State-provided childcare, and the existing global inequalities where low wage labour is being transferred from poorer to wealthier countries on the other hand. Fiona Williams and Anna Gavanas (2008) point out that even though childcare is supplied by the State sector, the cost of State-provided nurseries is expensive and does not always provide the hours necessary for parents in full-time employment. Only some parents have the advantage of drawing on the 'voluntary care-givers' (mainly relatives and friends) and therefore it is not a reliable tool to address the needs of every parent. As a result, parents are put in a situation where they have to look for the most financially sound solution, which Cox (2011) refers to as the marketised childcare economy.

The UK au pair placement immigration category was modified in 2008 and is now part of the 'Points Based System'. This change implies that au pairs coming to the UK either fall within the European Freedom of Movement Act, or in the case of non-EU citizens,[2] they can obtain a visa under the new 'Youth Mobility Scheme'. Despite these recent legislative changes, by and large an au pair refers to any young person (guidelines advise between 18 and 30 years old) of single status and with no dependants. Au pairs live with an English-speaking host family, help with light housework and childcare for up to a maximum of five hours a day and might be asked to babysit for up to two nights per week. In exchange, the host family provides free accommodation in the form of a private room, free board and 'pocket money', currently recommended at between £70 and £85 per week (BAPAA 2013[3]).

Up until now, research conducted in relation to au pairs has mostly been done either as a part of scholarly work on the feminisation of migration or the division associated with the sphere of domestic service (Hess and Puckhaber 2004; Parreñas

---

2 Referred to as Tier 5* Youth Mobility Scheme, eligible nationals who can apply for the au pair visa include Australia, New Zealand, Canada, Japan, Monaco, Taiwan and Republic of Korea, see also the web site of the British Au Pair Agencies Associations, BAPAA, http://www.bapaa.org.uk/displaypage.asp?page=1 [accessed: 24 April 2014].

3 For more information regarding the au pair scheme see Home Office (2013) or BAPAA site above.

2001, Williams and Gavanas 2008). Within the UK, attention has been given to the au pairs' personal experiences (Burikova and Miller 2010; Williams and Balaz 2004), the living conditions and interactions between the au pair and her/ his employer (Hess and Puckhaber 2004), the representation of au pairs in the British Press (Cox 2007) and, more recently, on the subjectivities of au pair visa immigration control (Anderson 2009). The above research raises significant issues concerning the employment of au pairs, namely the inequalities that persist within the sphere of domestic work employment. Approaching this topic from the viewpoint of relationships between au pairs and host parents, Rosie Cox and Rekha Narula (2003) explored the quasi-familial complexities and suggested that household rules are a key factor in shaping the relationship between the au pair and her employer.

In general, domestic work theories focus on the concepts of gender, care and migration. In other works they centre on issues such as inequalities, value of care and feminisation of migration. Through this lens, domestic work research has helped to illuminate many problematic areas that are located within this sphere, such as the vulnerable position of migrant domestic workers, their exposure to exploitation and the invisibility of such work. The interconnectedness of these issues is clear, as it is the invisibility of the private sphere of home that to a degree influences this type of work as either low paid or unpaid altogether. Au pairs are undoubtedly part of this migrant domestic work network. For example the invisibility of au pairs is further underlined by government policies which label this scheme as a 'cultural exchange' and this is also reflected in the low remuneration as au pairs receive 'pocket money' rather than wages for their labour. The studies highlighted above demonstrate that classing domestic workers (in this case, au pairs) as family members poses difficulties in the way power is distributed and managed within the employer/employee relationship. As a result, domestic workers experience decreased working conditions as employers view their 'family membership' as a means of gaining control of working hours.

The interest of this chapter, however, lies in the changes that occur as a result of au pair employment on the larger host family dynamics, as well as the means by which the host family and the au pair negotiate their new circumstances. In order to do this, the next section will highlight the scholarly field of family studies.

Overview of Family Theories

When considering the diversity of contemporary family forms, sociological literature has paid attention to nuclear (Crompton 1997), extended and multigenerational (Bengston 2001), single-parent (Silva 1996), divorced (Smart et al. 2001), transnational (Zontini 2006), ethnic minority families (Collins 1990) and reconstituted families (Ribbens McCarthy et al. 2003) or same-sex partnerships (Cheal 2008).

With this accepted diversification in mind, new theories of family as well as the reasons and motivations behind such diversity are emerging. For example, the thesis of individualisation or de-traditionalisation has been outlined in recent years as one of the explanations responsible for the current changes in family arrangements (Beck 1992; Giddens 1992). This process implies that people today have more choices in terms of their family lifestyle and are not necessarily following the 'traditional family form'. Within these lines, Anthony Giddens (1992) argues that individuals are 'reflexive' authors of their own biographies, and similarly, Zygmunt Bauman (2000) comments that family relationships today are much more 'fluid' than in the past. Similarly, Ulrich Beck's (1992, p. 2) theory of individualisation states that it is the notion of 'reflexive modernisation' which impacts on the traditional way of life such as family life, identity and gender relations. Ulrich Beck and Elizabeth Beck-Gernsheim (2002, pp. 2–3) refer to the increased fluidity and individualisation as a 'loss of security' and imply that 'familiar concepts such as "marriage" no longer apply'. In other words, due to the condition of individualisation, what was previously perceived as a traditional family with set roles and obligations now becomes questioned as there are more choices individuals face in relation to family living. Within these lines, David Morgan (1999) suggested looking at families as fluid and flexible entities rather than as static units of analysis, as the way to truly understand the current diversity of family life and family practices. Emphasising change, fluidity and flux, Morgan also highlighted that 'family represents a constructed quality of human interaction or an active process rather than a thing-like object of detached social investigation' (1999, p. 16).

Contrary to the thesis of 'individualisation and reflexive modernity', Graham Crow (2002) points out that despite the impact of increased individualisation on family life, the notion of family and family values remain rather powerful in contemporary society. Other scholars critiqued 'de-traditionalisation', suggesting it overrates the process of social change amid the persistent importance of tradition (Ribbens McCarthy et al. 2003), but also in light of how 'individualisation' refers to family as a culturally universal notion (Smart and Shipman 2004). That is, instead of increased 'individualisation', scholars highlight the continuous influence of social rules. For example, Catherine Marsh and Sara Arber (1992, p. 10) note that the concept of family involves not only biological and legal ties, but also a range of relationships that impose norms of behaviour for each member. Social rules within the family unit are a key part in prescribing obligations that are imposed on each member. Moreover, the feminist literature on domestic work examines patriarchal roles within the household unit and critiques the inequality of roles between men and women (Anderson 2001). Jon Bernardes (1997) notes that the prevailing ideology of the traditional family and its associated roles has a huge impact on what individuals perceive as what should be an appropriate type of work for each member (1997, p. 27). In this way, the 'abstract' idea of gendered division of labour in households becomes concrete as it is women who are taking on the majority of domestic and childcare work. Each set of roles (father/mother) brings different expectations of behaviour and actions that altogether imply diverse outcomes for individual opportunities and achievements.

Existing research on family studies, whilst acknowledging the diversification of contemporary family forms, does not focus on families with au pairs, and the mainstream literature on domestic work constricts itself mainly to issues of inequalities experienced by migrant workers. Very little attention has so far been given to families, which include an au pair. Are there any adjustments that host parents experience as a result of au pair hire? What impact does living with an au pair have on the host parents' relationship?

Methodology

Applying a qualitative approach, semi-structured interviews were conducted with 18 host parents (11 host mothers and seven host fathers), and 18 au pairs, together with an analysis of au pair recruitment advertisements. Additionally, follow-up interviews with five host parents were conducted over the period of one year in order to obtain deeper insights into relationship changes which occurred over time. All of the interviews were carried out in the East Midlands region of the United Kingdom. This chapter is based partly on my PhD thesis entitled, 'Au pair family dynamics'. The aim is to understand family members within their own context of family life, family roles and relationships. This chapter explores how their perspectives are constructed within an area where multiple and individual meanings are being simultaneously created. According to Gill Valentine (1999), some of the conventional family studies research, although claiming to study families, actually employs the perceptions from only one family member. More often than not, this family member is a woman (mothers/wives), as they are usually easier to gain access to and also because families tend to be perceived as a female domain (Valentine 1999).

The perceptions gained from au pairs, host mothers and host fathers also allowed us to investigate beliefs and perceptions relating to the gendered nature of family practices and the gendered roles represented within the family, as well as the effects on couple relationships that living with an au pair has.

Host Mothers' Perceptions

The host mothers interviewed all shared the view that their au pairs are there to help 'them', with 'their' work and 'their' domestic and childcare responsibilities. For example, host mother Samantha gave the following reply when asked to summarise what having an au pair meant to her: 'In a way, for me, it is like having a wife, another wife, because she [au pair] does all the things that a wife would do for her husband' (Samantha, 42 years old, part-time real estate manager).

This statement summarised rather fittingly the prevalent view of traditionally gendered family roles, where women were perceived as the main housekeepers and childcarers, whilst emphasising the notion of the husband's main role as the breadwinner. As such, the au pairs were perceived as an extension of women's responsibilities in families.

During the interviews with host mothers, there was a mixture of tones regarding the husbands' involvement in domestic tasks. For some host mothers the rather rigid gendered role separation was accepted and perceived as something much more 'natural', as a 'way of family life'. For example, host mother Debbie described her husband thus: 'When he is travelling, he is gone, and that is one of the reasons why I decided to get an au pair. Of course he comes from work and he does his best, but no picking up, no taking, no nothing' (Debbie, 45 years old, part-time assistant manager).

What is interesting with this statement is the fact that even though Debbie's husband was apparently unable to carry out domestic or childcare duties, he was still described as 'doing his best' in this regard. The reality of her husband's persistent absence described as 'no picking up, no taking, no nothing' seems to contradict with the belief that the husband is still 'doing his best'. One could ask why there is such a contradiction between the reality of the absence, and the belief that placed the husband as imaginatively present. In this regard, Pamela Stone also found that the stay-at-home mothers in her study 'tended to advantage their husband's absence by this false egalitarian principle, simply pushing away the reality of an unequal power balance of domestic work and childcare between couples' (Stone 2011, p. 367). According to Sophie Bowlby et al. (1997), issues with domestic and caring responsibilities based on gender are linked to debates surrounding femininity and masculinity. In this way, as childcare and domestic work is linked to female responsibilities, host mother Debbie could be producing and drawing on her femininity, and in turn creating her own authority and control within the family. Additionally, according to Scott Coltrane's (2000) review of housework literature during the 1990s, research also demonstrated that when husbands work longer hours in paid employment, wives are more likely to perceive the division of domestic labour as fair, even though they are responsible for the majority of it.

Such observation was also apparent in interviews carried out with four host mothers who were, at the time, either on maternity leave or stay-at-home mothers, whereas the rest of the group (seven host mothers) were employed full time. Sociological studies concerning housework have shown that it is physically and emotionally difficult, and women are responsible for unpaid domestic work even when employed outside of the home. This occurrence has been since referred to as the 'double burden' or the 'second shift' (Hochschild 1989; Oakley 1974). In terms of this research, the interviews with host mothers also revealed how the 'double burden' has encouraged them to employ an au pair. For example, host mother Anna commented:

> She [au pair] does lots of the things the nanny used to do, but it is outside of my work time which helps me the most ... When I did not have an au pair, I would come home, then I would have to spend hours preparing the food and the

kitchen, so it is nice to come in now, and have things ready (Anna, 39 years old, physiotherapist).

From the examples stated above, be it the host mothers who explicitly see the domestic work and childcare as their sole responsibility, or the host mothers who felt resentful regarding their husband's absence, it is noticeable how the gendered division of domestic work operates and creates extra demands on host mothers. Stone (2011) noted in her study of elite stay-at-home mothers that their husbands' lack of involvement was one of the main reasons for giving up their full-time work. However, in the case of this research, such absence and the unequal power dynamics in the form of the 'second shift' between host mothers and fathers resulted in the hiring of an au pair. By doing this, the primary responsibility of childcare and housework still stayed with host mothers, as it was they who assigned the daily tasks to the au pair. In this way, host mothers were perceived as the person primarily responsible for the au pair. This new responsibility revolved around different aspects of au pair associated work, starting with the practical aspects of preparing for and managing the au pair arrival as well as dealing with her on a daily basis.

Host Fathers' Perceptions

Various researchers have pointed out that contemporary fathers in developed countries are increasingly more involved in parenting activities compared to half a century ago (Coltrane and Adams 2008). For example, Tina Miller (2010) notes that contemporary discourses surrounding fatherhood in the UK are linked to concepts of 'emotional engagement, involvement, sensitivity and intimacy' compared to previously associated notions of 'absence and economic provision' (Miller 2010, pp. 7–8). Indeed, she refers to this change as a 'shifting understanding of masculinities' which in turn was described as the 'de-traditionalisation of fatherhood' (Ibid., p. 9). However, despite these changes, there is still a prevalence of fathers having a significantly lower proportion of responsibilities regarding childcare and domestic tasks compared to mothers (Doucet 2007). Reflecting on this, Miller (2010, p. 8) also acknowledges that: 'whilst shifts in discourses and policies may imply change, research findings continue to highlight entrenched and gendered practices in the division of domestic labour and paid work between the "logic of cash" and "care"'. Within this research, the ways in which host fathers related to their familial roles could to a large degree be associated with the traditional breadwinner/fatherhood model. For instance, host father Walter commented:

So, if it would not be for our au pair Monika, I would get sucked into looking after the children much more during the day, and I love spending time with them during the weekend, I love it, having sort of the time after work to spend with them, from sort of five thirty in the evening onwards (Walter, 47 years old, managerial director).

Such statements clearly demarcate the separateness of the time host father Walter spent at work (paid employment) compared to the time spent caring for their children. The time spent with children, although perceived as very important, was clearly separated from the paid employment, and almost considered as a leisurely activity to be carried out during the weekend. The perception of fairness of splitting childcare was undermined by the fact that it only occurs at certain times, and thus women are still perceived as the primary care-givers.

In the previous section, it was apparent that host mothers were perceived as the ones responsible for managing au pairs, which involved practical as well as emotional aspects of work. Similarly in the interviews with host fathers, there was a general consensus that it was host mothers who were normally in need of employing an au pair, and who were 'responsible' for recruiting, dealing with and communicating with au pairs. As host father Jeremy rationalised:

> We first got an au pair when Anna (wife) was expecting our second child. So we, Anna, could cope and we could cope as a family unit with one child, sort of with one year old, but when we had a second child, it became apparent that, yeah, Anna, needed some help. That was sort of the bottom line of it (Jeremy, 44 years old, IT consultant).

In this interview extract, it became evident that when host father Jeremy referred to the reason why he and his wife decided to hire an au pair, the connotations of 'we', as a married couple, became actually associated with the wife only, as it was Anna who could not cope with the demands of caring for two small children and the house. Again, similarly to the host mothers' interviews, such a view resonates with the idea of families with traditionally divided roles, the stay-at-home mother and the breadwinner father. Among the host fathers interviewed, they often made remarks such as: 'you would have to ask my wife if she actually went to the agency or on-line', or 'I am not sure if we did any interview on skype' or as host father Paul reported: 'I can go days without seeing her [au pair], my wife is in the forefront of the relationship and I am very much the secondary'. This disconnectedness with the au pair described by Paul contradicts the proximity of the relationship described by host mothers. The sense of dis-involvement continues when host fathers were asked about house rules:

> I try to stay little bit detached, so if something is not right, I would try to feed my concern to my wife ... I think it is more appropriate that there is one voice and it is my wife who is the key host and I don't want to be having to tell the au pair that some room is untidy or that she is not doing something with the children (John, 38 years old, business owner).

Statements such as the ones above suggest the belief in gendered separation of family roles. In the case of this research, the host fathers that had the most distant relationship with their au pairs seemed to be based on the fact that they saw their au pairs as the representation of female domestic labour, something they, as men, had nothing in common with.

The Concept of 'Family Time' in Au Pair Families

As mentioned previously, based on the principle of cultural exchange, au pairs are to be treated as 'family members' rather than 'employees' by their host families. It is the aim of this section to examine how the 'family member' emphasis of the au pair programme is interpreted by host parents. How does living with an au pair impact on family time?

Whilst a pseudo family arrangement is emphasised by the au pair scheme, in reality research studies in the past have demonstrated the economic aspect of this agreement, where the host parents' decision to hire an au pair was affected by the relative affordability in comparison to other forms of childcare such as nannies or nurseries (Burikova and Miller 2010; Cox 2007). As such, it could be said that there are competing subject positions within the scheme, one set up on the ideal of the family member model and one set up on the reality of the host parents' needs for a domestic worker. The majority of the host parents interviewed recognised the cultural exchange principle, however at the same time admitted that the au pair programme was a suitable means of getting low-cost childcare and housework. Having said this, the notion of cultural exchange was still embedded in the host parents' view of the programme, as ten host parents described their au pair as a 'visitor' to the UK and as such would be likely to be interested in visiting different cities/places and taking part in local events (goose fairs, local craft and garden markets, sports events) and national events (Halloween, Guy Fawkes night, Christmas fairs and so on). Similarly to Cecilie Øien's (2009) study of the Norwegian au pair scheme, 'host families may not per definition be disinterested in cultural exchange although they have the au pair for other reasons' (Øien 2009, p. 84). Therefore, whilst some host parents seemed to be fairly confident in involving their au pair in sufficient cultural activities, others simply felt that giving the au pair 'plenty of free time' ensured there was no extra pressure in creating 'compulsory family time'. Actually, it was the issue of 'family time' that seemed to generate 'mixed feelings' during the interviews. In one way, host parents seemed to conceal themselves behind the ideology of a 'happy family'. Half of the host parents would proudly announce at the beginning of the interview that their au pair lived with them as part of their family. But what does this actually mean? How was the family membership interpreted by host parents? The following quote from host father John describes his way of understanding, as he told me at the beginning of our follow-up interview, 'Yes, you know, everything is going great, Lena [au pair] is really now like a member of our family and the kids really love her, she is just lovely, you know' (John, 38 years old, business owner).

In this way, it seems as if denoting au pair Lena to family member status implied interconnectedness, where Lena was viewed as someone 'more' than simply caring for the children. Perhaps it also symbolised the longer length of time Lena spent with the host family? Later on, John was asked to explain in what way Lena was considered a family member, to which he replied, 'No, that is not what I meant, you know, it is just a nice thing to say, I thought it sounded nice you know, of course she is not family member, she just lives here and helps out' (John, 38 years old, business owner).

In this way, to perceive Lena as a family member is seen as something that is almost expected. As au pair regulations stipulate, 'an au pair must be welcomed as a member of the family' (BAPAA 2013); John felt as if he was supposed to say that Lena was a family member, but in reality, as he mentioned later on, Lena is 'just living' in their house and 'helps out'. In other cases, host parents seemed somewhat confused when asked whether they would describe their au pair as a family member. For example, host mother Amelia replied:

> Well, she is like a, like a daughter almost really in a way. You know, daughter but not a daughter, you know what I mean. Not that close, because as I said she is very different to me, with her culture and all of that, but she is lovely, lovely person. Like a cousin, that is really good analogy, like a cousin. You know, someone you would care for great deal and whatever, but not so close as your own (Amelia, 44 years old, stay-at-home mother).

In this instance, Amelia was at first not sure where in the 'family scale' she should place their au pair Magda, and then resolved this dilemma by placing Magda in the cousin category, which was not perceived as the closest circle of intimate family members, but still close enough to the family realm. Abigail Bakan and Daiva Stasiulis (1997, p. 10) described that 'the personalised relations and non-work related bonds of attachments that commonly exist between employers and employees are a feature of paid domestic service' and it is this intimacy that goes hand-in-hand with the often heard phrase by host parents stating that au pairs are 'just like one of the family'. What is more, when referring to au pairs as family members, host parents often contradicted themselves at various points within an interview. The view of au pairs as being 'like part of our family' would be later contradicted by claiming that the au pair was not invited to join the rest of the host family for holidays because that was 'the real family time'. Bridget Anderson (2000) notes that:

> Being told that you are 'part of the family' often serves to conceal the real power relationships at work, and this leads to confusion and exploitation. Employers can

switch from considering the relationship as contractual or familial, depending on what is most convenient for them (Anderson 2000, p. 31).[4]

For instance, host mother Joan continuously talked about their au pairs as family members, and when she was asked in what ways she sees the au pairs as family members she replied:

> We just involve them [au pairs] with anything we do as a family, on a family level, like family occasions. Like, when [au pair] Nora came, I took her to Derby to meet my mother. When I go to visit, my mum lives in a bungalow and we all went over and I said to Nora that we are going, but I don't invite her all the time because the bungalow is too small. And it is almost too small to have all of us and her in that small space. But, I mean I would not be going to my mum and not introducing her, I mean she knows the circumstances. So, it is very much to make her feel like part of the family. Like, we had a party on Friday night and the neighbours came and everybody who came, they were like: 'hello Nora!' (Joan, 38 years old, part-time HR coordinator).

In this statement, Joan described taking their au pairs to 'anything we do as a family', however later on she also described not inviting the au pair every time because 'the bungalow is almost too small' to have all of the family and the au pair in such a small space. Such contradictions were also apparent in nine other interviews with host parents. Clearly, the construction and negotiation of family time influenced host parents in such a way as to create two versions of family time; one would include all of the family members and the au pair and the second version would exclude the au pair from the rest of the host family. The following is an extract from interview with host mother Trish. When asked about spending time with the au pair she replied:

> We don't want them really involved in our days at the weekend. I don't mind if she is around during the hours she is off during the week, some of them are off, like I am finished and that is it now, others, they are much more flexible like that. And if they want to get involved coming and spending some time with us during a Saturday or Sunday, I am very happy about that, but I would not want it for all Saturdays and Sundays. And my husband is also, he is looking for a job now, but he is looking for a job all day, so he doesn't want to be entertaining the au pair and include her in our weekend and our time together as a family. So we don't do that, whereas some people are probably more inclusive, but we don't do that (Trish, 37 years old, general practitioner).

---

4   Other scholars have also documented the classification of domestic workers as family members, such as Burikova and Miller (2010) and Cox and Narula (2003),

The contradiction between two sets of family time, one as genuine (excluding the au pair) and one as general (including the au pair), is clearly discernible in Trish's comments. Therefore, 'our family time' could either exclude the au pair, whilst at other times the au pair is 'welcome' to spend time with the family. Pei-Chia Lan (2003, p. 525) also described how the employment of a domestic worker turns 'the private home into a contested terrain where employers and workers negotiate social boundaries and distance from one another on a daily basis' and concluded, that the notion of 'other' is constructed and redeveloped by the employers in order to exclude and include their domestic workers within their family, and, by this, these families develop multilayered boundaries (Lan 2003). Similarly in this study, the concept of 'family time' was reconstructed by host parents in order to welcome the au pair to either all of the family activities whilst at other times the 'our time as a family' was indicative of excluding the au pair from the rest of the host family. In this way, by renegotiating the notion of 'family time', host parents generated different levels of boundaries that either imply inclusion or exclusion of the au pair.

One particular family occasion, which 12 host parents highlighted during their interview, was 'the Sunday lunch'. Also referred to as Sunday roast, Sunday lunch is generally perceived as 'the family meal' in the UK (Jackson 2009). It was almost as if host parents separated the working week from the weekend, and as such managed to navigate the complexity of positioning au pairs as family members. Thus, the invitation to Sunday lunch was mentioned frequently as an example of how host parents would spend family time with the au pair. For example, host mother Debbie noted: 'You know for Sunday afternoon, it is very very family, and you know, we always invite the au pairs' (Debbie, 45 years old, part-time assistant manager). Similarly, host mother Beverley said, 'During the weekends I cook and we sit to eat together for Sunday lunch, she is either with us, or I put her portion on a plate to have later on' (Beverley, 48 years old, stay-at-home mother). Other host parents also used this example as 'weekend family time'. Yet, in other cases host parents expressed how family time is not an activity they want their au pair to feel forced into, rather they left it up to the au pair to decide whether to join the host family or not. For instance, host father Richard commented:

> We always say to them [au pairs]: on the weekends, don't feel that you can't spend time with us, we will take you to Sunday lunch or anywhere, you can come with us, but if you don't want to see us during the weekend, we are fine too. If you feel like you want to go to Sunday lunch with us, we will always take you, but if you don't feel like that it is fine. Some of our au pairs always did come and some would rather chill out by themselves (Richard, 52 years old, lawyer).

Even though some host parents seemed to be clearer about when and why to include au pairs into their family life, others were not so specific. At the same time, all of the host parents interviewed found the boundaries between employer/family members rather complex. Not surprisingly, during the interviews, the au pairs' position was being referred to as: employee, young cousin, daughter, older sister, nanny, family friend, second wife and helping hand. Host parents described how the balance of living with au pairs whilst employing them was difficult to negotiate.

Within the research on au pairs and domestic workers, Sabine Hess and Annette Puckhaber (2004) have focused on Germany and the United States and have analysed the working/living conditions and interactions between au pairs and their employers. Their findings suggest that those au pairs who were more integrated within their host families were discouraged from criticising the unjust working conditions, because mutual responsibility and cooperation as a means of belonging to the host family were being employed to the au pairs' disadvantage. Anderson (2000) also notes that the notion of 'being a family member' within the employment of domestic workers is often deemed as the easier option for employers. This is because in this way employers find it easier to refer to their domestic worker as 'a family member', and as such an association acts as a coping mechanism on issues relating to status. Anderson (2000, p. 236) also suggests that referring to domestic workers as family members, and as such negating the reality of their position, happens because the live-in domestic workers share the 'home' with the family, and are thus witness to many intimate details of family life. Domestic workers are often referred to as family members as this position has clear advantages for the employers. For example, within the interviews with host parents, host mother Jean noted:

> I mean, the weekends are free, but because we encourage the au pairs to be part of the family, if they do go out, that is fine, but it is almost like we don't expect that, we expect them to spend time with us. You know, I would often ask, can you do stuff for me? Like this weekend we had a party and I said to Astrid, I have got a party, would you help me just with the preparations, and I gave her little bit of extra money for doing that. You know, she said 'yes, I enjoy doing it', so you know. I always get this when I am answering the au pair's questions, when they want to come to us, they would be like: 'what is this? And what is my rate of pay? And what are my hours?' and like that. And I am like: 'well, you are a member of my family so yes, you do have two days off work, but as a member of my family it is not like, oh now you are working and now you are not working, you live with us, so it is not that exact'. So I always, I am aware that they are supposed to be working for 25 hours a week and I don't go over that (Jean, 41 years old, part-time IT developer).

Jean's view of au pair Astrid being treated as a member of the host family implies that Astrid should be readily available as a 'helping hand'. Whereas in reality, the family time involves Astrid working for the host family with whatever tasks are needed. Anderson (2000, p. 235) also describes how the negotiation of working hours, wages and other working conditions is undermined by the fact that domestic workers are considered as part of the family. This is because when domestic workers would want to negotiate better conditions, such an act is then considered an 'insult to the family'.

Concluding Remarks

This chapter has focused on the dynamics of au pair families, from the perspectives of family and domestic work research. The combination of these approaches allows for an increased understanding of au pair families; not only as a category of the domestic work sector, but also how host parents understand and negotiate the meaning of family in their own lives.

Taken as a whole, the degree of association, communication and involvement with au pairs, although varied, appeared to be very different in relationships between host mothers/au pairs and host fathers/au pairs. Associated with the gendered division of roles and responsibilities within families, the interviews with host mothers and host fathers revealed that the au pairs were perceived as mainly the responsibility of the host mother. In this way, the host mothers were observed as having to navigate between the roles of employer, host, friend and mother. On the other hand, the host fathers were negotiating what was perceived to be an appropriate distance, underlined both by their detachment from domestic duties and their role as main breadwinner.

Moreover, the negotiations of family time, in particular the weekends and Sunday lunch, all pointed to the blurred boundaries of au pair work, and host parents' endeavours in creating the 'au pair family'. Even though some host parents invited their au pair to family gatherings and cultural events, this was not necessarily meant as an inclusion in 'family time', but rather as fulfilling the 'cultural exchange' principle of the au pair scheme. Although some host families adopted the 'domestic work' model in how they structured their relationship with au pairs, other host parents described their difficulty in fine-tuning the dimension of domestic worker/cultural exchange/family member. This was highlighted by the host parent's negotiation of family time, where 'general family time' consisted of spending family-related activities with the au pair, and 'genuine family time' meant that the au pair was not invited.

In conclusion, when examined through the lens of gender, the interviews with host parents revealed rather traditional organisation of family roles. This is contrary to the thesis of individualisation which emphasises the fragmentation of traditional family structures (Beck 1992). Yet, if we were to adopt the meaning of Morgan's (1999) 'family practices', the au pair presence in itself could represent yet another family adaptation – the au pair family. In this way, the concept of de-traditionalisation and fluidity is helpful in examining host parents' negotiations and reinvention of family time, where they either include or exclude the au pair.

Adopting the perspective brought forth by family studies into the analysis of au pairs as a category of domestic work allows us to gain new insights that go beyond domestic work discourse into the interplay of family dynamics, and how they in turn relate to the impact that an au pair presence has on the family.

References

Addley, E., 2002. Not Quite Mary Poppins. *The Guardian*, 28 November 2002. Available on-line at: http://www.theguardian.com/g2/story/0,3604,849114,00. html [accessed: 14 April 2014].

Anderson, B., 2009. 'What's in a name?' Immigration controls and subjectivities: The case of au pairs and domestic worker visa holders in the UK. *Subjectivity*, 29, pp. 407–24.

Anderson, B., 2000. *Doing the Dirty Work? The Global Politics of Domestic Labour*. London: Zed Books.

Bakan, A. and Stasiulis, D., 1997. Negotiating citizenship: The case of foreign domestic workers in Canada. *Feminist Review*, (57), pp. 112–39.

Bauman, Z., 2000. *Liquid Modernity*. Cambridge: Polity Press.

Beck, U., 1992. *Risk Society: Towards a New Modernity*. London: Sage Publications.

Beck, U. and Beck-Gernsheim, E., 2002. *Individualisation: Institutionalized Individualism and Its Social and Political Consequences*. London: Sage Publications.

Bengston, V.L., 2001. Beyond the Nuclear Family: The Increasing Importance of Multigenerational Bonds. *Journal of Marriage and Family*, 63(1), pp. 1–16.

Bernardes, J., 1997. *Family Studies: An Introduction*. London: Routledge Publications.

Bowlby, S., Gregory, S. and McKie, L., 1997. 'Doing home': Patriarchy, caring, and space. *Women's Studies International Forum*, 20(3), pp. 343–50.

British Au Pair Agencies Association (BAPAA), 2010. Available on-line at: http://www.bapaa.org.uk/ [accessed: 14 April 2014].

Burikova, Z. and Miller, D., 2010. Au pair. Cambridge, MA: Polity Press.

Cheal, D., 2008. *Families in Today's World, A Comparative Approach*. London: Routledge Publications.

Collins, P.H., 1990. *Black Feminist Thought: Knowledge, Consciousness, and the Politics of Empowerment*. New York: Routledge Publications.

Coltrane, S., 2000. Research on Household Labor: Modelling and Measuring the Social Embeddedness of Routine Family Work. *Journal of Marriage and Family*, 62(4), pp. 1208–33.

Coltrane, S. and Adams, M., 2008. *Gender and Families*. Plymouth: Rowman & Littlefield Publishers.

Cox, R., 2011. Competitive Mothering and Delegated Care: Class Relationships in Nanny and Au Pair Employment. *Studies in the Maternal*, 3(2). Available on-line at: http://www.mamsie.bbk.ac.uk/documents/Cox_SiM_3(2)2011.pdf [accessed: 14 April 2014].

Cox, R., 2007. The Au Pair Body: Sex Object, Sister or Student? *European Journal of Women's Studies*, 14(3), pp. 281–96.

Cox, R., 2006. *The Servant Problem: Domestic Employment in a Global Economy*. London: I.B. Tauris Publishers.

Cox, R. and Narula, R., 2003. Playing Happy Families: Rules and Relationships in Au Pair Employing Households in London. *Gender, Place and Culture*, 10(4), pp. 333–44.

Crompton, R., 1997. *Women and Work in Modern Britain*. Oxford: Oxford University Press.

Crow, G., 2002. Families, moralities, rationalities and social change. In: A.Carling, S. Duncan and R. Edwards (eds), 2002. *Analysing Families: Morality and Rationality in Policy and Practice*. London: Routledge Publishers, pp. 285–96.

Doucet, A., 2007. *Do Men Mother? Fathering, Care, and Domestic Responsibility*. Toronto: University of Toronto Press.

Duncombe, J. and Marsden, D., 1999. Love and Intimacy: The Gender Division of Emotion and 'Emotion Work'. In: G. Allan (ed.), 1999. *The Sociology of the Family; A Reader*. Oxford: Blackwell Publishers, pp. 91–111.

Ferguson, D., 2013. How to cut your childcare costs. *The Guardian*, 29 January 2013. Available on-line at: http://www.theguardian.com/money/2013/jan/29/how-cut-childcare-costs [accessed: 14 April 2014].

Giddens, A., 1991. *Modernity and Self-Identity: Self and Society in the Late Modern Age*. Cambridge: Polity Press.

Hess, S. and Puckhaber, A., 2004. 'Big Sisters' are better domestic servants?! Comments on the booming au pair business. *Feminist Review*, 77(1), pp. 65–78.

Hochschild, A., 1989. *The Second Shift: Working Families and the Revolution at Home*. London: Penguin Books.

Home Office, 2013. *Au pairs: Employment Law*. Available on-line at: https://www.gov.uk/au-pairs-employment-law [accessed: 22 April 2014].

Jackson, P. (ed.), 2009. *Changing Families, Changing Food*. London: Palgrave Macmillan.

Lan, P.C., 2003. Maid or Madam? Filipina Migrant Workers and the Continuity of Domestic Labor. *Gender and Society*, 17(2), pp. 187–208.

Marsh, C. and Arber, S., 1992. *Families and Households: Divisions and Change*. Basingstoke: Palgrave Macmillan.

Miller, T., 2010. *Making Sense of Fatherhood: Gender, Caring and Work*. Cambridge: Cambridge University Press.

Morgan, D., 1999. Risk and family practices: Accounting for change and fluidity in family life. In: E.B. Silva and C. Smart (eds), 1999. *The New Family?* London: Sage Publications, pp. 13–30.

Oakley, A., 1974. *The Sociology of Housework*. New York: Pantheon Books.

Øien, C., 2009. *On Equal Terms? An Evaluation of the Norwegian Au Pair Scheme*. Oslo: Fafo-report.

Parreñas, R., 2001. *Servants of Globalization: Women, Migration and Domestic Work*. Stanford, CA: Stanford University Press.

Ribbens McCarthy, J., Edwards, R. and Gillies, V., 2003. *Making Families: Moral Tales of Parenting and Step-Parenting*. Durham: Sociology Press.

Seccombe, W., 1995. *Weathering the Storm: Working Class Families from the Industrial Revolution to the Fertility Decline*. London: Verso.

Silva, E.B. (ed.), 1996. *Good Enough Mothering? Feminist Perspectives on Lone Mothering*. London: Routledge Publishers.

Smart C. and Shipman, B., 2004. Visions in Monochrome. Families, Marriage and the Individualisation Thesis. *British Journal of Sociology*, 55(4), pp. 491–509.

Smart, C., Neale, B. and Wade, A., 2001. *The Changing Experience of Childhood: Families and Divorce*. Cambridge: Polity Press.

Stone, P., 2011. The Rhetoric and Reality of 'Opting Out'. In: A. Skolnick and J. Skolnick (eds), 2011. *Family in Transition*. 16th Edition. Boston: Allyn and Bacon, pp. 362–70.

Valentine, G., 1999. Being seen and heard? The ethical complexities of working with children and young people at home and at school. *Ethics, Place and Environment*, 2(2), pp. 141–55.

Williams, A. and Balaz, V., 2004. From private to public sphere, the commodification of the au pair experience? Returned migrants from Slovakia to the UK. *Environment and Planning*, 36(10), pp. 1813–33.

Williams, F. and Gavanas, A., 2008. The intersection of childcare regimes and migration: A three-country study. In: H. Lutz (ed.), 2008. *Migration and Domestic Work: A European Perspective on a Global Theme*. Aldershot: Ashgate, pp. 13–28.

Zontini, E., 2006. Italian Families and Social Capital: Care provisions in transnational world. *Community, World and Family. Special Issue: Families, Minority Ethnic Communities and Social Capital*, 9(3), pp. 325–45.

Chapter 12

A Fair Deal? Paid Domestic Labour in Social Democratic Norway

Guro Korsnes Kristensen

In this chapter, some of the paradoxes and ambivalences related to the increase in paid domestic labour in Norway will be explored. The focus is on the role of employers and their perceptions and experiences of paying others to undertake what has traditionally been perceived of as gendered family tasks within the private home. The main question that is examined in this chapter is how employers align this organisation of family life and domestic work with Norwegian cultural ideals of social equality and sameness.

The Norwegian Context and Research Questions

In the post-war era, the use of paid domestic labour in Norway was not particularly widespread relative to many other European countries. This has often been explained by the comprehensive Norwegian welfare model, which, among other things, aims to reduce the need for private care solutions (Isaksen 2010; Sollund 2010). A concurrent explanation is that social democratic ideals of social equality led, more or less, to an extinction of the 'servant category' in the 1950s, which made paid domestic services in the private home both socially and morally unacceptable for large parts of the population (Sogner 2004; Sollund 2010). In line with this argument, social anthropologist Marianne Gullestad claimed that social equality, in the sense of sameness, is at the core of Norwegian culture and what it means to be Norwegian (2006). This is evident in Norwegian tendencies to downplay the significance of social class and racism in Norwegian society (Gullestad 2006), and also in the typically Norwegian (re)presentation of Norway as a haven for gender equality (Kristensen 2010).

However, over the past few decades, there has been a steady increase in demand for both domestic cleaners and au pairs, which are the most common forms of paid domestic labour in contemporary Norway.[1] Whereas 6 per cent of the population reported paying someone to clean their home in 2000, this

---

1   The official intention behind the au pair scheme is cultural exchange, rather than work; however, in practice, au pairs perform a considerable amount of domestic work in many Norwegian families.

number increased to 13 per cent in 2007 (Kitterød 2009). Currently, the two most prevalent users of personal cleaning services are the middle class, dual earner urban families (in which both adults work long hours[2]), and single, elderly men (Kitterød 2009). In line with this, the Norwegian cleaning industry is steadily growing; however, as 46 per cent of those who purchase private cleaning services pay cash-in-hand (Lindal 2011), it is difficult to gauge the exact size of the industry (Torvatn 2011).[3] What is known, however, is that home-cleaners are mostly women, and a vast majority of them are immigrant women from Eastern Europe (Alsos and Eldring 2010).

Norway has traditionally been a source of au pairs, in the sense that it has long been popular for young Norwegian women to pursue au pairing in order to travel to another European country, learn a new language and experience a foreign culture.[4] In the 1990s, however, the balance tipped when Norway became a receiving country for au pairs from around the world. Whereas 277 au pairs acquired an 'au pair visa' to enter Norway in 2000, 1,600 au pair visas were awarded in 2012.[5] Of these, the majority were granted to women from the Philippines (Øien 2009). Unlike the job of home-cleaning, au pairing is not defined as work, but as cultural exchange, whereby a young adult is able to learn another language and culture as a guest of a family in the host country. In compensation, she or he is expected to do light housework and help with childcare, up to a maximum of 30 hours a week. In Norway, au pairs receive a monthly pay (approximately 600 euros before tax) in addition to food, lodging and Norwegian classes.[6] According to national regulations, au pairs must be between 18 and 30 years old, and they must not have children.[7] Further, in order to obtain an au pair visa, a candidate must demonstrate that he or she will likely return to his or her home country after a maximum of two years. These regulations do not officially apply to residents of Schengen countries, as they are able to travel freely across borders. Thus, residents of the Schengen Area are not counted in national statistics, and this makes it impossible to determine the exact number of au pairs currently working in Norway. Despite the explicit focus

---

2   In families where both adults work more than 40 hours a week, 21 per cent are reported to use personal cleaning services; this statistic rises to 26 per cent for those who work more than 45 hours per week (Kitterød 2009).

3   The Norwegian private cleaning industry is dominated by a small set of large enterprises that employ a large proportion of the cleaners and a vast number of small and very small enterprises comprised only of an owner, or one or two employees (Torvatn 2011).

4   Au pairing was formalised in 1969, when the Council of Europe instituted the European Agreement on Au Pair Placement. Norway signed the European Agreement, and UDI (the Norwegian Directorate of Immigration) is responsible for managing the scheme.

5   Available   on-line   at: http://www.udi.no/Global/UPLOAD/Publikasjoner/ Aarsrapport/2012/Aarsrapport2012/Aarsrapport2012.html [Assessed: 13 March 2014].

6   Until 2012, the minimum pocket money for au pairs was approximately 500 euros, which is why some of the interviewees reported paying their au pair this amount.

7   The restriction that au pairs must not have children was added to the au pair scheme in 2012. Four of the au pairs who had stayed in the host families interviewed had children.

on cultural exchange, research has documented that au pairs living in Norway perform considerable amounts of housework and childcare (Bikova 2010; Sollund 2010; Øyen 2009).

There are several ways to understand the increasing occurrence of paid domestic labour in Norway, and most theories point to a combination of increased feminised migration, which is found in many European countries (Cox 2006; Lutz 2007, 2011; Lutz and Palenga-Möllenbeck 2012), the higher income level in Norway (Alsos and Eldring 2010), and the 'time bind', which, in a Norwegian and Nordic context, is strongly associated with the dual earner model for gender equality (Bikova 2010; Isaksen 2010; Sollund 2010; Stenum 2010; Øyen 2009). Another theory is that the increase in paid domestic labour has been caused by a growing acceptance of social stratification, which, according to criminologist Ragnild Sollund, might also be an effect of the au pair scheme, as the scheme makes servants more normal and tolerable (Sollund 2010).

The increase in paid domestic labour means that more Norwegian families have an extra pair of (typically female) hands to perform what Andersson (2000) labelled the 'three Cs': caring, cleaning and cooking. Or, to put it another way, more Norwegian families are outsourcing traditionally gendered family tasks to immigrant women, who, for a shorter or longer period of time, have left their home country to live with a Norwegian family, work and experience Norwegian culture.

Although paid domestic labour has become more widespread in recent years, the practice is highly controversial in Norway, as illustrated by a comment from the former leader of the Liberal Party: 'people should wash their own dirt' (Sollund 2010). In line with this, Norwegian politicians submitting proposals for tax breaks and financial refunds for domestic cleaning[8] are often criticised for supporting systems that lead to greater social stratification, social dumping and a new category of servants. In relation to au pairing, public debates have focused both on global inequalities and the potential exploitation of underprivileged women from poor countries, and on au pairs' insecure working positions in private homes (Bikova 2010; Isaksen 2010; Sollund 2010; Øyen 2009). In the wake of several lawsuits involving hosts who have seriously assaulted their au pairs, the former Norwegian Minister of Justice, Grete Faremo, made the following statement:

> Many of us notice that the au pair arrangement has evolved from cultural exchange to an arrangement that has many severe weaknesses. I am not satisfied. I have to admit that as I see it the au pair scheme might not be maintained. We will pay close attention to it in the future (Vårt Land, 24 April 2012).

Another controversy in the Norwegian au pair debate relates to good and bad parenthood, and whether recruiting an au pair implies that parents are outsourcing care or making more time for care.

---

8   Such systems have been introduced for example in Sweden, Denmark and Finland.

Building on this contextual background, the following sections will explore the cultural conceptions that Norwegian parents of relatively young children relate to and (re)produce when they explain their decisions to outsource domestic labour in their private homes; and when they present their particular interpretations and practices of the somewhat open and unclear au pair scheme. How do families frame their decisions to employ domestic cleaners or au pairs? How do they bring their interpretations and practices of outsourcing in line with Norwegian cultural ideals of social equality and sameness? Furthermore, what do families' narratives of home-cleaning and au pairing tell us about contemporary Norway, and about what now seems to be at stake when cultural ideals of social equality and sameness have been potentially destabilised by feminised migration, increased global differences, social stratification and the time bind?

Empirical Data and Methodology

This chapter is based on qualitative research conducted in 2012 and 2013 on the employment relations of Norwegian domestic workers. The material consists of 22 interviews with 39 adults who were either hiring or about to hire a domestic cleaner or an au pair.[9] Half of the interviews were with au pair families, and the other half were with employers of domestic cleaners; however, the majority of the au pair families had also had experience with home-cleaners.

The interviewees lived in different Norwegian cities, and had various kinds of family and work. Whereas seven were in co-habiting relationships, four were single parents (women). All interviewees were parents of relatively young children. The number of children in each household varied from two to five, with a predominance of three. All interviewees were employed, but their working hours ranged from average to very long. In relation to social class, interviewees' salaries implied that all the employers of domestic cleaning services and half of the au pair host families could be classified as middle class, whereas the other half of the au pair host families could be classified as upper class.[10]

The families' experiences with home-cleaning included both regulated legal employment (obtained from registered companies) and illegal employment (arranged on the black market). A vast majority of the interviewees' home-cleaners were immigrant women. Au pair families also had quite varied experiences. Whereas seven families had previously had one or more au pairs, three families

---

9   The couples were interviewed in pairs, with one exception in which the husband did not want to take part in the interview.

10   As social class is generally not discussed in Norway, it is difficult to categorise the interviewees in this way. However, this classification is grounded on the fact that all interviewees have yearly salaries above the average salary in Norway, which in 2012 was approximately 45,500 euros. In the category upper class, the couple's total yearly salaries are above 250,000 euros, which is well above the average salary.

were employing their first au pair and one family was waiting for their first au pair to arrive. Altogether, the families had hosted 26 au pairs. These au pairs had come from different countries (15 from the Philippines, five from other non-European countries and six from Europe [within the Schengen Area]). All au pairs were women, and their ages ranged from 19 to 30 years old, with the majority between 25 and 30.

The interviewees were recruited through snowball sampling, using colleagues, friends and acquaintances as mediators. Each interview lasted between 45 minutes and two hours, and was organised into four parts. In the first part, interviewees were encouraged to describe their family's everyday life and to comment on their daily experiences. In the second part, they were asked about their decisions to hire domestic labour, focusing on their explanations and justifications. In the third part, interviewees were encouraged to share their reflections on the home-cleaner(s) and au pair(s) they had employed and/or wished to employ. Finally, they were asked to share their positive and negative experiences with paid domestic labour.

The interviews provided rich and varied material on multiple aspects of employment relations. Each was recorded and transcribed, and analysis followed a reflexive close reading technique, according to which the data analysis was theoretically informed.

Theoretical Inspiration and Analytical Tools

When analysing the data, the interviews were perceived as a collection of co-produced narratives; this allowed for the recasting of the interviewees (and the interviewer) into accountable, moral subjects in a given context. In the interview a number of co-constructed personal narratives were articulated, and they drew on different cultural narratives. We interpret each narrative (both personal and cultural) as performative, as if they *did* something to the narrator. Having to account for themselves, the interviewees were held accountable for their actions, and as the practice of paying someone to perform domestic labour in one's private home is commonly perceived as morally questionable in Norwegian culture, this is affecting both how she or he is perceived.

These perspectives were partly drawn from symbolic interactionism, which uses a similar perspective to interpret qualitative interviews and has been applied by researchers such as Margareta Järvinen (2001, 2005) and Dorte Marie Søndergaard and Dorte Staunæs (2005). From their research, we were inspired to view qualitative interviews as opportunities for people to give accounts of themselves, and to appreciate that these accounts can not only give information about the narrators, but also about the social context in which the interviews take place and the narrators live. In addition, we found inspiration in Judith Butler's theories of the ways in which discourse of normative subjects constructs 'livable' or 'unlivable' lives by granting social recognition to some ways of living and everyday practices over others. This also has implications for the narratives that people do and do not produce (Butler 2005).

To operationalise Butler's more philosophical theories of the ways in which narratives are constrained by normalising processes, a modified narrative analysis was used. As Ann Phoenix asserted, 'narrative analysis allows personal accounts to be situated in their cultural context' (Phoenix 2007, p. 182). This means that, by focusing on what people say, we not only get to know the people we are studying, but also the social context they are part of.

In this study, a focus on storytelling and self-presentation was applied to an examination of the accounts of persons who, on the one hand, can be classified as part of the Norwegian elite, and, on the other hand, can be thought to challenge important cultural ideals and norms. We were particularly interested in the ways in which interviewees related to their contested and somewhat non-normative organisation of family life, and the work they did to make these contested and somewhat non-normative practices and lives intelligible in the particular context of the interview, and in contemporary Norway, more generally.

'Because We [Desperately] Need It'

Although the families interviewed led rather varied lives and seemed to practice home-cleaning and au pairing differently, the ways in which they framed their decisions to employ home-cleaners or to host au pairs were surprisingly alike. The most striking likeness was found in their tendency to explain their decisions as consequences of a more or less desperate need for help in managing the family/ work balance. Listening to the interviewees speak, one gets the impression that, without the home-cleaner or the au pair, interviewees felt that their family would fall apart, or that they would have to make big changes in the ways they organised their working and family lives, and adjust to a busier daily life in a less tidy house.

The most striking examples of this need-orientated perspective were found in interviews with au pair families. To illustrate, we will start with an interview with Anne and Arne, a couple with three children and two-and-a-half years of au pair experience.[11] Their current au pair was scheduled to leave the family in one month's time, and she would not be replaced. When I asked Anne and Arne why they had initially decided to host an au pair, I was immediately presented with a vivid narrative of the very difficult and exhausting situation that the family experienced when the three children were under the age of three and they had no family or friends nearby to help with childcare:

> The situation was absolutely chaotic when the twins were born. It was just crazy ... There were constantly so many things that needed doing, day and night. We just didn't have enough hands to manage it all. That is why we decided to have an au pair (Arne, married, father of three).

---

11   Due to anonymity requirements, aliases for all interviewees have been used.

This feeling of desperate need was confirmed in the couple's explanation of their decision to terminate the contract with their au pair six months earlier than was planned:

> The situation is not so chaotic any more. Little by little we have retained control and now I really feel that things are going fine. The last six months have been much better. Lately we have had the feeling of surplus. That we are not drowning in domestic work and paid work (Anne, married, mother of three).

Anne described the decision to have an au pair as a solution to a problem, and when the problem was solved, she and Arne neither needed nor wanted the au pair any longer. To put it another way, the disadvantages of having an extra person living with them eventually outweighed the advantages:

> Now we would like to have the house to ourselves. Finally we are able to take care of our family, and we would like to do that. Now we want to be together the five of us … It has been a great advantage to have an au pair for two and a half years, but now we are ready to go on by ourselves (Arne, married, father of three).

Anne and Arne perceived their au pair as a feasible and legal solution to a demanding life situation, but did not feel that life with an au pair could last forever. At least, they did not want it to last forever. Later in the interview we found out that the couple had also looked into home-cleaning, which they had used prior to hosting their first au pair. They were considering using home-cleaning again after the au pair left, and felt it was an arrangement that they needed, but would preferably do without, 'I do not want to employ a home cleaner straight away. First I want to enjoy having the house all to myself, and then maybe I will feel that we do not need it' (Anne, married, mother of three).

Another example of the need-orientated narrative was found in the interview with Berit and Børge, a couple with two children. Berit and Børge had decided to hire an au pair after Berit was offered a new work position with longer hours. Børge was also working long hours:

> Before having an au pair we used to employ a domestic cleaner. But when I got that new job we realised that we would not manage without an au pair. So, having an au pair was a prerequisite for me accepting that job offer (Berit, married, mother of two).

Listening to Berit and Børge's description of the childcare and housework their au pair took on, it was obvious that having an au pair made a big difference in their lives: 'She cooks dinner five days a week. She does the laundry. The ironing. Cleans the house and makes sure that it is neat and tidy … And she helps out with the children' (Berit, married, mother of two, date and place of interview).

According to the couple, they were also explicit about this need for help when they first applied for an au pair: 'To us this is not first and foremost about cultural exchange. To us this is about help to manage everyday life. Like it used to be 150 years ago, when young women from the countryside came to help families in the cities' (Berit, married, mother of two).

This perspective differs somewhat from the perspective of Anne and Arne, who, when asked whether they would consider having the au pair stay in their basement – which had then been let to someone else – they responded, 'We couldn't afford that. And besides, then it would be like having a maid' (Arne, married, father of three).

Although Anne and Arne explained their decision to host an au pair by pointing to their desperate need for help, they did not think of themselves as having a maid. In line with this, the couple also emphasised that the au pairs they had hosted had not performed work that was out of line with the au pair scheme, 'The au pair's tasks have primarily been to help out with the children and to do light housework. They have not been cleaning the floors and that kind of work' (Arne, married, father of three).

Three (out of four) single mothers interviewed felt that they desperately needed the au pairs. As fully (or nearly fully) employed single parents with young children, these women spoke a lot about the time bind and, more specifically, the challenges of balancing work and family. Gunn, a single mother of three children, described it in this way:

> The reason I have an au pair is that I can't manage. I don't have time to clean the house and things like that. And that is one of the things she does. And in addition she does the laundry, cooks dinner, and helps out with the children. And these are the things I cannot manage on my own. If I had a partner it might have been different. So the reason why she is here is that I am on my own (Gunn, single, three children).

Like Anne and Arne, the single mothers saw that having an au pair had some disadvantages, such as preventing them from having the house to themselves when their children were away, depriving them of the opportunity to be alone with their children and, of course, increasing their financial burden. Although none of the women portrayed themselves as economically strained, they did admit that having an au pair made a noticeable difference to their personal economy. However, as one of the single mothers described, 'I do not bother to think about the disadvantages, because to me the advantages are much bigger' (Gunn, single, three children).

Another variant of this need-orientated narrative was found in an interview with Siri and Sigurd. The couple had married five years previously and, together, made up what is often labelled a 'modern family', with both separate and common children. Altogether, their modern family led what they described as a rather busy everyday life. Sigurd had a demanding job and was away from the house for 12 hours each day. Siri described their reason for hosting an au pair in this way:

The reason we wanted to have an au pair was to be able to take care of all the children, to be able to spend time with them and with each other. We are sort of newlyweds and have hundreds of children and a lot of fuss, and then we really need to have time just together, and not running about, sweeping and cleaning and being grumpy ... If it weren't for the au pair, I would have been a bitch. Seriously (Siri, married, mother/stepmother of five).

In line with the need-orientated narrative, Siri and Sigurd were very clear that they were not as interested in the idea of au pairing for cultural exchange – which they perceived of as more appropriate for exchange students. Also, their decision to host an au pair from the Philippines was related to the fact that they needed help, 'We had this idea that people from the Philippines have very strong work ethics. Usually. Of course there are exceptions. And they have a very soft and nice attitude' (Siri, married, mother/stepmother of five).

In summary, these narratives show that the families' desperate need for home cleaning and au pairing was a reflection of their perceived need to manage their work/family balance and help their family stay together. This means that au pairs were perceived as employees, rather than beneficiaries of a cultural exchange, and as hard-working heroes, rather than exchange students from another country and culture. Because Norway offers no alternatives to au pair work, au pairing is considered legitimate and fair. Despite Norway's comprehensive welfare system, these families felt that they could not manage without extra help – at least when they did not have family members who were able to help with childcare.

However, these need-orientated narratives do not suggest that the au pairs gained no cultural knowledge during their time in Norway. Most of the families were also eager to demonstrate that their au pairs had had several nice and exciting experiences during their stays in Norway – including activities that are typically thought of as Norwegian, such as fishing, skiing and hiking (see Chapter 11 by Pelechova). Further, some families spoke positively about the opportunities that au pairs from other parts of the world had for learning about both democracy and gender equality during their Norwegian stays.

'Because We Can and Because We Wish for It'

In addition to the widespread desperate needs perspective, another perspective on domestic labour employment was identified that we labelled 'because we can and because we wish for it'. Compared to the need-orientated narratives, narratives with this perspective presented the employment of domestic cleaners or the sponsorship of au pairs as something the family could (easily) manage without, but something they pursued anyway because they wished for it and were in a position to actually achieve it. Whereas need-orientated narratives seemed more dominant among au pair host families, 'because we can and because we wish for it' narratives were more common among families using home cleaning services. But, as we will see, some of the au pair families had also adopted this perspective.

A typical example of the 'because we can and because we wish for it' narrative was found in the interview with Tone and Trygve, married parents of two children: 'It is so nice to come home to a clean house. And there are so many other things we can spend time on, like sport and spending time with the children, so why not?' (Tone, married, two children).

Another example of this narrative was found in the interview with Ole and Olga, who had had an au pair for ten months. As their au pair was about to terminate her contract with the family in order to take an ordinary job in either her home country or in Norway, the family had already begun the process of finding a new au pair to replace her. However, as we will see, neither the employment of the first au pair nor the planning of the second was explained or legitimised by an idea of (desperate) need. Quite the contrary, as this couple described, their life situation and experiences with au pairs indicated that they did not actually need an au pair's help, 'Of course, the au pair helps us out and makes everyday life easier, but we do not depend on her' (Ole, married, father of two).

Ole described the au pair as a positive contribution to the family, in the sense that she reduced stress and gave the couple better opportunities to relax, concentrate on their children and spend time together. According to Olga, the arrival of the au pair and the help the au pair offered was what she needed to finally get a more suitable job. An important argument in Ole and Olga's narrative is that their house was suitable for a resident au pair. But, again, as they expressed in the interview, they were by no means dependent on her.

This positive, though not dependent/need-orientated way of framing the decision to have an au pair was also found in an interview with one of the single mothers, Marit, who was the mother of two children. In contrast to the three other single mothers, Marit did not give the impression that she needed help taking care of her children and doing housework. Rather, her decision to have an au pair was defended by her wish to get to know another person and, not least, to take part in a young person's first interaction with Norwegian culture and language, as she stated, 'I enjoy watching them change from young and insecure girls into more confident, competent women (Marit, single, mother of two).

Whereas several of the other interviewees spoke about the somewhat challenging experience of having another person staying in their house, this woman described the experience as one of the main advantages of having an au pair, 'It is nice to have someone to talk to. To share experiences with' (Marit, single, mother of two).

So far, we have seen that au pair host families and employers of home-cleaners explained their decisions to hire domestic labour as a result of either (desperate) need or wish for some help in the house chores and caring work. In the next part, we will see that nonetheless our interviewees felt that this was not necessarily enough to make the arrangements socially and morally acceptable in social democratic Norway. Often, more explanations and justifications were needed.

'They Don't Know What They are Talking About'

Although most interviewees emphasised that their decisions to have au pairs were well received and quite often praised by people they knew and met, quite a few of the narratives related other peoples' lack of understanding of and negative reactions to the family's decision to employ a domestic labourer. They also responded to their own reactions to imagined and expressed criticism towards this particular organisation of family life.

According to Anne and Arne, who had decided to get an au pair to help them manage a difficult time with three small children, the reactions they had had from others in response to this decision had mostly been positive, with some even envious. Despite this, Arne admitted that he was not very happy to discuss anything about his au pair when he was back in his rural hometown:

> Arne: I do not think I would have liked talking about it back there ...
>
> Anne: You wouldn't?
>
> Arne: No. I might have felt rather uncomfortable.
>
> Anne: Really? I do not mind talking about it. But I have noticed that those who live there very often have the children's grandparents there to help out, and that is a very different situation.
>
> Arne: It is not that I'm ashamed. I don't know ... it's just ... a lot of people think that you have to be extremely rich to have an au pair. But actually it doesn't cost more than an old rusty car. It costs less than that. I'm sure there are people who spend more money on gambling than we spend on having an au pair (Arne and Anne, married, three children).

In this extract, we see that Anne refused to accept that she was morally inferior because she and Arne had an au pair. At the same time, she immediately introduced an explanation for their particular organisation of family life – namely that they did not have any family living close enough to help out. Arne, on the other hand, was more open about the uneasiness he felt with exposing his way of life in his hometown, and he was also open about what he was uneasy about – that he didn't want to be thought of as very rich or, worse, someone who proudly demonstrates wealth.

Interestingly, Anne claimed to have more difficulties with being identified as someone employing a home-cleaner, rather than someone hosting an au pair. She stated, 'I think the au pair thing is okay, but home cleaning. ... It is this idea that cleaning your house is something you should manage yourself'.

Another example of interviewees' experiences of criticism was found in the interview with Berit and Børge. Throughout the interview, the couple spoke extensively about how important au pair*s* had been for their happy family life. However, they had periodically been confronted with other perspectives on their organisation of family life:

> Interviewer: Listening to you, I have the impression that you are very happy with having an au pair. Do you have any objections whatsoever?
>
> Børge: Yes, because as we have already said, to us [au pairing] is not first and foremost cultural exchange. To us it is help. And that's like it used to be in Norway 150 years ago. People in the cities had girls from the countryside staying with them to help out. And then some people say that this is social dumping. But that is not our experience. We feel that those who mean that are people who have no experience with au pairing, themselves (Børge, married, father of two).

As we see here, Børge was familiar with the au pair critique that was most widespread in the media and most debated by politicians. But, similar to Anne and Arne, he didn't feel that the criticism was relevant to the contemporary practice of au pairing in Norway. Nonetheless, social dumping was not the only criticism the couple had met:

> Børge: Some people think that people who have an au pair do not give priority to their children. But as we see it, it's not like that at all.
>
> Berit: We have had some comments. In the beginning, the staff at the after-school was talking about 'the girl who is looking after your kids'. But in that situation it was rather easy to correct them. 'Hello, we have an au pair for a reason'. But sometimes I feel that I have to excuse myself and explain that the reason we have an au pair is to have more time together with our children, not to outsource time with them (Børge and Berit, married, parents of two).

In this excerpt, both Børge and Berit show that they did not accept being positioned as distanced, uncommitted and uninvolved parents. Their reply to such accusations was to explain that, to them, the au pair allowed them to avoid being such (bad) parents. In other words, Børge and Berit's account of their practice of hosting an au pair and their manner of parenting was in accordance with normative prescriptions for Norwegian family life, in which quality time with children is important (Bø and Olsen 2008).

As these examples indicate, host families defended themselves from criticism by claiming that those who were critical towards au pairing did not know what they were talking about, and that their criticism was not relevant to au pairing, in general, or to the specific family's interpretation and practice of the scheme.

'The Deal is Not so Bad After All'

Although the host families seemed very assured when they dismissed criticism that they had been confronted with or had imagined that they could be confronted with, several host families spoke about different kinds of worries and discomforts related to having an au pair in their home. In most cases, these feelings were related to au pairs who seemed unhappy – a problem that, in most cases, was explained by the personal characteristics of the au pair and/or her family situation, and *not* the au pair arrangement or the specific host family's au pair practice. However, in some interviews, a certain discomfort related to specific aspects of the au pair arrangement and the system of inequality it was part of were identified. As we will see, this discomfort was more or less immediately countered by reflections that presented the au pair deal as fair and established the au pair hosts as responsible, moral subjects. In doing so, interviewees would include the au pair scheme in larger formulations of what (in this context) was (re)presented as culturally intelligible.

An example of this was found in the interview with Anne and Arne. Towards the end of the interview the couple was asked whether they were familiar with the public debates on au pairing. Arne answered:

> The au pair scheme and the contract that goes with the scheme is really good and fair, so as I see it you do not abuse anyone if you stick to that contract. That's my opinion. [The au pair] gets 4,000 kroner pocket money every month that she can spend on herself. And that I do not think is bad. She only works five hours a day, and she has plenty of days off … But I do understand that it is possible to exploit an au pair … to make the au pair work many hours and not let them have any days off, and when they are asked to do a lot of cleaning and when they are refurbishing the house. … Then I do understand this kind of criticism. But if you stick to the contract I think the deal is fair (Arne, married, father of three).

As Arne saw it, the au pair scheme, in itself, was not the problem, as he felt it was quite good. Rather, the problem was with host families who did not stick to the deal. By demonstrating that he was fully aware of the content and intention of the au pair contract, and by disapproving of those who did not stick to the deal, Arne established himself and his wife as good host families.

In a rather similar vein, Børge also argued that the au pair scheme, in itself, was rather good. As we have already seen, Børge and his wife Berit were aware that the au pair scheme had been described as social dumping. When speaking about their own way of interpreting the au pair scheme, they also referred to the content of the contract and what the au pair was intended to do: 'When thinking of it, her working hours are 30 hours a week. I work 52 hours. And then she doesn't have any expenses. So the deal isn't so bad after all. And she has got plenty of spare time when she can do whatever she wants' (Børge, married, father of two).

Even though the au pair earned very little compared to her hosts, Børge did not see that as unfair. Quite the contrary – the au pair was thought to have every reason to be happy, and Børge felt that he and his wife had no reason to feel bad.

'As Long as You Are Kind to Her'

Another, often co-existing, manner of framing the decision to employ domestic labour as morally acceptable was to bring it in line with social democratic ideals such as fairness, kindness and generosity. As we will see, manifestations of fairness, kindness and generosity took on different forms.

When it came to home-cleaning, interviewees most commonly portrayed kindness through lowered expectations for the quality of services and flexibility over when cleaning was done. In au pair families, kindness was also expressed through money, a relaxed attitude, flexibility and social inclusion.

As we have seen, Siri and Sigurd wanted an au pair to offer them significant help in the home. In the interview, the couple told me that their au pair worked long hours, often in excess of her contractual limit. Furthermore, she had a lot of responsibility. However, this violation was not presented as problematic, but rather as a good deal for the au pair, as her primary objective was to earn money. Sigurd described their treatment of the au pair:

> We pay her for the work she is doing. And we pay her a lot more than we actually need to. We do it because we want to. Because we like her, because we think she is clever, and because we want her to be happy here. We also give her other things. And then I perceive of this as a win-win situation (Sigurd, married, father/stepfather of five).

In contrast to narratives arguing that the au pair deal was rather fair, this framing of the au pair scheme took a different approach – namely to establish the hosts as particularly kind. Siri and Sigurd not only stuck to the deal, but they went over and above because they thought the au pair deserved it and because they wanted her to be happy.

Also, Berit and Børge spoke about the importance of being kind to the au pair. In contrast to Sigurd and Siri, however, their kindness was not expressed primarily through money:

> We have decided not to pay a lot of extra … Instead we have chosen to invite them to go on holiday together with us, or to buy them some cosmetics or a nice soap … We always try to show the au pair that we love her and that we really appreciate the work she does and the help she offers (Berit, married, mother of two).

Another way of showing kindness to au pairs was found in Kari and Knut's narrative, in which they spoke of how they included their au pairs in their family.

They let their au pairs use the house as if it were their own, allowing them to invite over friends and even throw parties. In line with this, Kari and Knut reacted very negatively when I told them that one of the other couples I had interviewed had asked their au pair to stay out of the living room after nine pm so the couple could have some time to themselves.

> That sounded both rude and unfriendly. To be honest, they really do not sound like very nice people ... I would say that such a behaviour contrasts the Nordic ideal of being equal. Because, even though we do have an au pair, we would never have said such a thing. It would have been so rude. Like telling someone that you are second-rate family (Kari, married, mother of three).

Here we see Kari constructing her and Knut's practice of au pairing (which involved including the au pair in the family) as generous and in line with Nordic ideals of equality.

As we have seen, interviewees demonstrated different acts of kindness towards domestic cleaners and au pairs. However, what all these acts of kindness had in common is that they established the employers as very kind people. By emphasising their own genuine kindness, the families were able to frame their employment as compatible with social equality and sameness. This brings us to the final perspective in this chapter, that of the win-win arrangement.

A Win-Win Arrangement

Through the win-win perspective, both the home-cleaning arrangement and the au pair scheme were described as very good – not only by employers, who needed and enjoyed the help of the cleaners and the au pairs, but also to the employees. In win-win narratives, families were described as successful, fair and professional employers in need of extra help. The cleaners and au pairs were generally described as good workers, and descriptions often drew on stereotypical understandings of different nationalities and cultures, and, in some cases, the employee's character and family situation. As Sigurd explained:

> As I see it, when it comes to the relation to those who want to be an au pair and who maybe come from really poor countries where they would have been really, really poor, au pairing is a win-win arrangement. That is how we see it. Of course, if you force them to work really, really hard and only pay them what you have to according to the au pair scheme ... But that is something totally different. We do not do that. We pay here properly, and even more than we have to (Sigurd, married, father/stepfather of five).

This narrative of mutual help was also found in several other interviews, and interviewees often used the same win-win phrase. Kari and Knut formulated it as follows, 'In a global perspective, it is absolutely horrible that they have to leave their children behind to come here and give love to my children. On a smaller scale, however, it is a win-win arrangement' (Kari, married, mother of three).

Yet another example was found in the interview with Espen and Emma, who were waiting for their first au pair to arrive. Their decision to have an au pair was explicitly related to the fact that they needed someone to take care of the youngest of their two children, as they had not been able to find a kindergarten the child could attend. In line with this, they also spoke about the problem of not having grandparents to help out. But needing help didn't prevent them from also speaking about the arrangement as a gift from them to another person, and to another family who they did not yet know. When I asked Emma to reflect upon the paradox that Norwegian families are importing women from the Global South to help solve their time bind, she replied:

> I think that dual earner families need help. And in many families grandparents can provide this help. Or one can pay someone to do it. And as I see it, it is only positive if you, at the same time, can help someone from a poor country. Because, for her it is not only a job, but also something that gives both her and her family economic security, and that way it is important. So, rather than having someone from Sweden do the same work ... You can help more than just one family – a whole family ... And the families I know of, they treat their au pairs well (Emma, married, mother of two).

As we interpret this answer, Emma did not accept the implication that, by having an au pair, she and Espen were taking advantage of global inequalities. Quite the contrary; Emma believed that they were performing mini-aid by helping not only one person, but also a whole family on the other side of the globe. The consequence of this perspective was that they did not appear selfish, greedy and rich, but rather caring, kind and socially conscious, and they extended this beyond their part of the world.

Concluding Remarks

In this chapter we saw a variety of ways in which Norwegian families explained their decisions to employ home-cleaners or au pairs, and also a number of legitimising accounts aimed at establishing the employers as busy, adventurous, accountable, kind and caring. All of these accounts contradict the common but contested understanding that paying someone to perform traditionally gendered family tasks within one's private home is somewhat socially and morally questionable in social democratic Norway. When it comes to au pairing the accounts also contradict the negative pictures of misuse and abuse that have been presented in the Norwegian media over the past few years, and the idea that au pair parents do not care for their children as much as other parents. As the interview guide explicitly focused on interviewees' reasons for employing domestic labourers, it is not surprising that the interview material was crowded with stories that legitimised their decisions to employ domestic cleaners or to invite au pairs to stay in their homes. However, both the number and the presentation of those accounts indicate that the families were aware of the controversies and the negative attention and felt the urge to convince me (and possibly those who would read my research results), and possibly themselves also, that outsourcing domestic labour could be very positive, for the family, the cleaners and the au pairs. Further, the families sought to demonstrate that their decisions to outsource domestic labour were not necessarily in conflict with Norwegian cultural ideals of social equality and sameness since they believed that buying domestic labour can also be a practice of kindness and solidarity.

The fact that the need-orientated perspective seemed more widespread among au pair host families than among the employers of domestic cleaners might indicate that the latter group did not feel as desperate for help. However, it may also indicate that au pairing needs more justification than home-cleaning does in contemporary Norway. This is because the role of the au pair is perceived as being closer to the position of a traditional maid, a figure which more or less disappeared together with the rest of the 'servant category' in the 1950s. At the same time, the analyses also revealed examples of narratives in which home-cleaning was described as more problematic and socially embarrassing than au pairing. This might point to the fact that the somewhat ambiguous and highly controversial au pair arrangement does after all offer the employer a possibility to avoid the accusations that they are organising their family life in an unacceptable manner and that they are exploiting vulnerable non-Norwegian women, by means of alluding to the idea of cultural exchange and by embracing the notion of giving a helping hand from the Global North to the Global South.

References

Alsos, K. and Eldring, L., 2010. Husarbeid uten grenser. *Tidsskrift for kjønnsforskning*, 34(4), pp. 377–91.

Anderson, B., 2000. *Doing the Dirty Work. The Global Politics of Domestic Labour*. London and New York, NY: Zed Books.

Bikova, M., 2010. The snake in the grass of gender equality. In: L.W. Isaksen (ed.), 2010. *Global Care Work. Gender and Migration in Nordic Societies*. Lund: Nordic Academic Press.

Butler, J., 2005. *Giving an Account of Oneself*. New York, NY: Fordham University Press.

Bø, B.P. and Olsen, B.R., 2008. *Utfordrende foreldreskap. Under ulike livsbetingelser og tradisjoner*. Oslo: Gyldendal norsk forlag.

Cox, R., 2007. The au pair body: Appearance, sex object, sister or student? *European Journal of Women's Studies*, 14(3), pp. 281–96.

Cox, R., 2006. *The Servant Problem: Domestic Employment in a Global Economy*. London: I.B. Tauris.

Gullestad, M., 2006. *Plausible Prejudice: Everyday Practices and Social Images of Nation, Culture and Race*. Oslo: Universitetsforlaget.

Isaksen, L.W. (ed.), 2010. *Global Care Work. Gender and Migration in Nordic Societies*. Lund: Nordic Academic Press.

Järvinen, M., 2005. Interview i en interaktionistisk begrebsramme. In: M. Järvinen and N. Mik-Meyer (eds), 2005. *Kvalitative metoder i et interaktionistisk perspektiv: Interview, observationer og dokumenter*. København: Reitzel.

Järvinen, M., 2001. Accounting for trouble. Identity negotiations in qualitative interviews with alcoholics. *Symbolic Interaction*, 24(3), pp. 263–84.

Kitterød, R., 2012. Rengjøringshjelp som avlastning i barnefamilier. Fortsatt få som tar seg råd til vaskehjelp. *Samfunnsspeilet*, 4, pp. 64–70.

Kitterød, R., 2009. *Vaskehjelp vanligst; høystatusgrupper* (part of the LOGG study), Samfunnsspeilet, I. Available on-line at: http://www.ssb.no/kultur-og-fritid/artikler-og-publikasjoner/vaskehjelp-vanligst-i-hoystatusgrupper [accessed: 22 April 2014].

Kristensen, G.K., 2010. Trad eller trendy med tre? Om barnetall, likestilling og 'norskhet'. In: A.J. Berg, A.B. Flemmen and B. Gullikstad (eds), 2010. *Likestilte norskheter. Om kjønn og etnisitet*. Trondheim: Tapir, pp. 70–100.

Lindahl, N., 2011. Black market cleaning a major problem for Norway's cleaning industry. *Nordic Labour Journal*, 7 April 2011. Available on-line at: http://www.nordiclabourjournal.org/i-fokus/in-focus-2011/temporary-workers/article.2011-04-06.4261384317_[accessed: 13 March 2014].

Lutz, H., 2011. *The New Maids. Transnational Women and the Care Economy*. London and New York, NY: Zed Books.

Lutz, H., 2007. The intimate 'other'. Migrant domestic workers in Europe. In: E. Berggren et al. (eds), 2007. *Irregular Migration, Informal Labour and Community: A Challenge for Europe*. Maastricht: Shaker Publishing, pp. 226–41.

Lutz, H. and Palenga-Möllenbeck, E., 2012. Care workers, care drain, and care chains: Reflections on care, migration, and citizenship. *Social Politics: International Studies in Gender, State and Society*, 19(1), pp. 15–37.

Øien, C., 2009. *On Equal Terms?: An Evaluation of the Norwegian Au Pair Scheme*. Oslo: Fafo. Available on-line at: http://www.fafo.no/pub/rapp/20119/index.html [accessed: 13 March 2014].

Phoenix, A., 2007. Claiming livable lives. Adult subjectification and narratives of 'non-normative' childhood experiences. *Magtballader – 14 fortellinger om magt, modstand og menneskers tilblivelse*. J.o.S. Kofoed, Dorthe. København, Danmarks: Pædagogiske Universitetsforlag, pp. 178–96.

Sogner, S., 2004. The legal status of servants in Norway from the seventeenth to the twentieth century. In: Antoinette Fauve-Chamoux (ed.), 2004. *Domestic Service and the Formation of European Society*. Bern: Peter Lang AG, pp. 175–89.

Sollund, R., 2010. Regarding au pairs in the Norwegian welfare state. *European Journal of Women's Studies*, 143(17), pp. 143–60.

Sollund, R., 2009. Migrant au pairs in the Norwegian welfare state: Care chains and transnational care. *The Journal of Social Criminology*, 1(1), pp. 122–48.

Stenum, H., 2010. Au-pair migration and new inequalities. The transnational production of corruption. In: L.W. Isaksen (ed.), 2010. *Global Care Work: Gender and Migration in Nordic Societies*. Lund: Nordic Academic Press, pp. 23–48.

Staunæs, D., 2004. *Køn, etnicitet, og skoleliv*. Fredriksberg: Forlaget Samfundsliteratur.

Staunæs, D. and Søndergaard, D., 2005. Intervju i en tangotid. In: M. Järvinen and N. Mik Meyer (eds), 2005. *Kvalitative metoder i et interaksjonistisk perspektiv*. København: Hanz Reizels Forlag, pp. 49–72.

Torvatn, H., 2011. *Cleaning in Norway: Between Professionalism and Junk Enterprises*. Walqing (Work and Life Quality in New & Growing Jobs) social partnership series 2011.5. Available on-line at: http://www.walqing. eu/fileadmin/download/external_website/publications/WALQING_ SocialPartnershipSeries_2011.5_Cleaning_NO.pdf [accessed: 13 March 2014].

Chapter 13

Paying for Care:
Advantages and Challenges for the Employers

Sabrina Marchetti and Anna Triandafyllidou

Introduction: Focusing on the Employers of Paid Domestic Work

This book takes issue with the role of employers in paid domestic work and particularly in the normative and policy debate on paid domestic work. We look at how employers make sense of their caring and cleaning needs, how they relate to their 'employees', how they negotiate tensions in their daily family and working lives (such as tensions between perceived models of parenthood and long working hours, tensions between normative expectations of an adult daughter that cares for her elderly parents and the desire to break free from such family obligations). But we also consider how the formal arrangements of paid domestic work are developing in different European countries, through the mediation of employment agencies, the emergence of specific legal and policy frameworks which frame domestic work relationships, and the transformation of the 'employer' from a care provider to a care manager and hence employer of a domestic worker. It is our contention that we can fully appreciate the issues and challenges involved in paid domestic work for citizens, migrants and policymakers, only if we include in our study a focus on employers, and not just on workers or policies as has been hitherto the case. The contributions included in this volume shed light on the role of employers in the paid domestic work relationship from a perspective different from that of the (migrant) domestic workers and/or the policymakers.

It is actually somewhat paradoxical that although employers are part of the middle class in the countries studied, and hence command a certain level of socio-economic power, they have seldom been the focus of research on paid domestic work and also have remained at the fringes of the policy debate on domestic work and particularly on the employment of migrants (usually migrant women) in the care and cleaning sector. Without overshadowing the importance of understanding the experience of the migrants that are working for them, this volume puts forward an urgency to understanding employers as crucial political, social and economic actors in contemporary Europe.

The need to investigate the role of employers is emphasised by the increasing trend in paid domestic work registered in recent years. A study conducted by the International Labour Organization (ILO) on the occasion of the promulgation of the Domestic Workers Convention (C189/2011) illustrates the general growth of this employment sector worldwide as well as in Europe (ILO 2011). Although the biggest employers, at the country level, are Spain, France and Italy, interesting data also come from other countries where there was a reluctance to replace care services provided in kind by the State with allowances paid to families. Indeed there is an increased monetarisation of care also in Scandinavian countries as well as a concomitant increase in the number of families that decide to delegate certain house chores to paid domestic workers.

Manuel Abrantes (2012) estimates that the number of paid domestic workers has grown by 44.9 per cent in the EU-15 in the period between 2000 and 2010, that is from 1.655 million workers to 2.398 million. Abrantes discusses Labour Force Survey data (LFS) across the EU, looking at the growth of two occupational groups, the 'domestic and related helpers, cleaners and launderers' and the 'personal care and related workers'. Due to country-based differences in the normative frameworks and in the methods for the gathering of statistical data, we need to look at both categories of workers in order to have a reliable comparative picture of the employment of paid domestic and care workers in Europe. We see indeed that, between 2000 and 2010, workers categorised within the first group increased by 36.7 per cent in the EU-15. This increase was most prominent (over 100 per cent) in Sweden and Belgium, and also significant (over 50 per cent) in France, Greece, Italy and Spain. On the other hand, the second category of workers increased by 41.6 per cent. In this case, the growth rate has surpassed 100 per cent in Austria, Finland, Luxembourg, Ireland and Spain, and 50 per cent in the United Kingdom. In some countries like Greece, Italy or Spain this increase may be related to an 'emergence' into the formal economy of a previously informal economy sector (notably of paid domestic work that would take place through cash in hand and with no welfare contributions or registration of the labourer). In other countries, like Sweden for instance, this trend suggests an actual increase of paid labourers in the domestic work sector (Gallotti and Mertens 2013).

Table 13.1 below provides an overview of the migration policy framework and the number of households involved in paid domestic work employment, based on ILO data and the review of the relevant reports by the Fundamental Rights Agency (FRA). Discussing in detail issues of domestic work legislation and the rights of migrant domestic workers goes beyond the scope of this chapter (see also Triandafyllidou 2013; Gallotti 2009; FRA 2011).

Table 13.1   **Labour and migration policy concerning the employment of migrant domestic workers**

Country	Specific labour legislation for domestic workers	Application of general labour law	Possibility to hire domestic workers from non-EU countries	Au-pairs as main recruitment-channel	Household employers of personal services*
Austria	x		x		9,200
Belgium	x		x	x	15,700
Denmark		x		x	5,500
Finland	x			x	8,000
France	x		x		591,500
Germany	x				203,200
Greece			x		52,600
Hungary	x		x		2,700
Ireland	x				6,800
Italy	x		x		724,700
Netherlands	x			x	2,300
Poland[†]			x		26,400
Portugal	x		x		126,900
Spain	x		x		658,900
Sweden	x		x	x	800
UK		x	x		31,300

Sources: Compiled by the authors on the basis of ACTRAV/ILO (2013), FRA (2011) and ILOSTAT Dataset 2012, http://www.ilo.org/ilostat/faces/home/statisticaldata?_adf. ctrl-state=10tysjsmmx_4&clean=true&_afrLoop=3113659776889943 [accessed: 24 April 2014] (classification ISIC, rev. 4 on service occupations). Emphasis added to the countries addressed in the chapters of this book. It was impossible to obtain data on Slovenia and the Czech Republic.

Note: [†]In Poland, domestic work does not fall under labour but civil law, as it is not considered an employment relation but based on a service contract (see ACTRAV/ILO 2013).

Table 13.1 above shows that paid domestic work and the transformation of the family into an 'employer' is an important feature of the care economy developing in Europe, even if the actual arrangements differ (as we discuss in more detail below) among countries and may range from the informal hiring of a migrant domestic worker (live-in or live-out) in the home (as happens for instance in Italy, Spain or Greece), to the hiring of a care or domestic worker through formal care schemes managed by the State or by private agencies/providers of domestic labour force (as happens for instance in the UK) or actually to the provision of the services by the State (as is the case predominantly in Sweden or the Netherlands).

Let us however turn to discussing in some more detail who are actually these families that become employers in their own private homes.

Who Are the Employers?

This book is an attempt to navigate through the different types of paid domestic work and the different categories of employers with a view to shedding new light on the socio-economic features and the specific experiences that characterise them as a group. The book thus provides, in each chapter, an understanding of typical employers' profiles, in different national contexts. It looks for instance at the case of host parents of foreign au pair girls in the United Kingdom and Norway (discussed in Chapters 11 and 12); employers of working-class women as housekeepers in Slovenia (Chapter 10); mothers of young children recruiting nannies on an individual basis or through agencies in Spain, Belgium and the Czech Republic (studied in Chapters 3, 8 and 9); and finally relatives of sick and elderly people hiring 24/7 care-givers who would live and work in their homes in Italy and Spain (discussed in Chapters 2, 5 and 6).

Employers can be categorised in terms of the type of services they require (cleaning, caring, other household chores such as gardening or grocery shopping, or a combination of these); their relationship with the employee (are they the direct recipient of services or are they engaging the care worker or cleaner on behalf of someone else, such as an elderly parent); the type of work arrangement that they request (live-in, paid worker on a monthly basis, or paid worker on an hourly or daily wage).

In addition they can be categorised in terms of their family situation: thus they may include parents (or a single parent) with young children (in need of babysitting and help with cleaning); elderly people who are self-sufficient but need help in cleaning and caring for themselves; the 'sandwich' generation of people who are in their 60s with their children grown up but still in the home and with very elderly parents (in their 90s) in need of care assistance; they may include double career families with or without young children.

The combination of type of work, type of family, work arrangements and relationship with employee produces several schemes and types of paid domestic work that may verge more into the caring profession or more into cleaning and house or garden chores. Table 13.2 below offers a mapping of work arrangements, tasks and types of families/employers involved.

Table 13.2   Mapping work arrangements, tasks and types of employers

Hiring mododality \ Employers	Double career family with or without children	Double career family with children	Elderly people who are self sufficient	Elderly people who are not self sufficient
Live-in		Both cleaning and caring		Both cleaning and caring
Every day but live-out		Both cleaning and caring	Caring	Caring
Occasionally, once or a few times per week	Cleaning			
Au pair		Both cleaning and caring		

Source: Authors' compilation on the basis of the findings of the contributions to this volume.

The findings of the contributions to this volume suggest that we are witnessing a 'proletarisation' of paid domestic work. Whilst in the past the employment of a cleaner, housekeeper, carer, nanny or general domestic helper was a luxury that only few households could afford, during the last couple of decades employers increasingly come from the middle class and lower middle class; for them to employ someone is not a luxury but a necessity. The domestic worker fills in the gaps created by a changing family structure, a diminishing welfare state, an ageing society and most importantly an increased participation of women in the labour market. Indeed, the profiles of employers sketched and analysed in this volume suggest that employers are actually a varied group: they are people of various ages and family situations, with diverse professional and educational backgrounds, living in the most industrialised and urban areas as well as in rural areas and small towns. They may be university professors or housewives, factory workers or lawyers.

Yet, a crucial determinant remains that of gender. The relevance of women's predominance amongst employers is to be seen within a general feminisation in the realm of paid care: it is usually daughters and mothers who take up the role of the 'employer' within the family unit when it comes to employing a babysitter for the children or a care-giver for an elderly parent. This comes particularly to the forefront in the chapters by Vega Solìs, Pelechova, Goñalons-Pons, Humer and Hrženjak who confirm that, within the couple, although men participate in some ways, still women are those who are mainly in charge of the employment and personal relationship with the person they have hired.

A final remark is in order here as regards the methodology adopted by the different authors contributing to this volume. Authors of the chapters in this book have embarked on attempts to define the profile of employers in a qualitative manner. Getting close to these different people and listening to their stories, gathering their opinions, is a job that the authors have accomplished with great sensitivity and in respect towards ethical guidelines for social science research. Their emphasis has been on these people's narratives, on their subjective construction of their identities, on the way they told their biographies (and those of their employees, in the chapter by Kordasiewicz). The result is a very rich and complex material that has been differently approached by authors by looking at the way gender, race and class have differently shaped the experience and the opinions of employers from different parts of Europe.

The variety of the locations in which these studies have taken place is also an important aspect in this book as it denotes the importance of contextualising the employers' experiences. Despite the general trends in the reorganisation of the welfare system and the 'care economy' throughout Europe, it is still important to look at the specificities of each national context when it comes to actual opportunities that employers have as well as the legacies they inherit from their past.

Naturally neither the individual chapters nor the book as a whole raise a claim to comprehensively representing the situation, problems or prospects of employers of paid domestic workers in Europe in general. They rather cast light to the interplay between private arrangements and welfare policies (as discussed in the section below) and to the moral and emotional tensions that employers experience in their interaction with their workers.

Employers: Navigating Welfare and Migration Policies

The debate on the dismantling of the welfare state and the increasing monetarisation of care is taking place in all EU countries, even in those that had the most flourishing traditions of public support to households in their caring needs (see for instance the formerly Communist countries in this volume, notably the Czech Republic, Poland and Slovenia, as well as Norway from the Nordic countries).

This book thus sheds light on the difficult positioning of employers in the context of the changing welfare arrangements in contemporary Europe where States have largely withdrawn from the direct provision of personal care while keeping mostly the regulatory function, meaning a framework within which domestic work and care have to take place. The ways in which welfare support in care for elderly or sick people or for young children is being reorganised and reduced differently among European countries. Naturally also the point of departure is different in each country, ranging from systems that largely relied on the non-paid assistance of family members (particularly women) as in Italy, to Belgium or the Czech Republic where such assistance was fully in the hands of the State.

In a recent study by Franca Van Hooren (2012) on care arrangements for elderly people in Italy, the Netherlands and the UK, she argues that different welfare systems lead to different types of migration, care arrangements and specific 'care markets'. Thus she finds that the Italian familialistic care regime which provides cash allowances to families without enforcement on how they spend the funds provides incentives for the emergence of a 'migrant in the family' model of care whereby families become employers of migrant care workers. In the British care regime where care is increasingly transformed into cash payments, however, a double market emerges. Families that are more affluent receive no payments and hence resort to a private agency care market from which they hire care workers. However both migrants and natives are reluctant to take up such jobs which often involve night shifts and low pay. Additionally, in this market, the turnover of care workers is high as private providers compete with one another by offering slightly better pay (Van Hooren 2012, p. 141).

At the same time those families that are recipients of Attendance Allowance (AA) in cash use it to cover side costs like transport, food and fuel while they rely on adult family members, friends and only to a smaller extent on professional care services for the actual care work. Van Hooren notes that the British AA payments are less generous than the Italian cash benefits and that is why, in her view, they have not led to the emergence a 'migrant in the family' care system. The State also checks how the money is spent, so hiring an undocumented migrant care worker is not an option in the UK. Last but not least, the Dutch welfare system relies on the provision of actual care services that are publicly financed. Thus individuals rely on the public system for personal care or on family members. There is no market for privately purchased personal care services and the demand thus for migrant care workers is very low (Van Hooren 2012, p. 142).

While the study of Van Hooren concentrates on the provision of care for elderly people, her findings point to the interaction between welfare policies, the provision of public service vs cash benefits and immigration policies and their eventual shaping of different types of care markets. Indeed, these findings are confirmed albeit slightly nuanced in the study by Barbara Da Roit and Bernard Weicht (2013). They find that Germany, Austria, Italy and Spain rely mainly on migrant care workers employed in the household, while the Netherlands, Norway, Sweden and the UK tend to rely more on the formal sector and on services provided by public or private services. They partly confirm the distinction introduced by Van Hooren (2012) between familistic care regimes leading to migrant in the family care models, and liberal regimes leading to migrant in the market models. They indeed show that the migrant in the family model adopted in Austria and Germany is the result of limited publicly available services, cash for care programmes and the segregation of migrants in low skilled jobs (Da Roit and Weicht 2013, p. 479). In Italy and Spain, the cash for care programmes are complemented by a notable level of undocumented flows and informal work arrangements. Da Roit and Weicht find that the segregated labour market and the presence of undocumented migrants willing to work as domestic workers are sufficient factors leading to a migrant in the family model even in the absence of generous cash for care benefits. At the same time, Da Roit and Weicht (2013, p. 481) find that while the absence of uncontrolled cash benefits and of a large informal economy are strong predictors of a migrant in formal care model as they find in the Netherlands, France, Sweden and Norway, but they are not sufficient conditions. For example, the UK satisfies these conditions but is characterised by a strong presence of the private sector and formal care arrangements through private providers. It is probably a combination of the public expenditure on formal care services with the absence of uncontrolled cash for care programmes and the absence of an informal economy of care that lead to the specific national care models.

The above findings are confirmed by the findings of the individual country chapters in this volume where different authors show that a privatisation and monetarisation of care arrangements leads to an increased role for employers. Employers are indeed pivotal actors in setting the conditions of the rapidly expanding market economy which is developing around the care and domestic labour sector. Employers are, in this sense, what Maurizio Ambrosini aptly defines as 'care-managers' (Chapter 2). Ambrosini emphasises that the crucial role of employers is paying the care worker's wages and discussing contractual conditions, regularising the legal status of migrant employees (when they are undocumented), administering medicines and special treatments to the elderly and providing instructions about meals, rest times and outings for the elderly person(s).

Marchetti (Chapter 6) also highlights the skills that 'care-managers' need to have in order to satisfy the wishes and needs of care-recipients. Making do with the available public or private resources and navigating the domestic work 'market' (looking at cost, modality, and the specific access to paid care work) is necessary on the part of the employer. Likewise Cristina Vega Solís (Chapter 5) explains how paid domestic work may transform the lives of women who are daughters of elderly parents, enabling them to delegate care work that would traditionally be performed by them to paid care-givers and transforming their family role from care-givers to care managers.

There are however also additional mechanisms through which the State can frame the emergence and functioning of a private care market, notably through introducing intermediaries in the paid domestic work relationship such as employment agencies. An example is the voucher system which was introduced in Belgium in 2004. Beatriz Camargo (see Chapter 8) describes the policy of housework vouchers (*titres-services*) which allows households to officially purchase weekly housework services from an authorised agency, through vouchers. In so doing, the State determines the salary of the domestic worker employed through this system. This policy is aimed at guaranteeing, on one hand, better working conditions for the domestic workers and, on the other, quality of the cleaning service for the clients/employers. Camargo shows however that this system does not significantly alter the employment relationships that generally characterise the sector. Agencies can hardly control if the job is indeed realised and in how much time, nor can they verify the quality of the service given or the actual working conditions. In other words, the essential features of the relationship between employer and worker in domestic work, such as proximity and interdependence, are actually not challenged by this triangular arrangement. The intimacy of domestic work is maintained and housework tasks do not change essentially with the shift to a formal employment relationship.

Other examples show the resilient role of the State in the provision of home-care and domestic services. This takes particularly interesting shape in the case of former Socialist countries where the rampant growth of market-services is sometimes contrasted by institutional attempts to direct the demand-offer dynamics to promote the occupation of unemployed local women, as in the case of Slovenia discussed in Chapter 10 in this volume. Humer and Hrženjak discuss the initiative called SIPA (System of Household Assistance) through which the State aims to facilitate the interaction between demand and supply, ensuring that supply is sufficient and that employers can meet the costs by subsidising this form of employment. Households with small children, on one hand, and long-term unemployed women, on the other, were the main groups addressed by this project. The former found affordable care while the latter found a job. The authors argue that the project succeeded in highlighting the increased care commitments and needs of parents with young children (especially mothers) while it also prevented the exploitative conditions that characterise informal domestic work arrangements.

The interaction between welfare and migration policy discussed by Van Hooren (2012) is also taken up by Bernhard Weicht in this volume. Indeed some countries are reluctant to welcome foreigners in this sector. A paradigmatic case is discussed by Weicht in relation to the approval of the Austrian reform of the sector (Chapter 7). Weicht critically analyses newspaper articles and parliamentary debates that have accompanied the reform in order to show how the State was able to construct what he calls 'employment without employers'. The predominant discourses put the responsibility of regularising employment on the workers rather than employers, by portraying the latter as dependant people who just needed support and assistance. Employers as such disappeared, while the discourse turned around the needy Austrian families and the migrant 'angels' coming to help them.

In the third part of this book we discuss au pair schemes which actually border paid domestic work arrangements in that they are not full-time paid domestic work arrangements, but they do involve similar chores such as childminding/babysitting or light household work. Indeed au pair schemes appear to serve well the needs of double career families with young children. Such arrangements are discussed in the last two chapters of this book on the basis of interviews with Norwegian and British host parents of international au pairs by Lenka Pelechova (Chapter 11) and Guro Kristensen (Chapter 12). The United Kingdom and Norway represent the case of some of those countries were the formal employment of a foreigner full time as babysitter or housekeeper is made very difficult while not impossible by the normative framework on low-skilled labour migration (see also Human Rights Watch 2014). It is in this context that several households seek an au pair girl who stays for a year and fills the gaps of caring and cleaning that the parents cannot do. In the au pair programme, which aims at a cultural exchange programme in which a foreign young person is given the opportunity to learn a new language and culture and acquire some skills in their host country, she can also enjoy enough free time and learning opportunities. Au pairing, however, has been transformed into a part-time or indeed full-time employment arrangement in exchange for accommodation and pocket money. Pelechova and Kristensen (in this volume) aptly show the tensions in balancing family and work obligations and responsibilities among couples with young children where both parents work. The value issues that parents are confronted with, their own perception of what the au pair scheme is for and their efforts to ease the moral and practical tensions of receiving care and cleaning work from their au pairs is many times consoled by playing the host parent ritual on evenings and weekends.

Employers: Negotiating their Changing Needs and Values

Another important aspect of the rising interest on employers lies probably in the fact that, given the special nature of care work, the moral aspects of the employers' experience appear to be quite important for the employer her/himself. In fact, no employer hiring a worker in another sector poses to her/himself so many questions about whether having an au pair or a care worker is the 'right' thing to do. Nor do they question how it fits with the overall values about family life, intergenerational solidarity or indeed social equality.

One of the reasons for this can be found in the intimacy that characterises the setting in which the job is performed and the ambivalence that surrounds the relationships between employers, care-givers and other members of the household, notably elderly parents or children. Moreover, as Ambrosini also emphasises in his chapter, moral dilemmas arise for employers also because paid domestic work is often provided by undocumented migrant workers. Thus, the employers play a crucial part in helping their migrant domestic workers legalise their residence status. They are heavily implicated in the regularisation of the migrant worker and bear the administrative and financial cost that relates to it (with the exception of Austria, as Weicht illustrates).

Different *regional patterns* come to the fore when we compare the experience described by authors regarding moral and emotional challenges that being an employer of a domestic worker raises. First of all, there is a pattern typical of northern European countries where the private employment of care and domestic workers poses a challenge to the national culture based on equality principles and 'cleaning after oneself' ideals. Kristensen in particular very nicely shows how dominant social equality values prevalent in Norway clash with actual everyday needs for some help and how these are normatively and conceptually negotiated by young parents/employers of au pair girls so that they feel 'ok' with their role as au pair employers. Some parents interviewed by Kristensen adopt a narrative based on their 'objective' need of help to run their homes with young children, while others instead defend the decision to host an au pair on the basis of their curiosity for young girls from other parts of the world and their wish to accompany them in their first contacts with Norwegian society. Others still argued that they were performing mini-aid by helping au pairs and their families from the Global South. Yet, several interviewees expressed discomfort for being negatively judged by others, especially in rural contexts, since employing help is stigmatised as going against the values of Norwegian society as based on equality and autonomy.

A similar pattern can be found in post-Soviet countries where, as mentioned earlier, there has been in the last decade a profound transformation towards the privatisation of care services and the 'precarisation' of employment. This has been accompanied by the breaking down of values based on equality and fair distribution of care commitments between women. This is analysed in the chapters by Humer and Hrženjak about Slovenia, by Souralová about the Czech Republic and by Kordasiewicz about Poland; and they all use different approaches for their analysis. Kordasiewicz in particular discusses in-depth the 'class guilt' that Polish employers express as a reaction to the above transformations. She describes the relationships between employer and employees as inter-class contacts that are problematic. In the employers' views they are problematic due to their lack of acceptance of the class gap that separates them from their domestic employees. This leads Polish employers to adopt a biographical justification and legitimation narrative, whereby the life of the domestic worker is presented as full of hardship, failure and personal problems and their employment in the household, while it actually symbolises their downwards social mobility, is presented as a way to save them from all these dramas and to find a solution for them.

In the Southern European country cases studied in this volume (see Chapters by Ambrosini, Marchetti and Vega Solís, in particular) the situation is quite different. Employers do not experience any value tensions as regards their commitment to social equality. Employing a paid care worker clashes with their family values and with the moral and emotional importance attributed to providing care for an elderly or sick parent or other close relative. Indeed in the Italian familialistic care regime and culture, care is performed inside the home, by family members, notably women. As times have changed and women have increasingly been employed outside the home, and society has been ageing leading to the creation of a 'sandwich generation' of middle-aged *children* (in their late 50s or early 60s) who find themselves physically and emotionally unable to look after their very elderly parents (in their 80s or 90s), deciding to delegate this care work to a migrant domestic worker is experienced as a necessary practical arrangement fraught with moral dilemmas and emotional concerns. Thus these new care employers strive to maintain control of the care work.

Sabrina Marchetti elegantly illustrates how the employers of elderly carers that she has interviewed tend to emphasise the importance of the job of supervision and management that they do, in comparison to their employees who instead carry on with the everyday tasks, often without the necessary emotional involvement. The distinction, in their view, is between a form of care that needs a sincere and profound interaction with the care-receivers, the preoccupation for his/her general wellbeing and the improvement of their mental and physical conditions. This attitude is perceived as a prerogative of employers insofar as they are connected to the care-givers by relationships of love and affection. These sentiments are not shared by employees who, especially in the case of migrants, are generally portrayed as money-interested and unable to understand the 'real' wishes of the care-receivers. The moral dimension of paid domestic and care work and the expectations and prescriptions of employers on what is a morally accepted behaviour by their migrant domestic workers is highlighted also by Lena Nare in a recent study on Ukrainian and Polish domestic workers in Naples (Nare 2012). The construction of a moral dichotomy is functional in the employers' narrative to emphasise the importance of family bonds and intergenerational solidarity. This is very important in the Southern European contexts, even in households which decide to delegate to others a great part of these commitments (see also Vega Solís in this volume).

Finally, another specific moral and emotional pattern comes to sight when one considers the relationship between employers and employees as a women-only relationship. Here we see the heaviest emotional work as quite a few women appear not to feel guilty for entrusting to a carer many of their 'traditional' tasks since this allows them to have a professional career. Again, employers are keen to draw limitations on the impact that employing someone else has on their own care commitments as mothers. Pelechova in her chapter on host parents of au pair girls in Britain and Gonalons-Pons on Spanish middle-class women hiring a full-time nanny elaborate on this impact. Host parents interviewed by Pelechova tend to emphasise that although they feel a commitment to welcome the au pair 'as part of the family', there are still some parts of their 'family life' from which they prefer to keep her outside. This includes for instance Sunday lunch or visits to relatives. In some sense, employers do negotiate their uneasiness in having a 'stranger' inside the house and delegating to her parts of child-rearing, by establishing a dimension which is 'more about family' than the general everyday life. This is a dimension based on privacy and intimacy which remains exclusive to people connected by a kin relationship and in which mothers do maintain their traditional roles.

Investigating these different moral and emotional tensions that employers studied in the chapters of this volume face, we suggest that employers of paid domestic workers may be distinguished into two main categories: 'employers as agents of social change' and 'employers as preservers of traditions'. The first category includes employers such as the working mothers of young children or the daughters of elderly parents interviewed by Goñalons-Pons, Vega-Solis and also partially by Camargo. The (partial) delegation of their caring tasks to paid workers is a way for them to pursue new models of parenthood and family life, which do not forcefully entail a long daily physical commitment towards their family members. Gonalons-Pons talks about the search for a 'modern' version of domesticity that combines the responsibility towards the loved ones with engagement in paid work and a professional career and which inevitably reduces the amount of time spent by the *mater-familia* in the home.

The second category of employers include those who have to delegate the actual performance of care and domestic work to paid workers, but who would probably prefer to do the work themselves. Lack of time and energy, distance from their children or parents and commitment towards other family members are usually the reasons why these employers cannot directly take charge of the care of their relatives or even to clean their own apartments. Thus employing someone is a second best option which does not save them, however, from a feeling of guilt or betrayal. This perspective comes into view especially in the chapters by Marchetti and Kordasiewicz where interviewees express their discomfort in the employment relationship. In so doing, they put forward traditional views on commitment towards their households. Here again, women employers are particularly sensitive actors who hold a pivotal role in the preservation of family life and values.

In conclusion, contributions to this volume suggest that paid domestic work is a gendered sector not only as regards employees but also as regards employers. It is an important sector that is intertwined with basic issues of (re)productive and care work as well as labour and welfare policies. It tends to balance out the needs of employers, albeit this comes at a price of contesting values of equality and solidarity and challenging the concepts of family and care.

References

Abrantes, Manuel, 2012. Yes, but what about numbers? A quantitative contribution to the study of domestic services in Europe. *International Labour Review*. Available on-line at: http://onlinelibrary.wiley.com/doi/10.1111/j.1564–913X.2012.00004.x/pdf [accessed: 22 April 2014].

Actrav/ILO, 2013. *Decent Work for Domestic Workers: The State of Labour Rights, Social Protection and Trade Union Initiatives in Europe*. Geneva: ILO.

Da Roit, B. and Weicht, B., 2013. Migrant care work and care, migration and employment regimes: A fuzzy-set analysis. *Journal of European Social Policy*, 23(5), pp. 469–86.

Fundamental Rights Agency (FRA), 2011. *Migrants in an Irregular Situation Employed in Domestic Work: Fundamental Rights Challenges for the European Union and its Member States*. Vienna: FRA.

Gallotti, M. 2009. The gender dimension of domestic work in Western Europe. ILO International Migration Papers, 96. Available on-line at: www.ilo.org/public/english/protection/migrant/download/imp/ip96.pdf [accessed: 24 April 2014].

Gallotti, M. Mertnes, J. 2013 Promoting integration for migrant domestic workers in Europe: A synthesis of Belgium, France, Italy and Spain. International Migration Papers no. 118, International Labour Organisation (ILO). Available on-line at: http://www.ilo.org/wcmsp5/groups/public/---ed_protect/---protrav/---migrant/documents/publication/wcms_222301.pdf [accessed: 22 April 2014].

Human Rights Watch, 2014. *Hidden Away. Abuses against Migrant Domestic Workers in the UK*. Available on-line at: http://www.hrw.org/node/124191 [accessed: 9 April 2014].

ILO, 2011. *Convention Concerning Decent Work for Domestic Workers n. C189*. Geneva: ILO.

Näre, L., 2012. Moral encounters: Drawing Boundaries of Class, Sexuality and Migrancy in Paid Domestic Work. *Ethnic and Racial Studies*, 37(2), pp. 363–80.

Triandafyllidou, A. ed., 2013. *Irregular Migrant Domestic Workers in Europe. Who Cares?* Aldershot: Ashgate.

Van Hooren, F., 2012. Varieties of migrant care work: Comparing patterns of migrant labour in social care. *Journal of European Social Policy*, 22(2), pp. 133–47.

Index

Research in Migration and Ethnic Relations Series

Full Series List

Inside Immigration Law
Migration Management and Policy
Application in Germany
Tobias G. Eule

European Immigration
A Sourcebook
*Edited by Anna Triandafyllidou and
Ruby Gropas*

Ethnic Diversity and Social Cohesion
Immigration, Ethnic Fractionalization and
Potentials for Civic Action
Merlin Schaeffer

Irregular Migrant Domestic Workers
in Europe
Who Cares?
Edited by Anna Triandafyllidou

Migrants and Cities
The Accommodation of Migrant
Organizations in Europe
Margit Fauser

The Bosnian Diaspora
Integration in Transnational Communities
*Edited by Marko Valenta and
Sabrina P. Ramet*

Negotiating National Identities
Between Globalization, the Past and
'the Other'
Christian Karner

Security, Insecurity and Migration in
Europe
Edited by Gabriella Lazaridis

Media in Motion
Cultural Complexity and Migration in the
Nordic Region
*Edited by Elisabeth Eide and
Kaarina Nikunen*

Managing Ethnic Diversity
Meanings and Practices from an
International Perspective
Edited by Reza Hasmath

Muslim Diaspora in the West
Negotiating Gender, Home and Belonging
*Edited by Haideh Moghissi and
Halleh Ghorashi*

Inclusion and Exclusion of Young
Adult Migrants in Europe
Barriers and Bridges
*Edited by Katrine Fangen,
Kirsten Fossan and
Ferdinand Andreas Mohn*

Irregular Migration in Europe
Myths and Realities
Edited by Anna Triandafyllidou

Paradoxes of Cultural Recognition
*Edited by Sharam Alghasi,
Thomas Hylland Eriksen
and Halleh Ghorashi*

Labour Migration from Turkey to
Western Europe, 1960–1974
A Multidisciplinary Analysis
Ahmet Akgündüz

The African Diaspora in the United States
and Europe
The Ghanaian Experience
John A. Arthur

Minority Rights Protection
in International Law
The Roma of Europe
Helen O'Nions

Diversity Management and
Discrimination
Immigrants and Ethnic Minorities
in the EU
John Wrench

Cities and Labour Immigration
Comparing Policy Responses in
Amsterdam, Paris, Rome and Tel Aviv
Michael Alexander

Immigrant Women and Feminism in Italy
Wendy Pojmann

For Product Safety Concerns and Information please contact our EU
representative GPSR@taylorandfrancis.com Taylor & Francis Verlag GmbH,
Kaufingerstraße 24, 80331 München, Germany

Printed and bound by CPI Group (UK) Ltd, Croydon, CR0 4YY
01/05/2025
01858359-0005